Advance Praise for *Miracl[*

"If courageous and creative spiritual leaders like Norm Carroll do not share their biblical wisdom, I fear Christianity will become insular, sectarian and largely self-serving. Reflect, therefore, on these pages and be astonished by what you did not know. Be transformed and be grateful for your new life and for what you now know."

    —Richard Rohr, OFM, Founding Director for the Center for Action and Contemplation, Albuquerque, New Mexico, and Founder of New Jerusalem Community in Cincinnati, Ohio

"If you are tired of abstract interpretations of Scripture, I highly recommend Deacon Norm Carroll's *Miracles, Messages, and Metaphors.* You will experience the familiar characters who map the biblical landscape…[and] feel the passionate resonance sparked by the Living God breathing in each of these biblical persons. The chapters are brief and to the point, allowing the reader to move succinctly through the heart of the Bible and personally meet the Word of God in the words of humans."

    —Joseph A. Iannone, PhD, Dean, School of Theology and Ministry, St. Thomas University, Miami, Florida

MIRACLES,
MESSAGES &
METAPHORS

MIRACLES, MESSAGES & METAPHORS

Unlocking the Wisdom of the Bible

NORM CARROLL

Synergy Books

Miracles, Messages, and Metaphors: Unlocking the Wisdom of the Bible
Published by Synergy Books
P.O. Box 80107
Austin, Texas 78758

For more information about our books, please write to us, call 512.478.2028, or visit our website at www.synergybooks.net.

Publisher's Cataloging-in-Publication available upon request.

Copyright© 2010 by Norm Carroll

LCCN: 2009902967
ISBN-13: 978-0-9823140-1-2
ISBN-10: 0-9823140-1-9

Please visit www.biblemission.net to learn more.

10 9 8 7 6 5 4 3 2 1

I dedicate this book to you, my beloved readers, who search for truth and inspiration in the book that has for centuries nourished our spiritual ancestors on their journey to our common promised land. May you discover therein similar food for your journey until the day all of us embrace in our joy-filled destiny.

"Carl Jung said that a human being 'never perceives anything fully or comprehends anything completely'… So how can we peek out beyond certainty's edge? Jung concluded we can only do it with symbols, with metaphors and images."

—Ellyn Sanna, *Touching God: Experiencing Metaphors For The Divine*

TABLE OF CONTENTS

FOREWORD

How refreshing to read the work of a respected Catholic theologian who draws upon the roots of Hebrew and Christian
Scriptures to define what should be humanity's values and virtues.
The lessons learned from Carroll's writings are invaluable, and I
believe help to strengthen the human psyche. This book does not
hesitate to focus on biblical myth and the Abba experience of Jesus.
The presentations about preserving the planet, the efficacy of prayer,
and the practice of loving-kindness are superb. The deacon's work is a
treatise on reality as seen through the eyes, heart, and mind of a pro-
ponent of interfaith understanding. His scholarship is impeccable.

Although you might find content upon which we might agree
to disagree, the essence of his scholarship is inclusive, regarding all
of humanity as the book seeks to resolve serious issues and dilem-
mas confronting the soul of every citizen on planet earth.

The author's ability to explore and explain the myths and messages found in the Hebrew and Christian Scriptures and their values

has made this work a must-read for people who seek to comprehend the Judeo-Christian ethic. You will recognize Jesus as a true human being and a Jew who believes in one God.

Ending each chapter with a prayerful lesson creates within the human heart and soul a deeper comprehension of the purpose of this text, which is an act of discovery applicable to our own journey through life.

Peppered with Hebrew words, Norm Carroll does not deny or denigrate the roots of the Christian faith, but challenges you to consider the rigid practices, positions, and posturing in your own faith, which demonstrates the courage and honesty of this author. The author's vast research of Jewish and Christian sources adds an even greater credibility to this work. Miracles, Messages and Metaphors is a must-read. It is to be explored, enjoyed, and expressed in our daily lives.

Rabbi Robert P. Frazin D.D., Founding Rabbi Emeritus of Temple Solel, Hollywood, Florida; Professor of Comparative Religions in the Life Long Learning Institute at Nova Southeastern University, Davie, Florida; Secretary of the Southeast Holocaust Documentation Center and Museum; Member of the Board of Regents of the Hebrew University of Jerusalem

PREFACE

Essential Preambles

During the last twelve years, I have been privileged to present nearly two hundred parish biblical missions throughout the United States. Helen Rourke of Baltimore represents one of those who in nearly every church has asked the same question, "Norm, why don't you write a book on the real messages of the Bible?"

I demurred at first, but then began reflecting on the wisdom of the Bible and how so few seem to be able to draw upon it. Finally, today's powerful but puerile fundamentalism (the literal acceptance of the text) convinced me of the desperate need for a book that would explore God's wisdom hidden beneath the surface meaning of the Word. John 8:51 states, *"whoever keeps my word will never see death."* The hour of decision had come for me, and John's words from nineteen centuries ago had helped me arrive at this choice. Therefore, three years ago I began writing this book.

About that time, Mark, my adult son, asked me as he had many times to go bowling with him. Embarrassed at my inability to throw a heavy, unwieldy ball in anything near a straight line, I had always deferred. However, finally yielding to his persuasive powers, I agreed. Just as I had feared, the results destroyed whatever fatherly authority remained. His score was two hundred eight; mine, ninety-seven. The proprietor of the alleys had been watching my debacle. When I returned my rented bowling shoes, he remarked rather acidly, "You know, before bowling, you ought to learn how! Would you care to sign up for a how-to session this Wednesday night?" The three of us then enjoyed a hearty chuckle, and I slinked away into the night.

What he said, however, carried truth and applied, I realized, even to exploring the Bible. Before searching for biblical wisdom, we must learn how to search. The books comprising the Bible were written in foreign languages, necessitating translations and varied editions over many centuries. They derive from ancient peoples who are as nearly distant from us as Martians, and whose cultures, in many cases, are just as unintelligible. Although we can understand clearly most biblical texts, some are disconcerting. In one of many such examples, the first book of Kings tells us in chapter 11 that Solomon had seven hundred wives and three hundred concubines, and he is not even criticized (1 Kings 11:1ff.). One can only imagine how a wife today would react to a husband who followed Solomon's behavior. Yet, some preachers continue to claim that we must derive our morals exclusively from the Bible without regard for cultural or historical differences.

Why Seventy?

We shall consider seventy (some manuscripts indicate seventy-two) outstanding biblical characters and themes in rough chronological order as they appear in the Bible. Why seventy? In the Hebrew Testament, the Lord God bestowed the spirit he had given Moses on seventy elders (leaders) of the people, and they prophesized (Num.

11:25). In the Christian Testament, Jesus appointed in the same spirit seventy to carry his unparalleled message of wisdom, love, and fulfillment to the towns he would soon visit (Luke 10:1). Furthermore, the number seventy carries the Hebraic meaning of complete fulfillment. In other words, the Risen Christ, having overcome space and time, is still dispatching these seventy to us with his message of wisdom. Raymond Brown, the eminent scripture scholar, writes, "These various characters had different types of encounters with Jesus reflecting their respective personalities and backgrounds. Yet in another sense, each is a representative of all women and men."[1]

Christ is actually sending each of us to become one of the steadfast seventy of today's society. I do not intend this book as a historical overview of the seventy. However, I do reflect on the role of each of the seventy in the meaning the biblical author intended and as they relate to our spiritual journey today. As light shines through a clear pane of glass, divine wisdom shines through the biblical seventy and invites you to become one of today's translucent seventy.

These seventy selections fall naturally into two sections: the Hebrew Testament, and the Christian Testament. Incidentally, instead of temporal references to BC and AD, we shall use BCE (before the Common Era) and CE (the Common Era), in deference to our Jewish and other non-Christian readers. Our selections are not disparate and unrelated; rather, a double-fibered thread weaves through all seventy. The first fiber reflects humanity's ever-increasing understanding of God's Word until it reaches its fullness in the life of Jesus; for example, the book of Job, written about 450 BCE, proposes an incomplete solution to the problem of evil. Jesus, however, proposes a full and astounding solution of which few are even aware, and even fewer grasp. Refer to chapter 45, "Evil: A Stepping Stone to Success."

The second fiber traces God's seeking us through these seventy. Rather than employing sophisticated prose, God uses these humans, their experiences, and finally Jesus himself, to convey his wisdom to us. The success of our meditative reading should be measured in our greater understanding of God's Word and especially, as previously noted, in the adoptive divinization we live because of this understanding. As one of the seventy, you represent, in a real sense, God's continuing incarnation on earth.

Before digging into these seventy characters and events from the Bible, we must consider three fundamental preambles. First, the simple rules for its valid interpretation. Authentically interpreting the text carries huge importance because such understanding directly impacts our spiritual transformation. Ray Brown writes, "In some way, the readers...are to see themselves in each of these [biblical characters]."[2] In other words, we can place ourselves in their sandals, including those of Jesus, and derive immense spiritual insight from the experience if we have understood accurately the author's intended meaning.

Second, we must learn to resist the temptation to place any capricious interpretation on a biblical text. Rather, we must understand the Bible has sprung from an older tradition that is rooted in the person of Jesus the Christ. This tradition provides the grounding for exposing untutored and inappropriate interpretations.

Third, we reflect on today's simplistic fundamentalism that violates this tradition, ignores the Bible's relevant history and culture, and often provides meanings glaringly unrelated or even in opposition to the author's intended meaning of his text. In this process, we are thereby robbed of God's biblical wisdom hidden in the author's intention. *"Some people have deviated...and turned to meaningless talk, wanting to be teachers of the law, but without understanding either what they are saying or what they assert with such assurance"* (1 Tim. 1:6–7).

Understanding these preambles is essential for us to capture this jewel of awesome value: biblical wisdom. Their assimilation will empower us to feast on God's Words and become more easily transformed by them. And the Lord God spoke to Ezekiel (and to us), saying, *"Open your mouth and eat what I shall give you. It was then I saw a hand stretched out to me, in which was a written scroll which he unrolled before me"* (Ezek. 2:8b–10a). Truly, God's Words of wisdom are nutrition without which we suffer grievously and die eventually.

O God, father and mother of wisdom and all creation, we ask you earnestly to help us understand the depths of meaning in your Word. Grant that your wisdom may help us realize that whatever our faith or lack thereof, we are one human family drawn together in this space and time.

More importantly, excite us to reject apathy, suspicion, and violence. May this literary effort ignite our hearts to reach out in love to support avidly and appropriately all those with whom we share our beloved planet. Amen.

ACKNOWLEDGMENTS

I thank Mary Moran, who, in the midst of severe personal strife, encouraged, advised, and labored tirelessly for the publication of this book. Moreover, she joins me in believing that humanity, fortified with the supernal wisdom of the biblical word, is overcoming the primordial chaos of Genesis en route to its divine destiny.

I also thank Rev. Sean Mulcahy, and Jim Kerr, who, for one grand shining moment, helped to sow the seeds from which this book took root.

Finally, I must note the gift of my wife Joan and children, Mark, Joy, and Dawn. They have unknowingly blessed me with their tolerance and the genuine character of the lives they live.

INTRODUCTION

Fundamentalism, Deflecting the Search

The sins of that city are so scurrilous, I shall destroy all of it," said the Lord to Abraham, his walking companion.

"Wait, Lord! What if I go into the city and find fifty innocent people of wisdom—will you spare it?" asked Abraham.

"Yes, I will," said the Lord. So Abraham searched the city, but not finding fifty he said to the Lord, "What if I find thirty?"

"Yes," replied the Lord, "find me thirty, and I'll spare everyone." But Abraham could not even find thirty. Returning, he said to the Lord, "I know I'm 'leaning' on you, but if I can find just ten innocent people who will always seek truth and love, will you spare the city?" Again the Lord agreed. This time, Abraham searched all the public buildings, hospitals, courthouses, schools, and libraries, but could not find even ten.

"Lord, please don't be angry, but I'm certain I can find at least three people on whom you can always depend to live wisely despite whatever trial they suffer. If so, will you save the city?"

1

"Abraham, you are 'pushing' me, but if you find even three, I will save the entire city." Abraham went into every home and place of worship, but couldn't find even three who always seek their God of wisdom. Embarrassed, he returned to the Lord and begged, "Lord, what about if I find just one person who will always seek to live your wisdom no matter his pain? Would you still spare the city?"

And the Lord said, "Abraham, go and find me just one, and I will spare the entire city." (Gen. 18 and Ps. 14 paraphrased.)

Abraham continues his search in our cities to this day. Truly, the Lord is calling each of us in the midst of our self-doubt and seeming anonymity, to become that one. Accordingly, amidst our personal and societal tragedies, our need for divine wisdom could not be more acute. This biblical story, indeed the entire Bible, provides such wisdom. It can raise us from despair and loneliness to genuine fulfillment and joy. However, first we must appreciate the authentic meaning of the Bible and how to live it. Basic to this appreciation is the understanding of myth to which we often allude in the pages that follow. Myth does not mean a fictional story but rather a story that expresses a profound theological meaning. To explore that meaning often reveals the magnificence of God's wisdom.

Today, most of us drowse unaware of this vast biblical storehouse of wisdom plumbed so astutely by scripture scholars and in-depth seekers of various denominations. Such sleeping Christians stumble through life ricocheting from one painful uncertainty to the next, never understanding the Bible, its central hero, or the magnificent messages that could revolutionize their lives. Sadly, some biblical literalists, known as fundamentalists, are preaching a fast-food faith and call it Christianity. They are unwittingly rendering this greatest of books irrelevant and even anachronous. Worse, they are depriving their followers the in-depth spiritual wisdom that Christ desires for them. It's no wonder this brand of Christianity turns off non-Christians as well.

Such literalism has become so widespread that this book, by exploring the depths of biblical wisdom, implores to be written, and, for maximum credibility, must rise from the central characters and themes of the Bible itself, especially from Jesus of Nazareth. This is why we are exploring the biblical lives and messages through which God has expressed his profound being.

Biblical wisdom, when understood according to the sacred authors' intentions, provides that spiritual insight for which every human heart yearns. Additionally, it sows seeds of solutions for today's seemingly insoluble societal problems. Jesus remains the central bearer of this wisdom and seeks humanity's turning from personal despair, militarism, and unrestrained upward mobility to his wise and invincible truths. This book explores his wisdom with its precious and indispensable treasure.

Go for the Gold!

Jesus, whom Christians profess to be God's human presence, was a nondescript from the hills who would most likely be assassinated again today because of his compassionate pluralism. Still, he has impacted our society as no one else in all history. Given their stature, one can justifiably expect guidance from Jesus and the other central biblical characters and themes in addressing our monumental societal and personal challenges. This they do, but before learning from them, we must come to an understanding of Jesus and the book of which he is the centerpiece.

Why is the Hebrew Testament part of the Christian Bible? Does it point toward Jesus? What was his actual message? Do our churches reflect it accurately? Why is there evil in the world? Does God really dispatch people to hell? How can the Bible ease our pain? Must we change our lifestyles, and if so, why? Drawing from God's wisdom, this book responds to such monumental questions and many more in a powerful, educative, and prayerful way.

Your reading these words suggests you seek this biblical gold, but gold resides in the depths of the earth. Searching the stony surface, as fundamentalists do, may represent a childlike beginning, but one must dig into the earthen core to mine gold. John Chrysostom, a Church Father, writes about the year 400 CE, "The Bible is a well without a bottom."[1] The book of Proverbs even surpasses Chrysostom. "*How much better to acquire wisdom than* [even] *gold!*" (Prov. 16:16). This book will not only unearth such wisdom but also enlighten your individual search.

"I Live, No Longer I, But Christ Lives in Me!" (Gal. 2:20)

Jesus interpreted "Christliness" in terms of teaching, healing, and loving. He, as the Risen Christ, yearns to live this salutary life in the being and lifestyle of each of us. Thus, Jesus, the central character of the Bible, intends to transform us truly into other Christs. To promote such transformation is my purpose in writing. Therefore, I invite people of all ages and spiritual persuasions to these pages. If you are not Christian, I don't seek to make you one, but I do seek to prioritize the fulfillment of your human potential for surpassing goodness: your own "Christliness." This fulfillment represents the objective of a Christianity that is open, authentic, non-proselytizing, and inviting. Irenaeus, an ancient Church Father alluded to this: "The glory of God is the human person [not only Christians] fully alive."[2] Therefore, I shall not witness on behalf of any denomination but on behalf of you and the wisdom you seek. Each biblical character and theme of which I write expresses magnificent and unique facets of divine life; and finally, Jesus gathers all these emphases together in his life, the climactic crown jewel of our biblical treasure.

I trust that absorbing the biblical wisdom captured herein will draw you to the Bible itself, which I recommend as your companion in these chapters. As your literary servant, I write always with you first in mind, for you are more precious to me than any book. I suggest you embrace one chapter, or less, at a time. There is more than enough treasure in the life of each of these men, women, or themes to consume your rapt attention. Prepare for an amazing educative, and inspiring journey into the countercultural wisdom of God. Rejoice that, as you absorb and live this wisdom, you shall, like Jesus of Nazareth, become more fulfilled, more Christ-like. Welcome to God's biblical world of wisdom!

Dear Mother/Father of wisdom, grant these words of mine may never spring from any self-serving agenda. Rather, may they serve your daughters and sons who come searching for your living water to satisfy their thirst. Grant that, because of your Word, your beloved reader will determine to change dramatically some portion of her or his lifestyle so as to live more fully as another Christ. We ask this in the name of him who personifies biblical wisdom. Amen.

CHAPTER 1

SPIRITUALITY AND RELIGION

The great rabbi Abraham Heschel writes, "It is customary to blame secular science and anti-religious philosophy for the eclipse of religion in modern society. It would be more honest to blame religion for its own defeats. Religion declined not because it was refuted, but because it became irrelevant, dull, oppressive, insipid. When faith is completely replaced by creed, worship by discipline, love by habit...when faith becomes an heirloom rather than a living fountain; when religion speaks only in the name of authority rather than with the voice of compassion – its message becomes meaningless."[1] This helps to explain why many people today are "tuning out" organized religion while searching for spirituality. Elton John demonstrated this trend by calling for a total ban on organized religion, saying it "doesn't seem to work." John said he loves "the idea of the teachings of Jesus Christ," but organized religion "turns people into hateful lemmings."[2] Note Sir John considers spirituality and religion to be separate. A recent survey conducted by the Search Institute of

Minneapolis finds that 55 percent of people aged twelve to twenty-five say they are more spiritual now than two years ago, but nearly a third said they don't trust organized religion. Apparently, many people distinguish spirituality and religion. Do they really differ? If they do, why are people choosing one and rejecting the other?

Stephen Doyle, the Franciscan scripture scholar, describes spirituality as the love affair between God and humankind, and religion as the catalyst and celebration of the affair.[3] They do differ, and the distinction between the two carries great importance and stunning conclusions. Let's reflect first on spirituality.

Because we are human, you and I will always search for what lies beyond us, for the ultimate, for what some call God. Augustine writes of this, "You have made us for yourself, and our hearts are restless until they rest in you."[4]

True, a few of us deny God altogether, but that restlessness of which Augustine spoke still remains whether we practice religion or not. Biologist Edward O. Wilson writes, "The predisposition to religious belief is the most complex and powerful force in the human mind, and in all probability an ineradicable part of human nature."[5] If we weren't driven to search for what is beyond us and to relate to it, why else would have we launched moon landers and space probes into the unknown? We thirst by nature for the eternal and for immortality, and this thirst, when denied or ignored, often grows even more acute. Seeking money, fame, health, or any earthly good, as an end in itself, only reinforces this point, because acquiring physical ends never satisfies the human heart. We know this because many, despite their wealth, still seek more and more and more.

On the other hand, if the Bible is true, and God is love, the divinity also seeks us. This embrace between God and his beloved is known as spirituality; Doyle had it right. More importantly, Jesus, the Son of Man and the central character of the Bible, recognized this, for his first and last spoken words were centered on Yahweh, his Abba (his daddy) (Luke 2:49 and Luke 23:46). These truths "drive [us] beyond any religious system that claims to pose the truth of God in any ultimate sense. Religion…[must] be open-ended for me, and its forms can never be allowed to be final," states John Shelby Spong, the retired Episcopal bishop.[6]

Spirituality remains alive and well, and always will. But what about religion? Doyle maintains that religion serves spirituality both individually and communally. Its entire raison d'être is to invite all to prepare for, and celebrate, the ever-continuing spiritual wedding between divinity and humankind. When religion dedicates itself to this task, it prospers. When it seeks other goals, or makes itself the goal, religion fails. For example, the Catholic Church proclaims the real presence of Christ in Eucharist, and declares in its Canon Law (213) that Catholics have a right to this sacrament. However, it also rejects so many applicants for priesthood on the basis of gender or marital status that the church ends up denying many Catholics access to liturgy and Eucharist; this, in the face of Jesus preaching inclusion for all: *"Go out, into the main roads, and invite to the feast whomever you find"* (Matt. 22:9). Is the church serving the spirituality of its members by denying many of its own the opportunity to partici-pate in liturgy and the Eucharist, the sacramental Christ? The church surely has a right to regulate its sacramental system, but how does the church justify its denial of its own canonical declaration, the com-mand of its divine founder, and its justification for being: namely, to serve the spiritual wedding of its members and the divine?

Albert Nolan, the esteemed Dominican author writes, "One of the most significant developments of our time is the separation of spirituality from religion. Diarmuid O'Murchu, among others, argues that while spirituality has been with us from the beginning, religion was only introduced 5,000 years ago."[7] All religious leaders ought, therefore, to be asking themselves this crucial question: does my particular church teaching, principle, or practice serve true spirituality and my own community's self-interest or controlling power? Admission of such guilt by religionists demands tremendous courage; taking corrective action demands even more.

The Bible, Koran, Upanishads, and equivalent sacred writings fall under the aegis of religion, not spirituality. They are not, as fundamentalists would imply, objectives in themselves, because men and women who have not known any sacred writings have also worshipped God in truth. However, when religion and the Bible impassion us on our journey to our universal God, they become a mighty wind lifting us "on eagles' wings" to touch the divine. This represents religion at its best. From the heart of our being, we seek to touch the divine, and this illustrates why we treasure the Bible and why the Word of God has the power to transform us. We invite you to become a heroic member of your religion by striving with courage to propel it in serving spirituality.

Dear Abba, help us to expand our vision, even to realize that, before any religion existed, you were there; before life and death, you were there; after church, earth, and universe, you will be there. Give us the wisdom to understand that all creation and healthy religion serve to draw us to you. Finally, knowing that all else shall pass, help us to live daily your intimate embrace that constitutes true spirituality. I resolve to advocate for my religion and its leaders to serve this spirituality. I thank you with everlasting gratitude for inviting me to your eternal caress. Amen.

CHAPTER 2

TRADITION,
MOTHER OF THE BIBLE

Did you learn your faith from your parents, minister, teacher, another authority figure, or from the Bible? Many would answer, "At the knee of my loving mother, father, or grandparent." This son still happily remembers accompanying his mother to one of fourteen novena services every Thursday in the 1940s at St. Jude's Church in Paterson, New Jersey. She was teaching me her faith, and neither of us realized it. Truly, our forbearers often passed their faith along to us, and, most likely, their ancestors to them. Such passages are known as tradition.

Jesus initiated his own traditions, including baptism (which he probably learned from John), Eucharist, washing of the feet, and others. He never wrote a word; rather, he established a tradition and trusted his followers to pass it on. Christian parents, during those early centuries after Christ, handed down this tradition to their children, and teachers to their students. This tradition formed the headwaters of two rivers: one spoken, and later, the other written (the Christian Testament). Eventually, Christians divided tradition into two parts: Tradition in large case, and tradition in small case.

Tradition with a small *t* refers to unessential practices and teachings, such as the practice of married priests that existed for centuries in the Roman Catholic Church. Today, many churches struggle ordaining our gay brothers and sisters despite their baptism as children of God. Do you recall Catholics' eating meat on Fridays constituting mortal sin? These and many other traditions with a small *t* have been or can be changed. Tradition that refers to essential teachings, such as one spiritual God or the divinity of Jesus, is spelled with a capital *T* and will never change. God's inspiration of the Bible is such a Tradition. This is why any interpretation of a biblical text that violates the Christian Tradition becomes, to that extent, unchristian.

Many manuscripts were authored in these early centuries about Jesus. However, it wasn't until 393 CE at the Council of Hippo that the church selected the books that would comprise the Christian Testament. During those early years, heroes and "sheroes" gave their lives, not for this Christian Testament that still didn't exist, but for the Tradition that Jesus had started. One such martyr was Ignatius, Bishop of Antioch. While en route to Rome as its prisoner, Ignatius wrote, "Let me be food for the lions...I am God's wheat, and I shall be ground by the teeth of wild beasts to become a pure loaf for Christ."[1] His prayer for a holy death in terms of Eucharist was answered in 107 CE, nearly three hundred years before there was a Christian Testament. He died for the Christian Tradition.

Several weeks ago, I heard a television preacher exclaim, "We need no Tradition but only the Bible." Yet, without this Tradition, there would be no Bible and no standard for biblical truth. So, the inevitable has happened: absent Tradition, anyone can interpret any biblical passage in any way he or she desires. Naturally, such a one often declares his interpretation is the one and only true interpretation. For example, suppose I interpreted John 14:15–17 as meaning there are not three but four persons in God: the Father, Son, Spirit of Love, and Spirit of Truth. Exclude the Christian Tradition and the church that preserves it, and no one could authoritatively declare my error. Today, many preachers are justifying their interpretations of biblical texts on their own authority. Those who claim Christianity rests solely on the Bible don't seem to comprehend the priority of Jesus and the Tradition he founded. Indeed, if all the Bibles in the world were destroyed in a huge bonfire, Christianity would survive, because its Tradition lives in the hearts of Christians like you.

An amazing dimension of this tradition is its vitality. Even today, this tradition lives and grows in our understanding. When you witness Christianity to a friend, teach your child about Jesus, attend a church service, or give to the poor, you're passing on the tradition. Tradition, initiated by Jesus, appearing in written and oral form, and passed on by the People of God, has, therefore, the highest priority. The Bible achieves its dignity and authority not as much from its literary value or its antiquity but because it forms the written portion of this great Tradition. The Bible is inextricably bonded, therefore, to Tradition and Church. Losing sight of this bonding, which is the current theological myopia, can, as we have noted, cause unbridled license when interpreting God's Word.

We carry the responsibility of passing on our Christian Tradition. We accomplish this chiefly by living Christ's life in ours. How tragic that we, when speaking of the Bible, rarely consider the Tradition from which it derives, and by which our understanding of Bible must be judged. Without realizing it, we are thereby severing Bible from its moorings and insulting it and the Tradition for which Jesus and so many martyrs died. Let's never fall into the seductive trap of reducing our Christian way of living and worship to a mere book. Rather, we must firmly and forever rest on a person, Jesus, and his Tradition of which the Bible remains a partial record.

Lord Jesus, you gave us a powerful tradition, the heart of which states that we, like you, are called to give our all in the cause of goodness and compassion. We are filled with gratitude for your calling us to your tradition. Help us to appreciate this tradition and its heroes and "sheroes" because of whom we are privileged to proclaim, "The blood of martyrs courses spiritually through our veins." Grant that we may always be loyal to this Tradition by living daily in your presence until the day all of us join together with Abba in eternal embrace, the goal of our Tradition. Amen.

CHAPTER 3

HOW TO INTERPRET
THE BIBLE

This chapter is vital to understanding the rest of this book and the Bible because it establishes succinctly simple yet profound fundamental rules for interpretation. We urge you to give full attention to these principles as we begin to explore the depths of wisdom imbedded in our text.

Are there certain clear standards the church recommends for understanding God's Word, or are we left to our own whims or those of certain preachers? The church declares emphatically, "Yes, there are three basic principles." Joseph Fitzmyer, the eminent scripture scholar, writes of the first, "It is rather of supreme importance that the meaning of the Bible in the twentieth century have a homogeneity with that originally intended by the human author inspired by God to record His Word."[1] We seek, therefore, not the meaning *we* place on a text, but the *author's* meaning. For example, many would say that because of Genesis 1, the earth was made in six days; after all, that's what the text states. Christian biblical scholars tell us, however, the author composed this story primarily to point out that Yahweh created this universe, not how long it took him. It's absurd to impose an earthly timetable on our timeless God! Placing emphasis on a timetable before there was time ignores the objective of the sacred author. Therefore, we Christians have no valid theological objections to accepting scientific evidence indicating our cosmos is 14.5 billion years of age and our planet 4.7 billion years.

One can frame from such findings a profound spirituality of wonder, humility, and gratitude to our creator. Simply to look up is to peer into a tiny speck of divine mystery and munificence, and to look down suggests our God-given earthen solidity to which we cling while hurtling through space.

Other modes of interpreting God's Word—feminist criticism, canonical criticism, liberation theology, reader-response criticism, and others—have value, but we assert that no interpretation may destroy the author's intended meaning. Such hermeneutic models may derive from it, apply it, or parallel it, but cannot validly overturn it.

Wouldn't you like to ask Matthew and Luke why they disagree on the birth of Jesus; Mark and John why they don't mention it at all; or all four why they disagree on the details of the resurrection? However, in view of the evangelists' advanced age and questionable current physical condition, such conversation might prove difficult. Not to worry! This is the work of the scripture scholar, whose task is to search the author's intent by understanding his literary style, language, and culture as fully as possible. Therefore, when reading God's Word, a scripture scholar's biblical commentary is invaluable. *The Jerome Biblical Commentary*, *The Collegeville Bible Commentary*, and the Daily Study Bible Series by Barclay (though somewhat dated) all represent fine commentaries.

One Sunday morning many years ago, my dad gathered the family in our dining room before leaving for church. He placed what appeared to be a silver coin on the table and asked, "Tell me what you see." "A nickel," I guessed. Now it was my brother's turn, and I knew he would get it right. He got everything right. "It's a quarter!" he exclaimed confidently. Then dad showed us the coin, which turned out to be not a coin but only a silver button. He pointed out, "Remember we see things not as *they* are, but as *we* are. This goes for the Bible, too." My brother Joe, the curious fifteen-year-old, asked the question of questions, "Then how can we know what the Bible really means?" William Blake, a well-known English poet put it this way, "Both read the Bible day and night, but thou read'st black where I read white."[2]

Therefore, our second principle for understanding God's Word is that whatever interpretation we draw from a text must agree with the essential unchanging truth of our Christian Tradition. For example, the Catholic Church mandates a certain interpretation in less than ten biblical passages, and most of these passages form the scriptural Basis of its sacramental system. Other Christian denominations also allow freedom of interpretation, but always within that denomination's own essential Tradition. For example, imagine a minister of the Baptist Tradition preaching Jesus never baptized as is stated in John 4:2. His interpretation of that isolated verse would violate a core teaching of his Baptist Church, and to that extent, deny his own Tradition. Such an opinion could earn for him "tar and feathers" and possibly interrupt an otherwise promising career. Our interpretation of the Bible must agree with the essentials of our own particular Christian Tradition.

Thirdly, Mark Twain writes, "It ain't those parts of the Bible that I can't understand that bother me, it is the parts that I do understand."[3] Apropos of that, a theologian once told me the following story: "There was a scripture scholar whose intelligence and biblical knowledge were admired far and wide. He and one of his students, whom he had flunked years before, died at the same hour. They approached the pearly gates, and God said to the scholar, 'I'm sorry, but you can't enter here.' The scholar replied, 'But I studied and learned all my life about your Word.' Then the professor noticed his former student skipping through the gates, and asked God why such as he was acceptable. The Lord exclaimed, 'Because he lived what you merely taught.'" Jesus put it in a different way in Matthew 7:24, exclaiming, *"Everyone who listens to these words of mine and acts on them will be like a wise man who built his house on rock."*

Christ is calling you to be that wise person: Bartimaeus who receives sight (Mark 10:46–52); the paralytic who is healed (Mark 2:1–12); the arthritic woman who is freed (Luke 13:10–16); the Canaanite woman whose daughter is healed (Matt. 15:21–28); or even Jesus who tried to save whomever he touched. Place yourself in every story knowing that you are also spiritually blind, paralyzed, or arthritic. Encounter the events and emotions of each character therein as your own, and experience Jesus face-to-face.

God is calling you through the biblical page to spiritual greatness: that means living his life wherever you live yours. It's no wonder Jerome, the greatest scripture scholar of all time, exclaimed about 400 CE, "To ignore the Bible is to ignore the Christ."[4]

Eliminate, at this moment, all extraneous thoughts, and place yourself totally in Christ's presence within you. Admit to him your blindness, and, like Bartimaeus, tell him you want to see. Listen for his response. Can you promise him to begin every day with ten minutes of reflection on his Word? Do so, and you just may hear the same response he gave Bartimaeus: "Go your way; your faith has saved you" (Mark 10:52).

CHAPTER 4

DIG DOWN:
FUNDAMENTALISM EXPOSED!

One can't reflect today on biblical wisdom without first understanding and evaluating its powerful and insidious enemy, fundamentalism. Fundamentalism ignores the power and beauty of the wisdom to which the biblical words point. Rather, it's satisfied with the mere meaning of the words themselves. Ellyn Sanna, quoting Karl Jung, says, "A human being never perceives anything fully, or comprehends anything completely....No matter what instruments he uses, at some point, he reaches the edge of certainty beyond which conscious knowledge cannot pass. Jung concluded we can only do it with symbol, metaphors....[Those] allow us to prove something that has no literal explanation."[1] Fundamentalism insists only on the visible or palpable. It denies the symbol, the mystery, and thereby, the wisdom of the living God.

Fundamentalism ignores, in varying degree, the three principles we spotlighted in our preceding chapter, and still manages to attract multitudes of sincere and committed Christians, and even those of other religions. The fundamentalists I know are intelligent, good, and caring people, but one wonders how they can accept so passionately such shallow understanding. The great Lutheran martyr Dietrich Bonhoeffer refers to it as "cheap grace."[2] Phillips Brooks, the renowned nineteenth-century Episcopal clergyman, likened the Bible to a telescope through which one views God's transcendent world of beauty and wonder; but he added that the fundamentalist looks at the telescope itself and sees only it.

Let's now define and discuss this "traditionless" cultural phenomenon called fundamentalism. Biblical fundamentalism is a physical, common, literal way of understanding God's word.

Physical: Christian fundamentalists place their faith in the physical Bible, that is, in the words rather than the meaning to which the author points. For example, Matthew describes, in chapter 14:22–33, Jesus walking on water and assisting Peter to do the same. Fundamentalists would, with variations, marvel at this preternatural miracle, but this event means much more biblically. Genesis 1:2 describes the primordial waters of chaos; the flood in Genesis 6 threatens all mankind; the waters of the Sea of Reeds in Exodus 14 obstruct the Israelites as they leave Egypt. Water, in biblical context, often symbolizes chaos and pain. Matthew is really declaring through his watery analogy that Jesus the Christ will empower his readers, along with Peter, in their trials, whether spiritual, physical, financial, or relational. Are you facing the heart-wrenching pain of divorce, cancer, a death, or a similar tragedy? Matthew counsels you to keep your focus on the transcending Christ, and you will walk atop your swirling waters of chaos. Did Jesus actually walk on water? Perhaps, but to insist on its mere physicality is to miss the greater marvel: overcoming in Christ our own life-threatening perils. Instead of seeking solutions in miracles of our physical world, as Christians we acknowledge our doubts while still proclaiming, "I believe."

Common: "Fundamentalism is not a theological but a psychological problem," writes Rev. Eugene LaVerdiere.[3] It's rooted in our culture's unbridled uncertainty and fear; witness the most powerful nation on earth spending over fifty billion dollars annually to finance the Federal Department of Homeland Security. The more one has, the more one fears losing it. Similar fear explains the assertion of many fundamentalists that they are already saved. Such thinking seeks to eliminate doubt, but true faith dwells amid the darkness of doubt. So, I say to you my fundamentalist friends, "Seek not to play God by asserting your own salvation; rather, live as a Christ and trust in Abba's wise disposition!" Jesus never declared he was saved and, in fact, gave little attention to his security. Rather, he opened his martyred heart to all and trusted his Abba.

Many seek absolute answers to life's difficult questions. "What could provide more certain answers than God's Word, which is unassailable?" asserts the fundamentalist. These good folk, however, forget that each of us views God and the Bible from different genealogical and experiential backgrounds, and thus can, and often do, draw justifiably different conclusions from the same passage.

Few churches identify themselves as fundamentalist; however, fundamentalism reigns in the hearts of a great number of evangelical Christians, other Christian denominations, and Catholics as well. This is not surprising, for our entire culture reflects this insecure and consequent fundamentalist reaction. Scripture scholar Barbara King quotes the following depressing findings: "Sixty percent of Americans believe the Bible stories are word-for-word true; this includes the Bible's explanation of Moses parting the Red Sea, God creating the world in six days and Noah's Ark....and a fifth say that the sun revolves around the earth."[4] Fundamentalism is so pervasive today that those who struggle for the deeper spiritual wisdom of the Bible open themselves incredulously to suspicion and even charges of heresy.

Literalism: The soul of fundamentalism lies in accepting the words in their surface meaning and in ignoring the deeper wisdom to which they point. Heschel writes, "The surest way of misunderstanding revelation…is to imagine that God spoke to the prophet on a long-distance telephone. Yet, most of us succumb to such fancy, forgetting that the cardinal sin in thinking about such ultimate issues is literal-mindedness."[5] Does this not reflect the superficial dimension of our Western culture bespeaking instant gratification?

There's a story of Francis Bernardone who, in 1204, stopped at the broken-down chapel of San Damiano. Deep in prayer before the crucifix, he heard the words, "Go, Francis, and restore my house which is falling." He immediately began repairing the chapel. It was only later that St. Francis understood God was telling him to restore the universal church. Thank God, Francis grew mightily from and beyond his fundamentalism.

Most literalists don't realize they are participating in a powerful, but recent, twentieth and twenty-first century reaction to the mainline Protestant biblical scholars of the nineteenth century. These scholars applied sound principles of literary criticism to the Bible. Some churchmen considered such scholarship an affront to God's Word and ignited the massive retreat into the fundamentalism we witness today.

Fueled by their insecurities, men and women in all denominations have succumbed to fundamentalism's subtle seduction. Many sincere seekers seem unable to understand that faith lies in believing not so much in creeds or words but in believing when there is nothing in which to believe; for example, the faith of Jesus hanging on a cross. He had been stripped of all dignity; his dreams were smashed; he had left no writings; his disciples abandoned him; and still he believed in his Father, himself, and his followers. Jesus would never have been so abused if he had been a fellow fundamentalist or legalist as were most religionists of his day. Jesus called his followers not to prioritize words, books, or rules. Instead, he urged them to open their hearts in love. Jesus was no fundamentalist.

Simon Parke has penned the following marvelous lines of poetry, entitled "Desert Warm," which every seeker ought take to heart:

As any desert dweller will tell you,
when looking for firewood among the big sands—
and you will need to,
for it's very cold at night—
you should look beneath the sand.
Where the wicked wind has buried it.
Dig down.
Just because you don't see it
on the surface,
doesn't mean it isn't there.
If you want to keep warm amid the cold,
dig down.[6]

Lord Jesus, the demands of raw faith are of far greater challenge than the limited certainty of the literal word. Help us dig down through your words to their meaningful depths and accept your call to heroic faith. Grant that we may comprehend that we don't sail on vessels that have reached port, but rather on boats being tossed by massive waves en route. We trust not in ourselves, nor in our salvation. We entrust our entire selves and destiny to our Father in your words, "Father, into your hands I commend my spirit" (Luke 23:46).

CHAPTER 5

ABBA'S BREATH OF INSPIRATION

I f you have ever written, painted, designed, or composed, you are
aware your creation results from your being inspired by a person, cause, or idea. In authoring this book, I have been inspired
by one central objective: to be of spiritual service to you, my sister
and brother in Christ. Because I don't physically know you, this
sounds wildly idealistic, but you and I are serious seekers of truth
and love, and share thereby a certain profound spiritual bonding. I
thank God he has privileged us by sharing with us a remnant of his
biblical wisdom and mystery.

When considering biblical inspiration, a great danger looms:
namely, to believe that God forces his inspiration in varying degree
upon the biblical author, thereby controlling his thoughts, written
message, or even his literary style, and restricting the author's freedom. In this scenario, one must recognize the authors' every word as
literally true, even his geological and historical errors and disagreements with other biblical authors that frequently arise. The Second

Vatican Council asserts, however, "The Books of Scripture must be acknowledged as teaching firmly, faithfully, and without error, [only] that truth which God wanted put into the Sacred Writings for the sake of our salvation."[1] Literary devices therefore need not be accepted as literally true because they are not necessary for our salvation. For example, it is not necessary to accept five thousand Hebrews walking across a riverbed over one hundred miles wide, or Yahweh writing, in Hebrew, on stone tablets. This is not to say these events never physically happened, but they have deeper and more significant spiritual meanings that warrant our deeper reflection.

Christian Tradition does not affirm that God exercises external control over the sacred author. This preserves the freedom of the author, and our ability to evaluate critically his writing. Accordingly, the Catechism of the Catholic Church defines inspiration as follows: "That process by which God chose certain men who, with God acting in and through the authors, made full use of their faculties and powers."[2] Truly, the authors of Exodus, Luke, Galatians, or any biblical book wrote freely from their own thought process, style, and culture, to communicate consciously their own message and the others. Paul did not realize his letters were divinely inspired. Only centuries later did his church community so consecrate his words. This declaration provides us the assurance of God's authentic inspiration of the text. The author was completely free to write whatever and however he wished, and so extend the entire process of incarnation.

When one accepts this reasonable assertion, he or she understands why we must search out the meaning the author intends, for it is that salutary meaning that is inspired, not necessarily the literary device the author employs to convey his meaning. As an example, the author of Jonah intends to point out to the Jews that they must reach out even to their enemies with the good news of

Yahweh. The story of the great fish and Jonah's converting Nineveh, a city that had passed from existence at the hands of the Assyrians over 150 years prior, is a mere literary device by which the author attracts the reader to his or her mighty message. This message saves the entire book from becoming one grand fish tale. Hopefully, however, all of us will agree that our being inspired by God's Word is what's most important. If we profess the Bible as inspired but largely ignore its profound transforming message, do we really believe it's divinely inspired?

Inspiration means literally "to breathe into." You will recall God physically breathing life into the first human (Gen. 2:7), and Jesus breathing spiritual life into his disciples (John 20:22). The Risen Christ is now attempting through the Bible to breathe his life into us so that we might live his life daily and breathe spiritual life into others. We have the power to make it come true, and it all begins with our being inspired to immerse ourselves daily in God's Word for at least ten minutes.

St. Isidore of Spain lived and prayed for such an inspired life until he took his last breath. He composed the following deeply meaningful prayer for the Second Council of Seville in 619 CE that we now invoke, and which was prayed at Vatican Councils I and II.

"Holy Spirit of God, we, the followers of Jesus, have tended to ignore you through the centuries. Come now to inspire us not only with appreciation for the divine wisdom in God's Word, but also for your presence in our hearts when reading it. Be the inspiration of our intentions and the energizer of our actions. Help us develop a great devotion to you forever, for you alone possess a name equally glorious with the Father and the Son. Amen."

CHAPTER 6

IN THE NAME OF YAHWEH

My attempt to author a chapter on God reminds one of the wooden Pinocchio, who could not speak, trying to describe his creator, Geppetto, who began with a piece of wood and fashioned Pinocchio. Your creator and mine, however, began with total chaos to create an indescribably complex, dynamic, yet patterned cosmos. He accomplishes this while residing in another totally transcendent dimension yet, amazingly, dwells in every cosmological cell. My only hope, as one in a sense less than Pinocchio, is to seek understanding of God's words and actions partially recorded in the Bible and to pray for his tolerance and your acceptance. With that said, we proceed.

Picture a group of anatomically modern humans twenty thousand years ago. They are holding hands and encircling a fire as their "priest" leads chanting and praying. Anthropologists tell us mankind has always worshipped, from the very beginning, his god or gods. It's "natural" for us humans. Some (for example, Robert

Hutchins, former president of the University of Chicago) say this fact alone proves that God exists, for how else could we humans have possibly conjured up such transcendent divine meaning with our very limited, mundane cognition? The geneticist Dean Hamer found a human gene having an innate inclination toward faith in the divine.[1] We even sing of this supernatural yearning: "Shepherd Me O' God beyond my wants, beyond my fears, from death into life."[2] At any rate, we humans have surely "created" great diverse divinities. We have worshipped the sun, the moon, animals of all kinds, statuary from our own hands, and even other humans. Could nearly all of us from our human genetic roots be in total error? It's therefore rash, and in a sense inhuman, to deny God's existence. The better question is: what is God like?

About three thousand years ago, our Hebraic ancestors provided humanity with the greatest gift ever given humankind: recognition of one spiritual God. Their devotion to this God proved uniquely countercultural in many respects. Soon they developed a sacred library (the Hebrew Testament). A few, called prophets, claimed a special relationship with their God and gave their lives rather than renounce their bonding with God.

Their books told a sacred story concerning the naming and the character of God. Remember in the famed tale of the burning bush, Moses asking, "What's your name"? The voice from the bush responds, *"I am who am"* (Exod. 3:14). Hebraic religious culture maintained that one knowing another's name suggested the former enjoyed authority in relation to the latter. With this in mind, the audacity of Moses asking God for his name is indeed surprising; that God gives his name to Moses, astounding. This God is surely different from all those other gods, for he wishes to be with, in, and for the Hebrews and us. God provides the name "Yhwh," meaning in Hebrew, "I am present to you in a continuing presence or relationship." This name refers not as much to an existential meaning (I really exist), as it does to a relational meaning (I am in relation with you, or, I am here at your service). Yhwh, later spelled *Yahweh*, explains his name more fully to Jacob in Genesis 28:15: *"Know that I am with you; I will protect you wherever you go....I will never leave you until I have done what I promised you."* Yahweh is promising Jacob and his spiritual and physical progeny, including you and me, that he will be with us through all our pain and joy. However, some tend to recognize only what they can see or touch. Others believe tragedy and pain preclude his supportive presence and therefore ignore or reject Yahweh's name and presence. Would that we might perceive his pervasive presence and thus live in his name!

We can learn from Jesus, who accepted, from the very core of his being, Yahweh in his fullness. Jesus developed such an intimacy with Yahweh that he referred to him as Abba (usually translated as "Daddy"). Incidentally, he did not intend to eliminate the feminine, mommy, from Abba. *Abba* is derived from the ancient word *Ab*, which meant "the ungendered one." In fact, Jesus understood Abba as having the outstanding qualities many associate with females, such as compassion, tenderness, and sensitivity. Is it possible that, in the end, his intimate communion with Abba and his consequent lifestyle became the actual cause of his murder? After all, the Hebraic clerics refused, in unholy reverence, even to speak the name of Yahweh. And Jesus dared to call him Daddy!

As his disciples, do we thirst for Abba? Are we willing to embrace intimacy with Abba, meaning that worry, fear, and death no longer play a substantive role in our lives? If so, we can truly exclaim with Jesus, *"Father, into your hands I commend my spirit"* (Luke 23:46).

I have a widowed and lonely friend who suffered from insomnia and consequent fear of going to bed. She was "anxious and worried about many things." Then after spiritual counseling, she began the nightly meditative practice of envisioning herself being held and soothed by Abba as a mother does her babe. She never realized she was praying contemplatively. Soon, she found herself looking forward to bedtime with its warmth, deep sleep, and pleasant dreams.

Our searching for the meaning of Abba still remains, in the end, futile, for Abba dwells in another dimension. However, we shouldn't worry! The Bible tells the story of Abba searching for us in our dimension. Apropos of that, are the following lines of Abba spoken through Isaiah: *"Fear not, for I have redeemed you; / I have called you by name: you are mine. / When you pass through the water, I will be with you; /... When you walk through fire, you shall not be burned; /... Because you are precious in my eyes / and glorious, and because I love you"* (Isa. 43:1–2, 4).

By reflecting deeply and accepting fully these words of wisdom, you can overcome everything in this life, even death, and you have Yahweh's word on that. If you experience trouble sleeping tonight, try the practice of my friend. Picture your beloved Abba holding you to his bosom, for this is your real home anyway; despite your myriad concerns, you are truly safe and secure forever.

Lord God of this unimaginable cosmos, you are mystery to us: transcendent, unknowable, and wise beyond all our wisdom. Still, we believe you are afire with love for each of us, and you seek to inflame us in becoming as you are. Help us to dwell in your light and become a divine torch by living your life with wisdom and love. Amen.

CHAPTER 7

IN THE BEGINNING, WHEN GOD CREATED...

"In the beginning, when God created the heavens and the earth, the earth was a formless wasteland, and darkness covered the abyss, while a mighty wind swept over the waters" (Gen. 1:1–2).

Most of us are familiar with these words and the rest of the story; namely, God creating the cosmos in six days and resting on the seventh. We learned this story as children, and it has become "gospel." However, as adults, we accept the scientific truth that the origin of the cosmos dates not from six days in the divine workshop, but over fourteen billion years ago, and counting. We face, therefore, a titanic tension concerning the origin of everything that is. It appears we must choose between science and religion.

The problem is that the postmodern understanding of the universe as an incredibly expanding cosmos is creating a new incipient story. The more some religionists cling with closed minds to the literal interpretation of six days or some derivative thereof (the old story), the more irrelevant it becomes. Thomas Berry, the Christian ecologist, writes pointedly of this: "We are in trouble just now, because we do not have a good story. We are in between stories. The old story [from Genesis], the account of how the world came to be and how we fit into it, is [because of scientific findings] no longer effective. Yet, we have not yet learned the new story."[1]

A saving resolution of our perceived cosmic crisis is possible, and we approach that resolution by asserting that scientific truth does not diminish or negate the truths underlying the mythic Genesis story. We, as Christians, assert unequivocally that God did indeed create this cosmos and everything in it. Gerard Manley Hopkins writes of this with poetic beauty: "The world is charged with the grandeur of God,"[2] but this divine presence does not preclude scientific evidence of an evolving universe.

Who can measure with six days of time a God who is beyond time, whose "is-ness" always was, is, and will be? Isn't it more like our eternal God of love to create not in and by a six-day timetable but by preparing this cosmic and earthy magnificence in mystery and with exquisite, timeless planning? Creating remains an ongoing process from solar caresses to tidal torrents and shifting sands, and from human birth and growth even to this moment. Therefore, did God create in six days? Scientific truth, of which we Christians have no fear, exclaims, "No!" Christians with faith, courage, and respect for truth agree with such scientific evidence. However, we still assert that God created beyond fourteen billion years ago, and continues, through and with our help, in his earthen and cosmic dynamics. The biblical author tells the mythic story of six days of sacrosanct truth to affirm that God created all, and we ought to devote at least one day of seven to him.

This leads us to an even more compelling consideration. Did God create from outside, as a sculptor sculpts a block of granite, or from the inside (through constitutive generation), or both? Adult Christian thinkers point out that because God is perceived as an external force, he is thereby separated from his created beloved. Rather, they affirm that our God is love-energy, internal to all and therefore external to none. God is capable of and does reframe his presence in as many creative and marvelous ways as there are creatures. This munificence embraces the discoveries of quantum physics, according to which everything remains in some form of subatomic touch with every other being, symbolizing thereby the in-depth divine presence in everything, just as the poet Francis Thompson declares.

> *All things by immortal power,*
> *Near and Far*
> *Hiddenly,*
> *To each other linked are;*
> *That thou canst not stir a flower,*
> *Without the troubling of a star.*[3]

For Christians, this energy gives birth to human togetherness in a marvelous spiritual union called the Body of Christ. Such energy infuses even the non-human and non-living who replicate the divine in their own unique way. God resides, therefore, in all his beloved, both in their substantial and their accidental being (Thomistically speaking) as well as in their function.

Because God resides dynamically as one within all of us, we are called to continue co-creating with him, beautifying his planet, and increasingly, even the cosmos. Because of this "oneing" with God, each of us is divinely related to each other. We can thus respond to the Lord's question of Cain, "I am my brothers' (and sisters') keeper" (Gen. 4:9).

Creation cannot be a six-day effort, but a lifelong privilege symbolized by the six biblical days. Because of this role, your life and mine assume a new luster by which we can eat from all trees except that one by which we claim to be equal or superior to the creator himself. More positively, God finds fuller expression in you and me as we magnify his presence. As this divine spirit (mighty wind) of Genesis 1:2, continues "breezing" through us, God becomes ever more incarnate in us, and we are raised to the heights of the divine beyond, within and without.

Marvel at the ineffable greatness of our God, who initiated this ever-present creating process from a dimension of which we have the tiniest of knowledge. Consider also his profound thirst for peace and fulfillment that he engendered in his cosmos and especially on earth to image his own being. Realize his "need" for you to "make it come true." Finally, wonder that Abba in universal love resides up above, down below, and everywhere in between, but most meaningfully, in your own heart. By only looking up and not within, we miss this most intimate dwelling of God. In summary, God's first and supreme gift is creating; you have become his greatest co-worker, and the six days symbolize you and God in each other, creating order and beauty in our deeply troubled planet, day after day after day.

Ah, beloved Lord, you have given us this cosmos and planet of surpassing beauty of which we are a minute part. We thank you deeply and promise to cherish it tenderly and wisely. Give us the courage to generate gentle co-creativity with our sisters and brothers. May we nurture not a land of pollution or destruction but a planetary garden of loveliness reflecting your divine pastorate. Amen.

CHAPTER 8

EVE AND ADAM, ALIVE AND WELL

Sister Rose exclaimed to us third graders, "Now remember this: Eve and Adam are the names of the first woman and man." I still recall her clenching her right fist to emphasize the names of our first parents. However, as I grew into adulthood, I wondered about Sister Rose's adamant belief in them. Later, greater authorities questioned the physical existence of Eve and Adam. Cardinal Oscar Maradiaga of Honduras increased my tension by saying the faith of a child cannot support the life of an adult.[1] Accordingly, serious questions arose in my soul. Did Eve and Adam really exist? If so, what about scientific findings indicating our development from primates? Where do the cave people fit into this scenario? As we saw in our preceding chapter, by holding literally to the statement of Sister Rose, many relevant scientific findings are severely challenged, such as the indisputable evidence of the existence of cave people one hundred thousand years ago. I wonder what Sister Rose would believe today.

This I do know: according to the writings of our finest scripture scholars and theologians, the story of Eve and Adam is myth. Myth is not a story without truth, but a story designed to teach deeper truth than what appears. Eve and Adam designate the central characters in the myth and symbolize life (the meaning in Hebrew of the word *Eve*) and mankind (the Hebrew meaning of the word *A'dam*). Similarly, the word *Eden* (Gen. 2:8) derives from a Sumerian word *Eden*, meaning "fertile plain." Therefore, the author of Genesis is painting a picture, according to his primitive knowledge, of human life created in the form of woman and man with their origins on the plains. The scientific historic human trail certainly includes mankind's evolution from primates to cave people and then to more sophisticated types. "The [Christian tradition] has held that the Bible teaches not of scientific causes, or geological reality, or historical exactitude, but of God's purposes and intention and direction so that humans will understand how to live in order to be saved," declared scripture scholar Lawrence Boadt.[2]

Because this story from Genesis is mythic, we who believe in the truth of God's Word remain open and without fear (chapter 7) of the relevant discoveries of science. We do, however, insist on the theological truth to which the myth refers; in this case, that God created humankind, as is evident from both creation stories in chapters 1 and 2 of Genesis.

Other such theological gems from Genesis include our need for reverencing God regularly on the seventh day. The author also affirms clearly the equality of woman and man (1:27) by stating that mankind, female and male, were both created in the divine image. To support this verse, the author declares, *"The two of them become one body"* (2:24). This same myth describes God ordering this innocent couple not to eat of the tree of the knowledge of good and evil, or they would die (2:16–17). Despite this, they eat of it anyway, as if to say, "Lord, we give the orders, and we know what's good or evil for us better than you do." By seeking to reverse the power structure of the universe and elevating themselves above God, the author affirms clearly the foundation for all sin—theirs and ours. As we have discussed in chapter 7, God is the creator, not us; he merely invites us to join in his handiwork. In effect, like Eve and Adam, we abandon through sin and apathy the heights of intimacy with God and choose the depths of groveling with the serpent.

Now, the consequences! Shame (referring to the fig leaves covering their nakedness), guilt (their hiding from God), and cowardice (their refusal to accept responsibility and insistence on blaming another, even God): these three emotions begin their ceaseless residence in the human psyche.

We can trace, therefore, three stages in our ever-deepening understanding of Eve and Adam. First, we accept in a simplistic, childlike way two individuals from whom stemmed the entire human race. Second, we realize the author has woven a marvelous tale pregnant with response to some of the basic questions of life. Third, we discern that Eve and Adam have always lived, and do so today in the heart of every one of us. Their legacies, goodness and evil, battle daily in our own life experiences in which we seek not to replicate their "grab for power" but to maintain, as thinking human creatures, right universal order. We, like our first ancestors, remain good people but with a tendency to assert our independence from and superiority over our God of creative love. Such overreaching entices us, but shame, guilt, and cowardice remain its bitter fruits. Yes, Eve and Adam may not reflect historic persons, but they do live on as unwelcome harbingers of moral behavior in the lives of you and me.

Lord God, you took pre-time and eons of time to fashion so carefully your beloved humanity. We know Eve and Adam intimately, for they reside alive and well in our spirits, ever beckoning us to eat the forbidden fruit of overpowering and self-seeking. We also know you call us daily to fulfill the very best of the seeds you have planted in our soiled souls. As we journey precariously from Eden to your embrace, our promised land, we ask you in the prayer of the psalmist to keep us safe. "Keep me as the apple of your eye; / hide me in the shadow of your wings" (Ps. 17:8). For our part, we promise always to seek greater understanding of your Word and the wisdom to live its meaning. Amen.

CHAPTER 9

CAIN AND ABEL: BROTHERS IN BLOOD ONLY

We know the story of Cain murdering Abel, but one unanswered question has descended through the ages: why did God accept Abel's offering while rejecting Cain's when both seemed to offer appropriate gifts from their trade? The response to that question answers another: could this story carry any meaning for us today?

Abel, the shepherd, brought a calf, considered the choicest of all meats. He even offered God its fatty parts. These were the richest portions, and such were reserved in justice as temple offerings for Yahweh. Recall the loving father welcoming home his wayward son with a meal of fattened calf (Luke 15:23). Abel was giving his very best (as justice requires) to God, and so teaches us that from the very beginning we are to give the very best of ourselves to God. Cain simply *"brought an offering to the LORD from the fruit of the soil"* (Gen. 4:3). He offered whatever root he could find, implying he was unwilling to acknowledge, in justice, that God deserved his best. Cain kept the best for himself. Actually, he was following his parents' selfish pattern by refusing to accept the order of reality by prioritizing himself above his creator.

Therefore, it was eminently just that God would accept Abel's offering and reject Cain's. God does not force Cain or any of us at any time to acknowledge God's priority. Rather, as we have observed, God resides and functions spiritually within all creatures, including even the human freedom of choice. To acknowledge and reverence God's priority constitutes a basic and pervasive reality for us. How often do you and I, having received freedom gratuitously from God, then use that freedom to prioritize ourselves above God or neighbor? Is Cain living again in us?

God gives Cain in verse six another chance by asking him, "Why are you so resentful?" At times, we hear God asking us similar questions: "Why do you resent your friend's success?" "Why do you seek revenge?" Perhaps our self-interest sees our friend's success as a challenge to our own. At any rate, Cain retreats further into himself and begins plotting to kill his scapegoat, Abel, whom he perceives as the source of his trouble, when actually, his enemy is his own bloated ego. He is rejected, not because Abel is accepted, but because he insists on building his grandiose self higher than God. Finally, he murders Abel to protect his inflated self.

God asks Cain, "Where is your brother, Abel?" Note, from the beginning to the present, God considers all of us sisters and brothers. The truth is, because of the myth, both brothers can be found in each of us. The question remains, which brother's life shall we live? Cain continues his self-protection by lying: "I don't know; am I my brother's keeper?" In contrast to Cain's response, our answer must be, "Yes, I am my brothers' and sisters' keeper!"

God rejects, in this instance, "an eye for an eye" form of justice (capital punishment) by refusing to execute Cain. Rather, God, with flawless justice, gives Cain, according to the myth, what he merits: loneliness. Still, to protect Cain from those who might seek retribution against him, God puts a mark, probably a tattoo, on him and defies anyone to kill Cain. God has now twice rejected death as punishment. Does God still have hope for Cain? What does this say about our thirst for the retribution we call capital punishment?

This mythic story narrates the first murder mystery, and God's consequent dispensing of justice. The author concludes sadly in Chapter 4:16, *"Cain then left the LORD's presence and settled in the land of Nod,"* meaning in Hebrew, the land of nomads, or those who live alone. Upon leaving God's presence, Cain and the Cain in all of us suffer depression, loneliness, and guilt.

Samuel Taylor Coleridge, the famed English romantic poet, penned in his poem, "The Wanderings of Cain," the following lines about a young man, wandering alone and dejected beneath the unforgiving sun and elements.

> *Encinctured with a twine of leaves,*
> *That leafy twine his only dress!*
>
> ....
>
> *It was a climate where, they say,*
> *The night is more belov'd than day.*
> *But who that beauteous Boy, beguil'd,*
> *That beauteous Boy to linger here?*
> *Alone, by night, a little child,*
> *In place so silent and so wild—*
> *Has he no friend, no loving mother near?* [1]

Violence, murder, and war (organized violence) have, dear Lord, a long history among us humans reaching back to Cain; many say violence is essential to our human nature, but you have rejected violence even from the days of Cain. We have descended not from the violent viscera of Cain but from your spiritual loins of peace. Therefore, Lord, we know that peace is possible among us. We, as your progeny, dedicate ourselves to life: overcoming violence with peace, and hostility with love. Now we pause to reflect on what practical steps we can take to promote peace in our own relationships and on a national and international scale. Amen.

CHAPTER 10

NOAH THE MARINER

I f the Ark of Noah is discovered, it will be the greatest archae-ological find in human history, the greatest event since the resurrection of Christ, and it will alter all the currents of sci-entific thought,"[1] proclaimed Melville B. Grosvenor, fifty-five year president of *National Geographic*. A few years later, astro-naut James Irwin gazed at earthen beauty from the surface of the moon and was mesmerized by a "revelation" concerning God and Bible. Later, Irwin dedicated his life to discovering histori-cal artifacts to validate the Bible. He would organize a search party to find Noah's ark on Mt. Ararat in eastern Turkey; but like many before him, he failed. Even Marco Polo, the famed four-teenth-century Venetian traveler, searched for the ark to no avail. People of otherwise sound judgment have witnessed through the centuries their dreams of finding the ark turn into nightmares of futility. Finally, the Noah's Ark Alliance offered, in 1999, one million dollars to anyone who validates the ark's discovery. To my knowledge, that offer still stands today, but before setting out for Turkey, do examine the following biblical data concerning Noah and his ark.

The story begins in Genesis 6:5 and extends through 8:29. It contains very important inconsistencies. We are told in chapter 6 that God instructs Noah to take two of all animals, male and female, into the ark. However, Noah is told in chapter 7 to take seven pairs of all clean animals and one pair of all unclean. The total would compute to hundreds of thousands of animals. Interestingly, it was only many centuries after the putative Noah that Jewish law divided animals into clean and unclean.

The Lord tells Noah that in seven days, he will send rain for forty days and forty nights. After these forty days and nights, three times Noah sends out birds every seven days, and in twenty-one days (a total of sixty-one days), the waters recede. The story, however, also states in Genesis 8:3b that in one hundred and fifty days the waters receded. Could one or the other biblical assertion be false and therefore not inspired? Hardly. Rather, scripture scholars relate this story of Noah as representing the combining of two distinct traditions named J and P. These traditions had been orally passed on for centuries. One or the other is not wrong, but both traditions employ different nuances to convey the same or similar magnificent theological meaning. The author merely includes elements from both traditions in his story. We treasure the story of the obedient Noah, but all these prehistoric stories in the first eleven chapters of Genesis are mythic. As we have seen in previous chapters, biblical myths are not designed as mere historical records but as stories that symbolize powerful theological truths.

But where did the author find the story of Noah, the flood, and the ark? Scholars assert the author was familiar with at least the outline of the Epic of Gilgamesh. This Sumerian saga was written nearly two thousand years before Genesis. Flooding was frequent and very troubling in the land of the Sumerians and presented a natural backdrop to this epic that was known throughout the ancient world. Utnapishtim, the legendary hero of the flood, tells in tablet 11 the story of the gods seeking to destroy humanity with a disastrous flood. However, Ea, a god of wisdom, tells Utnapishtim to build a huge boat and gather the seeds of all living things on the boat. A great rain fell, lasting seven days. The boat settled on a mountain and a dove, a swallow, and a raven were dispatched. Surely, no one can doubt the author of Genesis uses the heart of this epic story as a device to point out his theological message: that Noah and his companions are saved because of his obedience and goodness.

The greatness of the myth arises from its ability to reach out to men and women through the centuries even to us today. The message of the Noah myth is his initiating a new holy people who are rewarded justly for their obedience and goodness. Hopefully, today, we comprise that people.

For us, the myth prefigures the new Noah, Jesus, the Noah of all generations, present to save us in our times of storm and flood. However, as disciples of Jesus, Noah also prefigures us, for we are also called to reorder God's world in overcoming today's forces of destruction. You can find not the mere physical ark but Noah himself. Don't search, however, on Ararat but in your own spirit. The myth concludes with the arching of the rainbow (Gen. 9:13) and God's promise that no storm or trial (symbolized by the flood) will overcome us if we remain faithful to God in the obedient spirit of Noah. Noah is calling us, his children, to be of the rainbow, children of hope.

Noah, you saved all earthen dwellers by your obedience and care for God's creation. We respect, with you, the right of all God's creatures to fulfill their time span in his providence. We reject all abuse and exploitation of Mother Earth and her children in the name of an indulgent lifestyle or negligence. Accordingly, we promise to support the "heart and soul" of at least one co-dweller on God's earth and can thereby rejoice that, through this pastoring, we shall join Noah in enriching our corner of the world from the floods that threaten. Amen.

CHAPTER 11

ABRAHAM, OUR FATHER IN FAITH

Abraham, the father of the Jews! Many know Abraham only in that capacity. However, our deeper understanding of his stories reveals Abraham as the father of the faithful. Even his name (*Ay brah-ham*) means "father of a multitude," and in his day, the Hebrews were not even established as a people, much less a nation; he is, therefore, the father of desert peoples—not only of Jews, but Muslims and Christians as well. Muslims traditionally trace their lineage through Ishmael to Abraham, his father: "We shall worship the God of our fathers: Abraham, Ishmael, and Isaac"[1] (Quran II, 133). As for Christians, Paul established early on the Christian claim, *"He* [Abraham] *is our father in the sight of God, in whom he believed"* (Rom. 4:17).

Because all three traditions claim Abraham as their father, why do we brothers and sisters in the same family kill and maim each other in the name of our common divine Father whom we and Abraham, our human father, worship? Why have we allowed this

49

savagery, common to all three, to persist through the centuries? Let's look carefully into our own hearts in this matter. Isn't it true that we, the children of these traditions, have petulantly ignored the lesson of our father Abraham; namely, that all of us walk in faith with the Lord God?

This lesson has two dimensions; first, the journeying. Some scholars believe our ancient patriarchal ancestors, including Abraham, derive from a people called Apiru. They were Bedouin wanderers who migrated into and among the more settled peoples of the Fertile Crescent. Whether true or not, Abraham was certainly a journeyman traveling through a large slice of this Fertile Crescent. His migrations through thousands of desert miles from Ur in Mesopotamia north to Haran and southwest to Canaan modeled physically the spiritual journey to which all three peoples, his progeny, are called. We three are nothing if not spiritual Apiru, en route from the deserts to our own spiritual promised lands.

Secondly, Abraham leaves us a monumental lesson of faith in the Lord. He repeatedly departed comfort zones to journey into the unknown with its terrors and hardships. Why? The author of Genesis answers during Abraham's first journey of over five hundred miles of steaming desert from Ur to Haran: *"Abram went as the LORD directed him"* (Gen. 12:4). Abraham had perceived, in some way, his God calling him to "move on." Abraham heard, believed, and departed in faith. God is also calling each of us, but are we listening and journeying in faith through our deserts? This is the challenge of our lifetime.

On another occasion, God summoned Abraham to climb Mt. Moriah (later known as Mt. Zion) to sacrifice his son, whom God himself had miraculously provided. Child sacrifice to gods was common in those days, and many believe this story represents God's rejection of such an evil. Abraham loved his son more than anyone.

God had promised him the greatest of contemporary male dreams: multiple future generations, but that depended on his son Isaac's survival. Imagine his tears of trembling and terror as he raised the sword to slay dear, precious Isaac. Nevertheless, Abraham was willing to, in total faith, carry out God's order when God suddenly intervened to prevent the slaughter. Father Abraham, how desperately we need your fearless faith in these days of crisis!

Our father Abraham through these mythic stories and others is telling us that no matter the cost or deprivation, we must follow in faith the clear directives of our God. Abraham's God, our God, is a God of love. His first command is to love him by loving each other. This love arises from our faith. All three traditions rooted in Abraham subscribe to this, but then seem to lose sight of it when they resort to defending their own turf, their own tradition.

God promised our common father, Abraham, *"I will make of you a great nation, / and I will bless you; / ...All the communities of the earth / shall find blessing in you"* (Gen. 12:2–3). If we of all three camps are to participate in that blessing, then it shall be insofar as we model the faith of our father Abraham. Abraham would be shocked to witness today the paranoia, revenge, and carnage his grandchildren inflict on each other in the name of possessing or defending the land he trod and the words he inspired. He stood for faith in Adonai, and we can find Adonai in each other. Surely, we of the same father in faith can join in brother and sisterhood by forgiving, reconciling, and trusting each other just as our common God requested of Abraham, our common father.

Father Abraham, whatever the cost, you believed deeply and fully in the Word of Allah and acted on it. We, your spiritual children whom you treasure, are experiencing deadly familial suspicion and hostility based on religious and ethnic divisions, while trying to live our faith. Please, intercede with our Father to empower us to see beyond our tunneled traditions, religions, lands, and biases, and embrace your faith in our Adonai, who transcends all borders and divisions. Help us to energize our journey through these deserts of danger to our promised lands of trust, community, and embrace of each other. Amen

CHAPTER 12

ISAAC, THE PASSIVE PATRIARCH

Because ancient patriarchs are often pictured as bizarre men with unreal experiences, why concentrate on them? Closer inspection reveals their lives carry profound significance and constitute a paradigm in some way for every human being. What if you, like Sarah, the mother of Isaac, were a postmenopausal woman married to a man of senior years! A visitor in your home says you will conceive and bear a son. Wouldn't you, like Sarah, laugh heartily? However, a year later, Sarah is nursing her son Isaac, and this has become no laughing matter. Consider, however, the relationships within this family, especially between Isaac and his half brother, Ishmael, born of Abraham and Hagar, Sarah's maidservant. Many of us are members of dysfunctional families; we can learn from the efforts of this biblical family and from their mistakes.

One explanation for this biblical story refers to the Hebrew tradition of describing an outstanding person as being born in an extraordinary manner. The author of Genesis may well be telling this story as a literary device to illustrate the point that Sarah's child, Isaac, is a special person in Hebraic history. A barren woman gives birth also in the stories of Rebekah and her sons Esau and Jacob; the same, for the mother of Samson; for Hannah and her son Samuel; and finally, Elizabeth and her baby John, known later as the Baptist. Curiously, there could be only one more surpassing mode of conception; namely, a virgin conceiving and giving birth. Isaac resides in illustrious company, but despite his anonymity to many, we shall see he deserves prominence.

Surely, the most well-known story of Isaac remains his near sacrifice by Abraham his father, as we discussed in chapter 11. We are accustomed to view this story as a portrayal of Abraham, a man of faith. This is certainly true, but Arabs call this event the *Akedah*, or the binding of Isaac. They emphasize justifiably the obedient role of Isaac. However, we now reflect on Isaac from a Christian point of view.

Abraham and Isaac were climbing Mt. Moriah when Isaac, who was carrying wood for the sacrifice, asked his father that poignant question: "*Where is the sheep for the holocaust?*" (Gen. 22:7). Did he suspect his father's intent? Probably not, especially when his father responded "*God himself will provide*" (Gen. 22:8). By now, they had climbed the mountaintop (to climb the mountain signifies, biblically, meeting your God). Suddenly Abraham seized Isaac and bound him atop the wood on the altar. He raised his knife threateningly toward the boy.

The author makes no reference to Isaac's feelings, but we can certainly imagine his terror. "Why? Father, why? What have I done?" Isaac must have been overwhelmed with horror at his father's behavior. Then Yahweh staid Abraham's arm poised to slaughter the boy.

There is no need to take this story literally, but its message is spiritual dynamite! No matter how horrific or hopeless our lives seem, God will ultimately deliver us. This experience also prefigures exquisitely a central event in the New Testament. The victim is the Son. He carries the wood, has no understanding of why, and becomes the lamb for the sacrifice. Truly, Isaac prefigures Jesus of Nazareth just as you and I also at times walk in the Nazarene's afterglow by suffering our own terrors without knowing the reason, but trustful in resurrection.

Isaac appears not as a powerful or flashy patriarch but as a naive, simple man. Rebekah was chosen to be his wife; still, he remains the only monogamous patriarch. The morality of our culture does not necessarily equate with the mores of another. Monogamy was so rare in his day that one must assume Isaac, as a rather self-contained family man, stands opposed to what we know today as a "macho man." "Macho-ness" couldn't be further from the Judaic-Christian ideal. Perhaps, men patterned on Isaac stand as the men of true faith and courage.

A second revealing story of Isaac arises from his family dysfunction. Rebekah, wife of Isaac, bore two sons: Esau, the elder and holder of the birthright, and Jacob. The birthright guaranteed the holder peer-preference, certain familial honor, and doubled the inheritance of the older. Rebekah, however, preferred Jacob, and Isaac, Esau. Family alignments can be powerfully destructive if we fail to address them.

The text (Gen. 26:28) describes Rebekah playing a conspiratorial role in Jacob's wresting the birthright from Esau. She conspired with young Jacob to deceive Isaac her blind husband, and obtained for Jacob, Isaac's deathbed blessing destined for Esau, his elder son. Isaac believed he couldn't "go back on his last words," and finally with a broken heart, the dying Isaac gave Esau an inferior blessing. The text fails to mention the pain and resentment that Esau surely must have felt toward his deceivers. For years, the two brothers remained embittered: all this, because of pathological family alignment.

Rebekah truly manipulated Isaac, but despite her conspiring and his naïveté, he is remembered as a patriarch of Israel. God teaches us, through Isaac, an astounding lesson that few are willing to accept. Even with all our neurotic fears and biases, God still accepts us just as we are. This is not to say we ought not to strive for daily resurrectional transformation, but it does say that at this very moment, despite our shadows, you and I are loved and embraced by this God of ultimate kindness. Finally, we read that after a full life, Isaac died. His two sons, finally bonded with Rebekah their mother, buried him. How unfortunate that the reconciliation of two or more family members follows only after the death of the mutually beloved! Beware of such heartbreaking delay in your family.

Place yourself in the presence of the Lord and of that family member from whom you have experienced greatest estrangement. Words and action may have delivered piercing hurt to both of you. Now, however, the Lord of forgiveness is present. You will need colossal courage and understanding to seek healing, but the Lord is present. Determine what you can do, perhaps by seeking professional help, to promote peace and reconciliation in your family in the name of Isaac; and the Lord is present.

CHAPTER 13

JACOB AND REBEKAH, FAMILY CONSPIRATORS

Make no mistake: loving and the joy of it are worth the pain. However, isn't it also true that no one can hurt us as deeply as the one we love? Loving carries its own "baggage," namely, vulnerability. Therefore, our family members, if so inclined, are uniquely positioned to plunge a dagger into our breaking heart. This certainly applies to the family of Isaac. We saw in chapter 12 that Isaac appeared naive and weak; Rebekah, wife of Isaac, headstrong and cunning; Jacob, compliant; and Esau, embittered. What an unholy, neurotic mix! Still, Jacob would eventually become known as the father of the twelve tribes, and it was founded on deception in a troubled and divided family. Yet, in this embattled biblical family, God was mysteriously present. He resides in the same way in our families despite our dysfunction. Drawing harmony from chaos seems to be God's chosen career from Genesis 1 through the final biblical page, and provides a model for our lives as well.

Jacob had just received his dying father's blessing. His brother, Esau, was furious with him for having stolen both his birthright and Isaac's final blessing. Now, with possible guilt, probable depression, and certain fear, Jacob traveled northeast toward Haran. True to form, Rebekah had conspired with husband Isaac to direct Jacob, because of Esau's anger, to their old home in search of a wife. En route, Jacob rested at a shrine in Luz where he dreamed of a stairway planted in the earth and stretching into the heavens (Gen. 28:10–22). Messengers from God were ascending and descending the stairway, and God stood next to Jacob at the foot of the stairway: a dynamic symbol of God communicating powerfully with Jacob and his descendants. God exclaimed that he would remain with Jacob, multiply his seed over the earth, and provide him the land on which they stood. Just imagine God selecting for greatness a man who had shown weakness and deviousness with his conniving mother against his own brother. God, however, knows in-depth the heart of each of us. Jacob responded to God that if he protected and supported him on his journey, "Of everything you give me, I will faithfully return a tenth part to you" (Gen. 28:22). This represents the biblical Hebraic justification for tithing. Jacob renamed the place Bethel, meaning "where God dwells." Consider your own life journey to this point, the Bethel of your life. Surely, you shall be open from this moment to God's dwelling ever more intimately in your heart. However, what does he ask of you, a spiritual child of Jacob?

Jacob continued on to Haran. There, he encountered his uncle Laban, whose daughter he wished to make his wife. He remained with Laban, working for him seven years for the hand of Rachel. Not surprisingly, Laban was able, by substituting Leah for her sister Rachel, to trick Jacob into another seven years due to his timidity. Eventually, after several harrowing experiences, Jacob acquired Rachael, and they departed Laban for Bethel.

The author of Genesis then relates one of the most famous and meaningful stories in the entire Hebrew Testament. Jacob learned that Esau, now estranged from him, was approaching with four hundred soldiers. Jacob had no war party to resist, but only his two wives, two slave girls, eleven children, and farm animals. Terrified, he dispatched his servants with all his flocks as a bribe offering to Esau. Fearful and alone, Jacob awaited Esau's wrath.

Jacob then had a dream with which biblical scholars have grappled for centuries (Gen. 32:23–31). A man (Yahweh's messenger) appeared and wrestled with Jacob the entire night. The combat became fierce, and Jacob would not "give in." Finally, in desperation, the man struck Jacob, and, as a sign of the combat, dislocated his hip. This symbolic struggle signifies the lifelong ferocious, psychological, and spiritual battles Jacob and each of us must wage in facing life's trials. Though injured, Jacob prevailed, and from this moment on, nothing could defeat Jacob's trust in God and self. Do you, though wounded, have the courage in your desperate challenges to trust as did Jacob and, like him, become a "winner"?

Jacob, now wise and courageous, saw Esau and his army approaching and threatening. The author describes an emotional and powerful episode. Alone, *"He himself* [Jacob] *went on ahead… bowing to the ground seven times, until he reached his brother. Esau ran to meet him, embraced him, and flinging himself on his neck, kissed him as he wept"* (Gen. 33:3–4). Trust had overcome fear.

This story of Jacob carries profound meaning for us, particularly in our darkest hours of weakness and insecurity. After taking all due precaution, we are called to persevere by placing our trust in God and going forward in his wisdom and power. We shall prevail in the end, for *"If God is for us, who can be against us"* (Rom. 8:31).

Consider that greatest worry with which you are today consumed. Have you done all you can to solve this worry? If so, place yourself in the presence of Jacob and your loving God. Now, comes your "Jacobian" struggle. Courageously, place your worry in God's hands; tell him you shall worry no longer. You shall not take that worry back, for you trust in him. You have done all you can, and now it's in the hands of the Lord. Remember the words of another who struggled with life: "Do not be afraid any longer, little flock, for your Father is pleased to give you the kingdom" (Luke 12:32).

CHAPTER 14

OUR JUDAIC-CHRISTIAN COVENANTS ENDURE

We referred in an earlier chapter to Pinocchio, the wooden marionette created by Geppetto, the wood-carver, from a story written by Carlo Collodi. Pinocchio had no value, nor rights, except those given him by Geppetto, who carved him from wood. Even more than Pinocchio, we have no value or rights except those given gratuitously by God, who continues to fashion us from utter chaos. He is more our Geppetto than Geppetto is to Pinocchio. Certainly, no one would agree to a contract with another who has, like Pinocchio, no value or rights, but our God has done exactly that. He has even inspired authors to detail his agreement in what is called the Covenant.

The parties to human or corporate contracts promise to exchange properties of approximate equal value; for example, you have contracted to purchase a house for one hundred thousand dollars, considered by both parties to be its true value. However, the biblical covenant (a covenant surpasses a contract) stipulates that

God promises a wonderful land flowing with milk and honey. His Pinocchio, the Hebrew tribes, must merely follow his law to which they are already obliged because he owns them.

The Lord God begins the foundational story of covenant by telling Noah and his family to enter the ark to be saved from the flood, which they do. As the waters subside, the author portrays the rainbow as God's sign of his covenant with all mankind: flood will never again destroy us. It's helpful for us to acknowledge that, centuries later, we remain as believing spiritual progeny of Noah, whom the waters of death and destruction can never harm.

The next pivotal episode in this journey of covenant occurs in Genesis 17: the Lord God exclaims to Abram, *"I am God the Almighty. Walk in my presence and be blameless. Between you and me I will establish my covenant, and I will multiply you exceedingly"* (vv. 1–2). He continues, *"I will give to you and to your descendants after you the land in which you are now staying, the whole land of Canaan* (v. 8)....*Circumcise the flesh of your foreskin, and that shall be the mark of the covenant between you and me"* (v. 11). God has now further detailed the provisions of this covenant and given its sign: circumcision. Each of us remains heir to the covenant with God. For those who believe they don't participate because they are not circumcised or Jewish, recall Paul's words to the Colossians 2:11: *"In him you were also circumcised with a circumcision not administered by hand...*[but] *with the circumcision of Christ."* God is inviting each one of us to a more significant circumcision of the heart that is symbolic of our personal and communal covenant with himself.

"Place the stones here," shouted Moses to his assistant. "This altar must go right here!" Moses was directing the building of an altar at the foot of Mt. Sinai as described in Exodus 24. It was the famed scene of the Ratification of the Covenant. Then Moses explained to the people all the *"Words and ordinances of the Lord"* (Exod. 24:3).

They responded, *"All that the LORD has said, we will heed and do"* (Exod. 24:7). Whereupon, Moses forced twelve stone slabs into the earth, one for each of the twelve tribes. He then had young bulls prepared for sacrifice. He splashed half their blood on the altar, and the people understood God had joined them in sacred covenant. Moses then sprinkled the remaining blood on the people, and they understood they were pledging their part in sealing this covenant. The Israelites struggled throughout their entire subsequent history to keep this covenant of doing whatever the Lord told them. You and I participate in this same struggle.

Jesus, however, improves on this Hebraic covenant, *"To that same degree has Jesus* [also] *become the guarantee of an* [even] *better covenant"* (Heb. 7:22). Jesus did everything the Lord had told him, and kept fully his part of the covenant, which elevates him above all humankind. He also formed, not in the blood of bulls, but in his own blood, a new covenant. This new covenant is written on the heart of every human being. It's no wonder the author of Hebrews writes, *"When he speaks of a 'new' covenant, he declares the first one obsolete. And what has become obsolete and has grown old is close to disappearing"* (8:13). Yes, by living the terms of the new covenant, we have fulfilled and surpassed the terms of the old covenant. This is our calling and privilege as members of the Christian Tradition.

Circumcision remains for Jews a sign of their covenant. Baptism is the sign of the Christian covenant, of our acceptance of God's terms: God gifts himself to us now and forever, and we modern Pinocchios covenant to live his life as embodied in Christ.

We suggest you and/or your families ritualize monthly a renewal of your covenant. This practice guarantees greater familial unity and love. One such ritual could include extinguishing all lights except for a lighted candle. Begin with a prayer; then read Exodus 24:3–8 and Luke 22:14–20. Pause briefly in silence after each reading to absorb the wisdom of its meaning.

Each person then renews silently or vocally her or his personal covenant with Abba. A final prayer from the heart of a family member commits you and/or your family in solemn covenant with Abba forever.

CHAPTER 15

THE EXODUS: BON VOYAGE!

We have all traveled on many journeys: some for business and some for pleasure, some brief and some for an extended period. Such journeys reflect the wisdom of the Bible's central theme: movement from the centrality of ego to the Lord. Serious reflection on the Hebrew Testament reveals the Exodus as its central event. Truly, this journey from slavery in Egypt to freedom in the Promised Land "paradigms" both the destiny of communal humanity and the destiny of each of us. Further, it portrays also the rigors of our journey, and its surpassing joy. Most importantly, the Exodus shows us how to navigate and reach this Promised Land.

Much of the history of the Exodus is shrouded in mystery: the number of Hebrews who actually departed Egypt, when they left, and what exact route they took, for example. However, most scholars place the final exodus of four to five thousand Hebrews during the reign of Ramesses II, about 1290–1250 BCE, but the historical facts surrounding the Exodus play "second fiddle" to its supernal meaning. The Exodus seeks to answer for every human that pivotal question arising in our daily journey and recorded in Exodus 17:7: *"Is the LORD in our midst or not?"*

The author of Exodus proclaims his response in chapter 4 verses 1–5. The Lord God had just told Moses to lead his people out of Egypt, but Moses resisted: *"Suppose they will not believe me, nor listen to my plea?"* (v. 1). Thereupon, the Lord transformed Moses' walking staff into a snake, saying, *"This* [the transforming staff] *will take place so that they may believe"* (v. 5). The staff and its transformation become in this story symbolic of Yahweh's enduring presence. From this moment, Moses and Aaron used this staff to overcome daunting obstacles. God is calling us to surmount our trials through the symbolism of the same staff: the presence of God in our midst.

The Hebrews departed Egypt only to encounter the Sea of Reeds. Scripture scholars discovered generations ago that the Hebrew word *Yam Suph* means not the "Red Sea" (a mistranslation) but the "Sea of Reeds." Thus, the Hebrews actually came to a vast marshy area (probably part of the delta of the Nile). Then the Hebrews spotted Pharaoh's army bearing down upon them from the rear. How wide was this marsh? How deep? Could they chance the crossing? They were hopelessly trapped. Have you ever felt such entrapment? Forced by very human circumstances, Moses encouraged his people to trust in the Lord and go forth into the fearsome waters. Holding his staff high, he led them through the murky waters to safety. Pharaoh's army tried to follow in their chariots, but the tidal waters rose, and the chariots sank in the mire: all this occurred as the Hebrews watched Moses extend the staff of the Lord over the waters.

The author of Exodus employs obvious symbolic prose. This writing style, as we have seen in previous events, does not preclude a natural explanation; however, the staff, symbolizing Yahweh's saving presence, always plays a leading role. The miracle was not so much a physical interruption of natural law as it was the realization by the Hebrews of Yahweh's presence in a natural event. The scripture scholar Gerhard von Rad writes, "The experiences of the world were for [Israel] always divine experiences."[1] Don't look for the miraculous in your life; seize the staff of God's miraculous presence and move forward in trust!

Later, the author describes in chapter 17 the event at Massah in the desert where the Hebrews complained bitterly to Moses of their terrible thirst. *"Why did you ever make us leave Egypt? ...to have us die here of thirst with our children and our livestock?"* (v. 3). Doesn't this sound like many of us blaming God or others for our wayward thirsts in our own dreadful deserts of desolation?

"Moses prayed, and God answered, 'Go over there in front of the people...holding...the staff with which you struck the river. (v. 5) ... Strike the rock, and the water will flow from it'" (v. 6). Water from rock—sounds unbelievable, even absurd, unless one is a Bedouin. These natives of the desert know that when one finds a spring in the desert, he marks it with a rock to benefit future travelers. Yes, Moses could have found such a rock, and by removing it, water gushed forth. Picture these Hebrew men, women, and children shouting with joy, dancing, and drinking midst the dry desert dunes. Again, the Hebrews see, with spiritual insight, the saving presence of Yahweh in a natural desert phenomenon. One can certainly interpret uncritically these events and others of the Exodus as miraculous preternatural happenings, but this does not explain the prominence of the staff of Yahweh signifying God's presence.

Does Exodus 17:7, *"Is the LORD in our midst or not,"* reflect the meaning of the entire Exodus? These events, understood with the "third eye of the spirit," trumpet lustily, "Yes, God is in our midst!" Furthermore, Yahweh is present, not only in the midst of the natural events of the Exodus, but today in our daily journeying through our deserts. The illustrious martyr, Oscar Romero, exclaims, "What God does for Israel, he wants to do for all peoples: [to lead all of us to the Promised Land.]"[2] Truly, the paradigm of all human history.

The Hebraic Exodus lasted forty years; just as Noah was forty days in the ark; just as Moses departed the people for forty days atop Sinai; just as Jesus was subjected to forty days of temptation in his desert. The number forty signifies more than just a numerical reference; it signifies a long period of trial. Consider their desert as not just a topographical reference but the desert of trial, discouragement, and desperation. Truly, all us humans tread through our own deserts of forty years en route to our promised land. And we hold in our hands the same staff: the presence of Abba.

Only two Hebrews, Joshua and Kaleb, made it to the Promised Land, and they alone demonstrated unconquerable trust in God's presence midst the storms of the desert. For most of the Hebrews and us, we find our promised land in the journey itself, in the mystery of seeing God ever present in the blinding, swirling storms of our deserts.

Yahweh, you were the staff to the Hebrews and now to us. As we, individually and as nation, family, and church, plod through our dark and stormy deserts, we know in our souls you are with us. Help us realize acutely your presence in our hearts so that we can, with resolute purpose and trust in you, complete triumphantly our journey. Joshua and Kaleb, guide us through the waters, thirst, and rock to our promised land of joy forever in Christ, our Messiah, our staff of God's presence. Amen.

CHAPTER 16

MOSES, THE TRANSFORMED JOURNEYMAN

Our previous chapter teaches that if the Bible is about anything, it's about journey and transformation; in this chapter, we see Moses as the greatest journeyman. We are surely aware of his leading the Hebrew exodus from Egypt to the Promised Land, which is the most renowned event of the Hebrew Testament. But wait! Many of us have not reflected on his personal journey of transformation, which proves even more impacting.

The origin of the three-month-old Hebrew male child (later to be called Moses) is remarkably similar to the origin of the pagan king, Sargon of Akkad, one thousand years prior. Sargon's mother placed him at birth in a basket sealed with mud and cast it adrift on the river. He was found and raised by another. Recalling that Sargon, an early empire builder, influenced culture profoundly for a millennium, the author of Exodus could well have modeled the story of Moses' birth on Sargon's.

The Pharaoh of Egypt ordered all newly born Hebrew males to be destroyed. Therefore, the mother of the infant hid her son for three months and then placed him in a basket lined with slime and pitch along the edge of the riverbank. One can not imagine a more demeaning beginning; however, Pharaoh's daughter found the infant and, unknowingly, gave him to his own mother to nurse. After weaning, the mother returned the infant to Pharaoh's daughter. This pagan woman named him Moses, and raised him. This schizoid beginning with its attendant insecurities surely impacted the growing Moses negatively, and perhaps contributed psychically to his later speech impediment. Like Moses, you and I stand largely as the product of both our genealogy and early experience. Consider objectively the light and shadows of your childhood and their influence on you today.

Years later, the adult Moses happened upon an Egyptian abusing a Hebrew slave. Furious, Moses looked furtively about. Seeing no one, he slew the Egyptian on the spot. Moses buried the corpse beneath the sands and slinked away. The truth has, however, a way of surfacing, and the next day, Moses realized someone saw the crime. Even Pharaoh had heard of it and was now searching for Moses, the murderer. Frightened and disheartened, Moses fled by night into the desert. Truly, a dark desert of despair awaits those who journey alone.

Eventually, Moses climbed Mt. Horeb (Mt. Sinai) and encountered the Lord God in a flaming bush. The Lord incredibly told Moses to return to Egypt and lead his people, the Hebrews, out. Moses was astounded and "begged off." After all, he was wanted for murder by the Egyptians, distrusted by the Hebrews, and could hardly speak clearly. Yahweh would not quit, however, and chose, as usual, the least likely candidate. Yahweh responded, "I will be with you!" Moses couldn't believe his God-given destiny but, in blind faith, followed its path anyway.

Do we not resemble Moses? Bruised by the perceived rejections of those we love and trust, we tend to lose faith and love of ourselves. "I'm too old or too young; I'm ill; I'm alone; I have no ability; it's impossible that God is calling me to lead my relatives, friends, and neighbors to goodness and peace." If we trust only ourselves, our self-doubt might be justified; but with God's presence within, our possibilities soar.

God responds to our self-doubt as he did to Moses: "I am with you." He fulfills to you his promise to Jacob in Genesis 28:15: *"Know that I am with you; I will protect you wherever you go....I will never leave you until I have done what I have promised you."* Whereupon, Moses realized finally his success did not depend as much on himself as it did on Yahweh's dwelling within him, which would endure always and through every desert. Moses had become a leader by giving himself up to divine leadership. You and I are also called to hear the Lord's voice from the flaming bush.

Elizabeth Barrett Browning writes of this exquisitely:

....

Earth's crammed with heaven,

And every common bush afire with God:

But only he who sees, takes off his shoes,

The rest, just sit round it, and pluck blackberries, [1]

....

Moses returned to Egypt, and with the staff of Yahweh in hand (symbolizing Yahweh's supportive presence), he inspired his people to leave Egypt for a land that he said Yahweh had promised them. What an amazing achievement for a boy of the mud who, flawed and distrusted, became a man of God. Moses led them on journey forty years through their physical and spiritual deserts. Therefore, the Hebrews were not the only ones who journeyed. Moses himself had transformed from murdering to saving; from fear to courage; from being self-centered to being Yahweh-centered.

Moses guided the Hebrews through myriad terrors, including thirst, hunger, snakes, and hostile armies, but he asserted their own fear and distrust had proven their most difficult enemy. Moses convinced them to overcome their self-doubt by trusting in Yahweh. Reflecting on their challenges should convince us that Yahweh encourages us also to continue our desert journey to wholeness.

Moses led the Hebrews east of the Dead Sea through the Plains of Moab to Mt. Nebo. Much of the book of Deuteronomy recalls this portion of the journey and the final event in Moses' life. Moses, now an aged and fragile man, climbed the mountain and addressed his beloved Hebraic brothers and sisters for the last time. He, who had extinguished life years before, called on heaven and earth to witness his words: *"Choose life, then, that you and your descendants may live, by loving the LORD, your God, heeding his voice, and holding fast to him"* (Deut. 30:19–20). Then, he blessed them, saying, *"Israel has dwelt securely, / and the fountain of Jacob has been undisturbed. / In a land of grain and wine, / where the heavens drip with dew. / How fortunate you are, O Israel!"* (33:28–29). Then, Yahweh showed Moses the Promised Land in the distance, saying, *"I have let you feast your eyes upon it, but you shall not cross over"* (34:4).

Yahweh's decision might seem harsh, but consider the events at Meribah in the desert (Num. 20:10–11). The Hebrews were dying of thirst and complained bitterly and threateningly to Moses. Moses prayed and remembered, as noted in our previous chapter, the desert tradition of marking a watery spring with a rock for future desert travelers. Moses found such a rock the next morning. Following Yahweh's intimation, he gathered all the people together and struck the rock with his rod, signifying Yahweh's presence. The author of Numbers declares, however, that Moses struck the rock *twice*, implying that Moses doubted the efficacy of the first blow, and therefore Yahweh's effective presence. This doubt subverted the fundamental theme of the entire Exodus experience; namely, to trust in God's saving presence despite whatever threatening circumstances they encountered. This doubt cost Moses his chance to cross into the Promised Land (Num. 27:14). Similarly, our lack of trust can prevent us from crossing into our promised land, which for us is the life of the Risen Christ.

Moses teaches us a precious lesson that, no matter how egregious our troubles, we can retain faith in the Lord, knowing he will lead us through the desert to our promised land. One can picture the venerable Moses viewing through tears of joy this land of bounty of which he had dreamed for so many years. Now, with his life's ambition fulfilled and journey complete, Moses died en route to another promised land (Deut. 34:6). To this day, Moses still calls each of us to transform in our deserts and to lead others through theirs.

Oh sainted Moses, you have told us to choose life by loving the Lord our God despite our desolate deserts. We understand this to mean that we must preserve and enhance all life wherever it is found. We shall cast down the walls of division erected through war, misunderstanding, self-doubt, hostility, and much more. We hereby consecrate ourselves to promote life from womb to tomb, and through this, we trust we shall find life and enter it with you in our eternal promised land. Amen.

CHAPTER 17

HAIL,
THE ARK OF THE COVENANT!

U zzah, don't touch it!" cried Ahio, but it was too late. *"God struck him on that spot, and he died there before God"* (2 Sam. 6:7). Uzzah and Ahio had been transporting the Ark of the Covenant on a cart pulled by oxen. When the cart began to tip, Uzzah reached out to correct the endangered ark, and it cost him his life. Surely, if we don't understand the real meaning of the aforementioned text, God's action is not only reprehensible but condemnable. The text challenges the literalism of our fundamentalist friends. Actually, the author, writing this story in typical Hebraic literary genre, is using hyperbole to inform his readers of the extraordinary reverence the Hebrews paid the ark.

One might question why we would include a chapter about a box carried by Hebrews over three thousand years ago that no longer exists. The answer lies in the aforementioned biblical story of Uzzah. If the Hebraic author of Samuel places such surpassing dignity on the ark, such that it can't even be touched, then certainly it ranks as one of the seventy most important components of the Bible.

The ark finds its origin in the famous "meeting tent" of the Hebrews. Exodus 33 describes Moses and his lieutenants erecting wooden frames and veils in a sizeable rectangular area outside their campsite in the desert to house the Ark of the Covenant. Any Hebrew could pray there, but when Moses entered the meeting tent, all remaining community members would stand before their tents and bow in worship toward the meeting tent.

A guard watched over the ark, which was really a gold-plated wooden box, about 4 x 4 x 2. When the Israelites moved camp, the ark was carried at the head of the column, and Moses would lead the community, chanting, *"Arise, O LORD, that your enemies may be scattered"* (Num. 10:35). Different traditions called it respectively the Ark of the Covenant or the Ark of Testimony, both titles indicating God's immediate presence among them. This belief may have come from its containing the two tablets of the law from Mt. Sinai, but more likely, from their growing belief that God resided on the two golden cherubim (angels) that surmounted the ark on each end. So, the ark, empowering them to overcome their enemies, led them through their desert. Picture the extraordinary sight of several thousand people with goats and sheep wandering through a forbidding wilderness while following a golden box carried on a litter. These Hebrews were so different from us, for they acted on their intense belief in God's presence. This empowered their incredible accomplishments.

As the Israelites prepared for their pivotal crossing into Canaan, priests carried the ark through the river Jordan, which they successfully bridged. They also carried it for seven days around the city of Jericho until "its walls fell," and the city was captured. Did its walls collapse physically? Not according to archaeologists, but the Israelites believed they overcame the city because of the presence of Yahweh in the ark, and so, for them, the "walls came tumbling down." Is it possible that our life-long battle consists of breaching and tearing down the walls that have been erected among us.

After occupying Canaan, the Israelites kept the Ark of the Covenant at Shiloh where the tribe celebrated their religious feasts. There, the ark served to center the tribal confederacy in the worship of Yahweh. The ark demonstrated their commitment to Yahweh, and when they were threatened, they turned to the ark for inspiration in Yahweh's saving presence. If only we, when severely challenged in our sands of struggle, would turn to Abba, to discover his courage has become ours.

However, as the Israelites' fidelity to Yahweh wavered, the ark was eventually captured by the Philistines, their ancient enemy. The Philistines then experienced severe reversals and came to believe the presence of the ark had caused such great havoc among them. They were relieved to return the ark. Finally, in a memorable scene, King David brought the ark to Jerusalem, his new capital city, with great fanfare and festival. Rejoicing, he danced in procession in the city streets before the ark. When criticized for this display, David replied, "I was dancing before the Lord!" It is sad that today so many of our liturgies with Christ really present generate little interest and no dance of joy. Eventually, the ark was placed in the temple, not to be moved again until its destruction by the Babylonians in 587 BCE.

Why do I share this history of the Ark of the Covenant? Consider its name. By housing the tablets of the law, the ark embodies the covenant between Yahweh and Israel and locates physically the heart of its relationship to Yahweh. For us, Jesus the Christ more than assumes the role of the ark by locating in his person the new covenant between Abba and humanity.

The history of the ark foreshadows the life of each of us and our institutions. It symbolizes the theme that good things happen in this life to those who follow the Lord. Jesus translated this to mean that following the Lord ensures final and full victory, not necessarily good times in the present life. Following Jesus, we struggle, fail, rise, and finally embrace Yahweh our Father, despite our appearing to become silent and lost beneath the sands. The history of the ark, also silent and lost beneath the sandy dunes, still speaks of Yahweh's presence in the Hebrews' lives and our wavering attempt to live his presence in ours.

Father of all ages and peoples, the ark symbolized your presence among your chosen ones. Help us, also your chosen, to realize our entire lives are shaped by the measure of our realization and response to your presence. Whether our days are spent in desert or oasis, you reside with us. Each of us stands as the ark of your presence, and I shall live today in its aura. Amen.

CHAPTER 18

OUR WARRIOR GOD?

How would you describe God in one word? Ask nearly any informed Christian, and he or she would respond, "God is love," referring to 1 John 4:16. Jesus especially conceived of God as love: *"Whoever loves me will keep my word, and my Father will love him, and we will come to him and make our dwelling with him"* (John 14:23).

Despite this, the Bible boldly preaches murderous violence by Yahweh in multiple texts; for example, *"When the LORD your God, delivers it [the city] into your hand, put every male in it to the sword; but the women and children and livestock and all else in it that is worth plundering you may take as your booty, and you may use this plunder of your enemies which the LORD, your God, has given you"* (Deut. 20:13–14). The Lord thunders menacingly even against his own chosen people: *"The corpses of this people [Judah] will be food for the birds of the sky and the beasts of the field, which no one will drive away. In the cities of Judah and in the streets of Jerusalem I will silence the cry of joy, the cry of gladness, the voice of the bridegroom and the voice of the bride; for the land will be turned to rubble"* (Jer. 7:33–34). Does our God of love really command violence in the same breath? We could ask in our vernacular, "Is God schizoid?" And what of similar texts from the Quran (the holy book of Islam) that might have led in some way to the notes the terrorists of 9/11 carried that fateful morning: "When boarding the plane, say 'This raid is for Allah!' Seconds before hitting the target, shout, 'There is no God but Allah!'" One such text from the Quran proclaims the following: "When you battle disbelievers, then smite their necks....If Allah willed, he could have punished them [without you]" (Surah XLVII, 4).

In the light of these texts from the Bible and the Quran, why do we Christians and Jews condemn only those from the Quran and ignore similar texts of divine violence from the Bible? Could this be one more psychological projection on Muslims? Hopefully, we can see more clearly the terrible need for followers of every religion to understand with ever greater wisdom the priorities of our God of love in our relationships with him and each other of different faiths.

In these days of often shallow and/or disordered religion, it's imperative for us, whether of East or West, to understand critically such sacred texts. They are written by human authors of varied cultures, struggling in religion's own evolutionary process to understand and touch our God of love in ever more authentic ways. It's not that our God is a God of violence; he isn't. But our understanding of the Lord, while maturing, is doing so at a lethally slow pace.

We noted in chapter 6 our human ancestors worshipped God long before any sacred texts were canonized. Consider the words of Percy Bysshe Shelley, the inspired nineteenth-century English poet: "The desire of the moth for the star, of the night for the morrow, the devotion to something afar, from the sphere of our sorrow."[1] Eons before writing was even imagined, a human-divine relationship was taking shape. This relationship has taken many varied forms, including today's Christian, Jewish, and Islamic denominations.

Most believers of all faiths describe human life as our journey into or at least toward the Divine. If we truly are journeying toward a God of love, we cannot allow egregious texts (even biblical) to steer us in an opposite direction. Despite certain fundamentalist beliefs, God does supersede our texts. Further, it's not surprising that biblical authors apply to God those triumphal dimensions they believe will help solve their contemporary cultural crises even if it includes aggression. Thus, the author of Deuteronomy posits, in the cited text, Yahweh commanding that all males, potentially soldiers, be slaughtered and everyone and everything else of value, seized. Furthermore, Jeremiah is trying desperately in our quoted text to convince the Judeans to forsake their wanton ways and return to Yahweh. He feels divine threat will prove the most effective argument in turning the Judeans' thoughts toward the security of Israel. We must critique all these texts in the light of the cultures of the authors' contemporary human religious impulse. How dishonest to lift a text from its context and an author from his context!

As humanity continues its intended journey into truth and love, it has taken many bizarre detours, often because of such texts. We have at times mocked Yahweh, Christ, Mohammed, the Bible, the Quran, the Torah, and other sacred writings by supposedly defending them with crusades, persecution, nationalism, terrorism, and excommunications. We continue, even at this moment, with destructive behavior in the name of God, while professing at the same time his love and forgiveness.

Let's not blame only our houses of worship or our national structures, for many of us either support or tolerate such policies in them and even in our own relationships. Search profoundly your own motives, convictions, and behavior. I recall standing next to a priest presider just before our Christian celebration when an apparently Christian woman approached and cursed him in the name of Christ for his being gay. Hurt and silent, he turned to begin anew his tortured journey toward the Table of the Lord. She spoke these words in the home of Jesus who said, *"Go out to the highways and hedgerows and make people come in that my home may be filled"* (Luke 14:23). As she projected her anti-Christian odium on him, I reflected on whether this could be considered a mini 9/11 attack and whether I harbored similar attitudes toward others.

In our challenging journey, we must acknowledge most importantly the nature of the journey, which is growth. If the biblical, Quranic, or Upanishadic author responds in his own crisis with savagery and claims God as its author, then surely we are compelled to examine this text critically. Akbar Ahmed, Chair of Islamic study at American University, stated as much when interviewed on August 12, 2006. Hopefully, our journey has carried us beyond simplistic acceptance of hate and vengeance being representative of our God of love. Our relationship with this God in his sons and daughters of all religious traditions stands preeminent, and we must never allow its fracture even by Church, Bible, Mosque, Quran, Torah, or whatever. Their task is to urge us onward along this path of approach to Divine Love, through human love.

Ours is *not* a "Warrior God," but a loving God, for love is the supreme dimension of human nature, and thereby qualifies best to approach the Lord. Our journey toward such a God of love constitutes healthy religion. Such religion seems in short supply these days, but *we* could decide this moment to reverse that in our lives by revering, as God does, all those whom we meet today, along the way. More specifically, we could reach out today to someone of another faith with the Good News of healing, admiration, and respect for his or her faith. We will then be playing our role in the universal, evolving process. The journey is long and arduous for all sisters and brothers, no matter our spiritual affiliation. However, we can temper its severity by heeding the counsel of Mother Teresa: "There is only one God and He is God of all....I've always said, we should help a Hindu be a better Hindu, a Muslim become a better Muslim, and a Catholic a better Catholic."[2]

Oh God of all healthy religion, help us to understand, with ever-growing wisdom, your heart of love. Although we do at times inflict our hostility on others in your name, forgive us. Despite this ignorance, we shall banish enmity and reach out in love to so-called enemies. We shall search, not for vengeance, but for appropriate ways to prove our love. In this way, we shall participate in overcoming the forces of evil and proving you are a God of love. Amen.

CHAPTER 19

SINGING PSALMS
AND LIVING LITURGY

Return to the time of Jesus and imagine yourself present in early October at the Feast of Tabernacles in Jerusalem. What a jubilant celebration of Yahweh's gift of rain that produced this year's rich harvest of grapes, wheat, and barley! You, with thousands of others, have come to the city with palms, branches, and willows. The faithful arch these above to form a canopy in the massive open-air courts of the temple and through the narrow streets of Jerusalem. Soon, the high priest approaches in solemn procession with many other priests and Levites from the temple to the Pool of Siloam about one quarter mile distant. He fills a golden goblet with water and returns with his priestly entourage beneath this leafy ceiling of green. You have been fortunate to find a spot, only three or four rows from the front of the multitude surrounding the grandiose, multi-tiered altar of sacrifice in the temple. Look! The high priest and his retinue are parading seven times around the pedestal beneath the altar. Now, he is ascending to its summit to pour the oil ceremoniously over the altar. You join, as one with the crowd, bending forward toward the altar with the fronds and willows in reverence.

Everyone is caught up in powerful song, singing with such volume the entire city seems to be bursting in sacred praise of Yahweh. The song is the "Hallel," Psalms 113–118. Praise! Praise! Jubilant praise! The multitudes are so caught up in this magnificent crescendo that it seems the very walls of the temple quiver, and your soul is exalted to heavenly heights. This is liturgy at its best, for we are participating and are consumed with our interaction and relationship to Yahweh. The scene reminds us of the admonition of the Second Vatican Council: "Mother Church desires earnestly that all the faithful be led to that full, conscious and active participation in liturgical celebrations which is demanded by the very nature of liturgy."[1]

Worship such as this bound the Israelites together as a people. They prayed the psalms throughout their glorious liturgies as well as in their personal lives. For them to ignore the Psalms was to ignore the soul of Judaism. It was no wonder that Jesus, a faithful Jew, prayed the psalms so fervently, and even intoned three psalms on his wooden bier. Following this tradition, thousands of Christian clerics and monks have chanted these psalms daily for two thousand years.

What are the Psalms? Songs—yes, and much more. The Psalms are hymns in prayer form, and prayers in hymnal form. The Psalms reflect the various relationships Israel and later mankind have with God and each other. Although praise, thanksgiving, and lament represent the usually quoted division of the Psalms, they actually reflect all our deepest moods: trust, hurt, desperation, joy, etc. This is why the Psalter is always current—because it tells the story of our deepest archetypes and ever-changing relationships to God and each other whether desperate, troubled, thankful, or joyous. We find in the Psalms challenge as well as solace. The Psalms, the prayer of the soul, reflect the soul of prayer.

David of the tenth century BCE is purported to be the author of at least seventy-four of the one hundred fifty psalms. All, however, reflect the human soul of antiquity. When praying the Psalms, listen carefully, and you will hear David, Jeremiah, John the Baptist, and even Jesus praying with you.

We of the West, especially of the United States, are strongly individualistic. This includes our relationship to God. We are easily entrapped into thinking in terms of "I and God." The Israelites, however, related to Yahweh primarily as members of Israel. Since the Covenant, they considered themselves as one body relating to Yahweh. The Psalms achieved their importance because they formed the official language by which the Hebrew family related to God. In a sense, the Psalms formed their bridge to Yahweh.

Because our concept of the Body of Christ, one family under God, is not generally appreciated, our bridge as a people to God and each other is more tenuous. We, as Christians, have liturgy as our foremost communal bridge to God. Unfortunately, our liturgy breathes too often of regulation, repetition, and coercion. Today's liturgy rises from the printed page and correct ritual. Consider the following example: You are suffering deep pain from a bitter divorce or terrible loneliness, or your family is embittered with hostility. You come to Sunday liturgy as though on your knees, desperately seeking counsel and support of God and community. Then, the liturgy repeats the same words you've heard for many years, read from the same book, by the same person, and with the same inflection. Forty minutes later, you are dismissed. Does this address your needs, soothe your anguish, challenge your soul, or encourage your return? Such an extreme scenario certainly does not always reflect our celebrations, but the truth is that, like the Psalms, effective liturgy has the power to touch our souls and carry us to human archetypal heights. When liturgy ignores the passion and depths of human experience, it ignores humanity. When it raises the human experience to the divine, it transforms humanity.

Do you have the courage to pray not from a book, but from your soul? If so, place yourself now in our Lord's presence and encounter your feelings, pain, and passion. Converse with the Lord, while being certain also to listen. Encourage the deepest part of you to feel, to touch the divine solace and challenge. Now open the Psalter to find an appropriate psalm. Feel its truth flowing toward and from your soul. You are praying from the heart as did Jesus, in the spirit of the Psalms.

CHAPTER 20

WISDOM AND HER CHILDREN

Whether we follow a particular religion or not, certainly all of us aspire to be persons of wisdom. Wisdom is not necessarily bound to a particular religion, but to all major world religions: Buddhism, Christianity, Hinduism, Islam, and Judaism. As an example, *Ramayana* (one of the two great epic poems of India) tells us:

> Wisdom is God in the world. It is on wisdom that justice always is built. It is in wisdom that everything is rooted. There is no higher level above that....In Buddhism, Wisdom is present in at least two images....[that] which perceives the dynamic and interdependent character of reality, [and] the mother, nourisher, and teacher of all Buddhists....Islam, despite its strict monotheism, has at least one theologian who wrote about divine Wisdom. To Ibn al-Arabi, who lived in the 12th and 13th centuries, is attributed a poem

about Nizam, a young woman whom he presented as an earthy manifestation of divine Wisdom.[1]

Plato, the Greek, says wisdom is the supreme science, and Cicero, the Roman, points to it as the high point of human development, but none of these really "nail it down." Even the seven Wisdom books of the Hebrew Testament don't define it clearly, but they can initiate *our* lifelong quest for wisdom. The Bible provides a seed for the growth of wisdom that each of us is called to nurture. We shall outline briefly this ever-maturing biblical understanding of divine wisdom by drawing from and expanding upon Karl Rahner's *Encyclopedia of Theology*. This is a story that builds to a great climax with a surprise ending.

We begin by considering that many ancients believed wisdom was beyond our attainment because it implied self-fulfillment, and no one was totally capable of that. Already, a certain transcendent dimension was attaching to the notion of wisdom.

The book of Proverbs, compiled six hundred years before Christ, laid a new foundation for wisdom; namely that fear (reverence) of the Lord is the beginning of wisdom (cf. Prov. 9:10). Thus, for Jews and Christians, the basis for wisdom is not found in self-improvement courses, such as *I'm OK—You're OK* (although these have value), but in the Word of the Lord. Later books on wisdom from the Hebrew Testament (Ecclesiastes, Sirach, and Wisdom) emphasize wisdom as God's gift. Importantly, throughout these Hebrew Testament manuscripts, wisdom is consistently considered feminine. Consider these revolutionary lines: *"Desire therefore my words / ... / Resplendent and unfading is Wisdom, / ... / he who watches for her at dawn shall not be disappointed"* (Wisdom 6:11, 12, 14).

Wisdom assumes not only the female gender but also the compassion and caring of woman. *"Wisdom has built her house, / ... / She has dressed her meat, mixed her wine, / yes, she has spread her table. / She has sent out her maidens; she calls / from the heights out over the city"* (Prov. 9:1–3). The foundation of wisdom is laid, and found, in the heart of woman; therefore, female wisdom empowers any love affair with God. *"She* [Wisdom] *produces friends of God and prophets....She is fairer than the sun / and surpasses every constellation of the stars"* (Wisdom 7:27c–29). James Robinson, the outstanding scripture scholar, advises, "Wisdom, in Greek 'Sophia' meaning God's wisdom, was a personification for God, a way of talking about God's action in human circles while at the same time protecting the sublime transcendence of God. Since, in both Hebrew and Greek (as well as in Latin) wisdom is a feminine noun; this provides the female dimension of God."[2] If we minimize the role of the female in contemporary church life, we are thereby implicitly attempting to diminish the very wisdom of our God—a chilling thought!

We turn the page to wisdom in the New Testament. There, wisdom appears firstly as a marvelous human virtue; for example, Matthew describes the people of Nazareth saying of Jesus, *"Where did this man get such wisdom?"* (Matt. 13:54). Luke details Jesus exclaiming to his disciples, *"I myself shall give you a wisdom in speaking"* (Luke 21:15).

Paul writes of the final climactic step in this journey into the heart of wisdom, *"It is due to him* [God] *that you are in Christ Jesus, who became for us wisdom from God"* (1 Cor. 1:30). Paul cries out that Christ Jesus does not only have wisdom but is God's Wisdom. Note the corollary: because Christ Jesus is Wisdom, his disciples are called by Wisdom to become Wisdom. That's wisdom! This dynamic may be likened to Jesus exclaiming, *"I am the resurrection and the life"* (John 11:25). Jesus is not speaking metaphorically; rather, he's saying that for his disciples, there is no spiritual resurrection or spiritual life without him. As well, there's no wisdom outside him because all wisdom is of God, and Christ Jesus reflects God on earth. "We dare not neglect the wealth of wisdom which the gospels offer us from Jesus himself, who is the divine Wisdom come among us in person," writes Gerald O Collins, the noted theologian.[3]

If you and I spend our lives seeking Christ Jesus, we are, in truth, seeking wisdom, which search in itself comprises wisdom and gives evidence of our becoming wisdom. This is what Jesus meant when he said, *"Wisdom is vindicated by all her children"* (Luke 7:35). We become the children to which Jesus refers. Yet, who of us seeks wisdom as our life-objective? Such seeking today would be considered countercultural and "outside the loop," but if you truly seek the divine, you are seeking wisdom and residing within Abba's family circle.

One final remark is in order. You will recall our referring to the female personification of wisdom in the Hebrew Testament. Couple that with Paul's identification of wisdom with Christ Jesus, and we have an amazing conclusion. Paul, who knew well that his Hebraic wisdom tradition focuses on the female, is really including, therefore, both genders in referring to Christ Jesus. In the order of wisdom, Paul is attributing to Jesus, the Son of Man, the best of the female heart, her wisdom. Therefore, Paul is calling all of us, males and females, to walk together on this journey into divine wisdom. Wisdom is summoning me, a male, to walk with the heart of a wise woman. This marks a divine approval of today's movement toward gender justice. Truly we are wisdom's children. "We are called," comments Monica Helwig, "to be Words of God and to be images of God that present divine Wisdom."[4]

Paul concludes our reflection on biblical wisdom by praying for you and me. His words pierce through centuries of time and place on earth, and neither age nor gender can withstand the power of wisdom. Contemplate in your heart his following verbal embrace:

"[I] do not cease giving thanks for you, remembering you in my prayers, that the God of our Lord Jesus Christ, the Father of glory, may give you a spirit of wisdom" (Eph. 1:16–17); to which we respond, Amen.

CHAPTER 21

JOSHUA, THE FOUR-STAR GENERAL

Do you remember our discussing the transformation of Moses from the banks of the Nile to the heights of Mt. Nebo; from fear to outrageous courage; from taking life to saving it? Transformation occurs also, as one might expect, in Moses' assistant and confidant, Joshua. His transformation, though very different from that of Moses, is profound and has powerful meaning for every era of mankind, particularly ours.

The author of Exodus introduces us to Joshua when Moses tells him, *"Pick out certain men, and tomorrow go out and engage Amalek in battle"* (17:9). Moses' selection of Joshua indicates the young man was already well-known among the Hebrews for his military skill. Joshua wins this battle decisively, and many more to come. We can certainly ascribe to Joshua, the seasoned militarist, a sense of order, discipline, and obedience. Although these same virtues are praiseworthy for the Christian, they comprise only a beginning of his or her journey to the promised land, which is not a physical land at all but a person, Jesus the Christ.

The author of Numbers tells a fascinating story that amplifies this disciplined way of thinking by Joshua. The tent of prayer was positioned outside the encampment. Moses placed seventy elders around the tent as he entered. The Lord then came down in the cloud and spoke to him. Taking some of the spirit that was on Moses, he bestowed it on the seventy elders; and as the spirit settled on them, they prophesied (that is, they spoke with raptured enthusiasm). However, two other men, not elders, remained in the camp and also prophesied. Joshua, with his mind-set of proper order, shouted to Moses, "My Lord, stop them!"

Moses responded, *"Are you jealous for my sake? Would that all the people of the LORD were prophets! Would that the LORD might bestow his spirit on them all!"* (Num. 11:29). Moses is suggesting that the younger Joshua must broaden his vision beyond obeying rules and regulations. Crossing the t's and dotting the i's do promote orderly human behavior, but the Spirit of the Lord flies beyond legalities and can't be contained or restricted by any mere human power, order, or law.

"Joshua," he says, "smash the shackles, and leap into the Spirit of the Lord!" Moses is calling Joshua from his military mind-set to the cloud and to the fire of the bush. Further, Moses is still calling each of us to this same soaring of the spirit, this flight of the phoenix beyond mere human regulations whether of church or state.

Later, as the Hebrews approached Canaan, Moses sent twelve scouts into this Promised Land. Joshua was among them (Num. 13:1–16). Upon returning, the twelve reported to all the people. The twelve confirmed the Lord's promise that this land flows with "milk and honey." However, ten of the twelve stated the residents were so fierce and well fortified they could never challenge them.

Joshua and Kaleb, the other two, asserted that, to the contrary, their defenses were weak, and implored, "We must trust in the Lord." Fearful, the Israelites cried out in anguish by day and night, threatening to stone Joshua and Kaleb, to replace Moses with a new leader, and to return to Egypt. Joshua and Kaleb spoke up again, saying, *"You need not be afraid of the people of that land;...the LORD is with us"* (Num. 14:9). Joshua was learning, as we all must, to rely not so much on physical solutions but to trust the spiritual. Moses supported Joshua and Kaleb, and eventually, the people did also. But of all those Israelites who departed Egypt, only Joshua and Kaleb set foot in the Promised Land. Truly, the Lord is calling each of us, our nation and all humanity, not to mere military power but to divine compassion.

After the death of Moses, Joshua led the Hebrews into the Promised Land. He suppressed the Canaanites' strongholds and is revered to this day as one of the great leaders in all Hebrew history. However, his greatest achievement was not of the West Point variety. This military commander had grown to realize the Lord's power of faith, truth, and courage was more effective than mere human militarism. One such outstanding victory is recalled in the spiritual hymn "Joshua Fit de Battle of Jericho" in the line "the walls came tumbling down." This African American spiritual recalls Joshua leading the Israelites to victory over the Canaanite fortification. However, military might was not responsible. Rather, Joshua dreamt of God's messenger advising him, not to lead the soldiers in bloody battle, but to have the priests march in faith for seven days around the city with the ark and the people. All would shout on the seventh day. The walls would collapse, and the city would be theirs. A crazy scenario! Joshua, the commander who gave orders and believed in strategic military power, followed the Lord's orders and achieved victory, just as the messenger had said. Archaeologists and historians have found no physical evidence of the crumbling of walls at Jericho. Could this be the story of a spiritual victory by Joshua? He had finally learned that commitment to Yahweh, even when it appears foolish and impossible, carries far greater import than his own military or physical prowess. His journey was nearly complete: *"Thus the LORD was with Joshua"* (Josh. 6:27).

Many years later, as Joshua himself was about to die, he addressed the Israelites, *"You have seen all that the LORD, your God, has done for you against all these nations; for it has been the LORD, your God, himself who fought for you"* (Josh. 23:3). *"Today, as you see, I am going the way of all men. So now acknowledge with your whole heart and soul that not one of all the promises the LORD, your God, made to you has remained unfulfilled"* (23:14). It is also true that, if fully understood, the Lord has also never failed you with any promise. The Lord still speaks to us through Joshua; his words of wisdom will never die.

Joshua had finished his journey from reliance on forceful solutions to trusting in the Lord. As for us, I hear echoes of Joshua in a letter Thomas Merton wrote the U.S. Bishops in 1963: "In spite of a universal desire for peace…governments contribute by far, the greater portions of their budgets to armaments….The modern world remains committed to force, and can, indeed, be said to believe in the primacy of power and violence."[1] Today, forty-six years later, is not Merton's insight still valid? Reflect with honesty on whether this applies to your nation. If so, will you become with your lips, pen, and actions, the Lord's prophet for peace?

Will we ever learn that force is not the way of Yahweh? Joshua teaches us in his life to trust patiently in the ways of the Lord both in our national as well as personal relationships. Is there a person whom we overpower: perhaps a child, a co-worker, a spouse? Do we continue to support our nation even in its aggressive mistakes? Joshua, lead us today not just in rejecting military solutions to human troubles but especially by embracing justice and non-violence. Can we accept the mind-set of Yahweh, our God of peace?

CHAPTER 22

SAMUEL, OUR WISE ANCESTOR

We are all aware that for a woman to conceive beyond her menopause is well-nigh impossible, but the early Hebrews believed the story of such a conception indicated a child's extraordinary closeness to Yahweh. As the story goes, Hannah, a holy woman of the eleventh century BCE, prayed with deep faith to the Lord for a male child despite her advanced years. Behold, she conceived and named her son Samuel. She brought her youngster to Eli, priest of Shiloh, the religious center of the day. In gratitude for this faith-filled gift, she requested him to raise her son in the service of Yahweh. Eli agreed, and Samuel grew under his priestly aegis. It's no wonder Hannah's song of praise to the Lord (1 Sam. 2:1–10) was immortalized by another mother who consecrated her son, Jesus, to the Lord which she celebrated in her prayer, the Magnificat (Luke 1:46–55). Have you who are parents ever considered consecrating with trust your children of whatever age to God for his gift to you of human life?

As the Hebrews completed their military dominance of Canaan (the Promised Land), they formed a confederation in which each of the twelve tribes received, by lot, a particular region. The tribes developed a quasi-administrator called a judge, who enjoyed military, judicial, and religious jurisdiction. Samuel became such a judge of the Tribe of Ephraim some thirty miles north of Jerusalem. He was the greatest, and last, of the judges.

Realizing Yahweh was calling him to proclaim the truth (as he does with all), Samuel even upbraided Eli, his mentor, for tolerating the evil behavior of his sons. The people recognized his wisdom and courage, and Samuel's name grew in stature throughout all Israel.

Suddenly, a great disaster struck. The Philistines, a powerful group of sea people who settled along the coast, slaughtered Israel in battle and seized the Ark of the Covenant (chapter 17). Eventually, they returned the ark, but were preparing a mighty force to destroy Israel forever. The Israelites were terrified and begged Samuel to implore Yahweh for help (even today, many turn to the Lord only in times of desperation). Samuel offered a pure and worthy sacrifice to Yahweh, and the Israelites annihilated the Philistines. Samuel became a hero and a judge for all the tribes, but he realized Yahweh was the real hero. This raises the profound question: How do we know today our warring is justified? Samuel would respond, "Would the Lord wage this war?" This is a powerful question that requires great courage from our generation of warriors to answer!

Now, the Israelites began to realize other nations had kings, and they had none. They had only Yahweh, whom they could neither see nor hear. Therefore, they asked Samuel to appoint a king for them. Samuel, believing they were rejecting the rule of Yahweh, was outraged. He warned them of the excesses and abuse a king would inflict on them, but they insisted. Samuel, in prayer, consulted Yahweh who told Samuel to grant their request. How many times do we also seek foolishly things for our own destruction, and when they are granted, we suffer.

Samuel anointed reluctantly a tall, handsome young man named Saul, saying, *"The LORD anoints you commander over his heritage"* (1 Sam. 10:1). One can feel the reluctance of Samuel to anoint Saul, but Samuel would, at any cost, follow Yahweh's command. One can also sense Yahweh's attitude: anoint this man, for my people must learn a lesson, and they surely will; it is a lesson we have been learning ever since.

We shall examine in our next chapter Saul's refusal to accept what Israel perceived as Yahweh's intent to make war "under the ban" and Samuel's consequent anger with Saul. Consider, however, Samuel's final bewitching appearance to Saul as described in 1 Samuel 28. Samuel had died, and Saul was preparing for battle with the Philistines. Seeing the vast physical superiority of the army of the Philistines, he *"lost heart completely"* (v. 5). Desperate and despite his previous banishing of all seers, he disguised himself and visited a witch, by night.

Saul implored her, *"Tell my fortune through a ghost; conjure up for me the one I ask* [Samuel]*"* (1 Sam. 28:8). With that, the spirit of Samuel appeared, and Saul begged his advice. Samuel responded from the grave, *"Why do you ask me, if the LORD has abandoned you?"* (v. 16). *"The LORD will deliver Israel, and you as well, into the clutches of the Philistines. By tomorrow you and your sons will be with me"* (v. 19). This strange tale contrasts Saul, bewitched and fearful without Yahweh as his anchor, and Samuel, always solid and safe in Yahweh. Yes, the story is bizarre, but many of us still place our trust in apparitions, coincidences, and omens. Samuel urges, not only Saul, but us across the centuries that, after we have given our best effort, we are called to trust our future to the Lord in faith. In the end, we must choose to be a Saul or a Samuel!

Samuel establishes a prophetic tradition of speaking the truth while not succumbing to threats or power. The authentic prophet will proclaim the truth of God despite danger to self. The Lord calls each of us from our baptism to be a prophet (an official representative of Abba in our relationships), to speak and live the truth with justice and courage. Do this, and you, as a prophet, shall be walking in the sandals of Samuel and of Jesus, the greatest prophet of all. Do you have the courage to live your prophetic calling?

Lord God, you sent heroic men and women, especially Samuel, as prophets to your chosen people. Then, you sent Jesus, who learned from your prophets and modeled his career on theirs. He then sent us, his followers, to learn of him and join this illustrious band of prophets. We ask you to inspire us to pursue avidly this, our calling. Help us to change our corner of the world to one of peace and justice, and "let it begin with me." We ask this through Christ, our Lord and prophet. Amen.

CHAPTER 23

THE TRAGIC SAUL

The Bible stands unquestionably as the most widely read book in all human history. Its popularity rises in part because it reflects not only the sacred but also the fullness of our human experience: love, hate, trust, betrayal, and even tragedy. As we noted in our introduction, God teaches us his wisdom through all human experiences, whether clear or muddied. Saul presents a profound biblical tragedy but, in his own way, teaches us wise lessons.

As we have seen, the prophet Samuel lived during the mid and later eleventh century BCE, in Shiloh, the village that had become the administrative and religious center for the tribes. The first book of Samuel describes in chapter 4 the aforementioned defeat of the Israelites by the Philistines and their seizure of the Ark of the Covenant, but chapter 7 records Samuel's celebrated victory over the Philistines and the recovery of the ark. Therefore, Samuel had become a primary figure in this loose confederation of tribes and the greatest spiritual leader of Israel since Moses.

Because he was ageing, the elders requested him to appoint a king. After communing with Yahweh, Samuel, as noted in our previous chapter, told them of the Lord's reluctance to have them suffer under the control a king would surely exercise over them. Did Yahweh's warning ever come true! We witness the same inequities of which Samuel prophesied when perpetrated by intrusive governments of today!

Samuel chose to anoint Saul as king because of his military prowess and imposing stature. The people ratified his selection. Samuel, however, warned the king and the people they must first have obedience to the Lord: *"If you do not obey the LORD...the LORD will deal severely with you and your king, and destroy you"* (1 Sam. 12:15). His warning extends to us also: we who support ungodly governments and leaders because of nationalism, party loyalty, or apathy.

After defeating the Ammonites in an early military campaign, Saul commanded wisely, *"No man is to be put to death this day, for today the LORD has saved Israel"* (1 Sam. 11:13). Saul recognized unselfishly the truth that the Lord had accomplished this victory through Saul, his servant. Saul is described in 1 Samuel 9:2 as standing *"head and shoulders above the people."* This may not have referred only to his physical stature. Spiritually, Saul was "at the top of his game." Centuries later, Paul would write in 1 Corinthians 10:12, *"Whoever thinks he is standing secure should take care not to fall."* All of us, including Saul, must be aware!

Saul waged many successful military campaigns. Samuel then ordered Saul in the Lord to attack Amalek under the ban, *"Do not spare him* [Amalek], *but kill men and women, children and infants, oxen and sheep, camels and asses"* (1 Sam. 15:3). The ban (*Herem* in Hebrew and human in origin) of destruction meant to kill all humans and animals in holy war (jihad). In light of centuries of hot and cold wars between the Christian West and the Islamic Near

East, the obvious question is, how could a God of love order total destruction of the innocent? The answer always remains that God orders not vengeance or violence but rather forgiveness and compassion. We, however, impose our vindictiveness on God claiming it's from God and retaliate against our enemy deceptively in his name. Our God loves all peoples, but understanding of this by Muslims, Jews, and Christians has proven woefully inadequate. Therefore, Herem, jihad, the crusades, 9/11, and other such violence in the name of God reflect negatively, not upon our God of love, but upon our lack of understanding of God. That understanding will hopefully mature because of my life and yours. War has been described as organized violence, and God plays no role in the violence and injustice inherent in nearly all wars. Oh, how obvious that most wars, planned chiefly by middle-aged men, and waged chiefly by young men, are anti-God!

According to the ban (chapter 18), we must consider Saul's behavior in the light of his own culture, which placed grave responsibility upon him to follow the dicta of the ban. Saul destroyed by sword the Amalekites, but spared Agag, their king, and their best sheep, oxen, and lambs for his army. Then, Saul erected a monument to his victory atop Mt. Carmel. Knowing he had violated the ban, why would he assume the role of a hero and construct a testament to himself while failing to recognize the Lord as he had previously? His ego had soared because of his position over the people and even above the Lord. Saul, in these dizzying heights, had lost his footing. How difficult it is for us to remember that God's presence affects whatever is worthy in us.

Samuel was infuriated with Saul and confronted him: *"Because you have rejected the command of the Lord, / he, too, has rejected you as a ruler"* (1 Sam. 15:23). Samuel abandoned Saul and never again set eyes upon him. Henceforth, Saul's mental state deteriorated rapidly until his servants suggested hiring a harpist to cheer Saul when he became depressed. So entered David upon this scene of royal melancholy.

David soon achieved great favor among the people in his well-known victory over Goliath, but Saul became jealous of David and, in anger, tried to spear him to death. Finally, Saul banished David and then sought to track him down in order to kill him. David became a hunted fugitive from the tortured Saul, whom many speculate suffered from bipolar disorder.

Saul tracked David and his followers obsessively throughout the land. He would visit soothsayers, admit his guilt in seeking to kill David, and then promptly resume his search for him. At the same time, Saul tried to maintain his struggle with the Philistines. Eventually, they chased Saul and the Israelites to Mt. Gilboa, where they slew the son of Saul. Saul himself felt the sting of arrows in his abdomen. Fearing he would fall into his enemies' hands, Saul ordered an aide to slay him with his sword, but the terrified man refused. In desperation, Saul took his own sword, and *"fell upon it"* (1 Sam. 31:4). Suicide was not then considered so pejoratively as today, but it will always remain an attempt to self-destruct, a surrender of self to the perceived pain of life. If only we could also perceive in our travails the saving hand of a loving God.

Often, we humans learn more from tragedy than success. Saul is a tragic figure who thereby teaches timeless lessons. Important status, an accomplished career, and charismatic presence—all these were Saul's. However, his was a tortured, self-serving soul that sought its own glorification rather than the Lord's, in whom he once trusted. Saul had descended from promising heights to darkened depths. The Bible ensures his life will always be remembered; thus we have the power, by learning from his mistakes, to make at least his legacy successful.

Mental, emotional, and spiritual distress present the most troubling human pain of all. What a shame that many stigmatize those who suffer such illnesses. Sadly, we who question ourselves in this regard therefore often hesitate to seek help. Will you join me in promising, here and now, that when confronted with habitual depression, anger, or anxiety, we shall seek the Lord's help through those who are professionally trained? May Saul rest finally and forever in peace. May he, and the Saul in each of us, rise from the ashes of pain to the heights of peace in the Lord. Amen.

CHAPTER 24

A SHEPHERD BOY:
THE TRUE GOLIATH

Samuel understood the Lord wanted him to travel to Beth-lehem to find a successor to Saul. This time, Samuel would not choose on the basis of appearance. Even Samuel had to learn the ways of Yahweh. He selected, not only the youngest of Jessie's eight sons, but a teenage shepherd, lowest on the Hebrews' socio-economic ladder. Even Bethlehem itself suggested lowliness: *"You Bethlehem–Ephrathah, / too small to be among the clans of Judah"* (Mic. 5:1). We could say David lived "on the other side of the tracks." Like many of us, David's story started at the bottom, unlike Saul's, which began on top.

David's career began as Saul's harpist when Saul summoned him to help ease his days of depression. Most can also remember the story of the boy David slaying, with a slingshot, Goliath the giant! I recall a recovering alcoholic telling me that when he tried initially to stop drinking, he felt like little David struggling with Goliath. Then, with a lilt in his voice, he reminded me of David's victory and his. To celebrate his gargantuan triumph, the man named his son David. Is there one among us who, as a David, has not struggled with one or more Goliaths in her or his life?

Picture David and Saul's glorious return from defeating Goliath and the Philistines. Many hundreds lined the streets while shouting, *"Saul has slain his thousands, / and David his ten thousands"* (1 Sam. 18:7). Saul's jealousy of David seethed within, and the next day, as David played his harp, Saul threw his spear at David, hoping to kill him. David escaped, becoming a fugitive until, as we have seen, the deeply troubled Saul took his own life in battle years later.

Meanwhile, Jonathan, son of Saul, placed himself in mortal danger by warning David of his father's hate for him. The two committed themselves to each other, *"The LORD shall be between you and me, and your posterity and mine forever,"* exclaimed Jonathan to David (1 Sam. 20:42). Do you have a similar relationship of eternal trust with anyone in your life? If so, how fortunate for you!

David exhibited outstanding courage in the face of Saul's murderous threats. Still, despite Saul's hostility, David always respected the person and office of the king of Israel.

Indeed, he could have, on several occasions, taken the life of his oppressor-king, but he refrained because Yahweh had chosen Saul. After Saul's death, the elders of the tribes anointed David the king of Israel. David, the shepherd boy, had come a long way, and did so without violence or manipulation but with courage and respect for another's office.

David would have made a consummate politician even in our own time, for he realized immediately the value of a central capital city. The tribes were essentially divided into northern and southern groups. Jerusalem lay on the border between and was still occupied by the Jebusites, one of the original Canaanite tribes. David knew that by its location and non-allegiance, Jerusalem was ideal for his capital. Despite being warned that it could never be taken, David's warriors entered the stronghold by night through its water shaft beneath the wall of Jerusalem and overwhelmed the city around 1000 BCE. It has come to be known even to this day as the City of David. To establish further its preeminence, David led, in jubilant dance, the procession bringing the venerable ark to its new home, Jerusalem. David now had a people, a capital, an army, and a central religious symbol. What more could any politician want?

However, as is usual in human experience, momentous heartbreak loomed, and this time it came from within David's own spirit: the Bathsheba affair. One day while walking atop his palace roof, David spotted a beautiful woman, Bathsheba, bathing. David discovered, not by accident, her husband Uriah was away fighting in David's army. So the king, despite his harem, proceeded to seduce Bathsheba, and she conceived. Even worse, David now began the familiar political cover-up. David summoned Uriah home to Bathsheba to make it appear Uriah was the father. Uriah, loyal to the laws of purity for a soldier in battle, refused to sleep with his wife. David descended further this slippery slope and invited Uriah's drunkenness at dinner in the palace. Imagine the scene of King David trying to persuade, with ignoble intention, a drunken Uriah to sleep with his wife. Still Uriah refused to violate the accepted rules of soldierly purity. The following day, David gave Uriah a sealed letter for Joab, his general. David knew he could trust Uriah not to open the letter. David wrote, *"Place Uriah up front where the fighting is fierce; then pull back, and leave him to be struck dead"* (2 Sam. 11:15). So, the murder by proxy occurred. Whereupon, David took Bathsheba, widow of Uriah, to be his wife in what seemed to be "the perfect crime."

We know nothing more of Uriah, but we need not wonder who, in God's eye, was the better man in this episode. The presence of Yahweh, the unseen witness, ensures no crime of any kind is perfect, and in this case, Nathan, his prophet, was about to proclaim it dramatically.

Nathan heard of this Bathsheba affair and approached David. He cleverly told David a parable with a character committing the same crime David committed. David responded to the parable, *"As the LORD lives, the man who has done this merits death!"* (2 Sam. 12:5). Picture Nathan with pointed finger and courageous heart, exclaiming dramatically to his king, *"You are the man!"* (2 Sam. 12:7). David dissolved in tears of repentance, but Nathan promised him, *"The sword shall never depart from your house"* (2 Sam. 12:10). And so it happened. Reflect on your weakest moment and picture Nathan pointing his finger at you with similar words.

Absalom, son of David, was bitterly estranged from his father. He therefore shrewdly organized an uprising against David. His forces marched toward Jerusalem, and David was forced to flee his beloved city and retreat across the Jordan as his own son moved against him. How David's heart must have been crushed by his own son's betrayal! Preparing for battle, David told his commanding officers, *"Be gentle with young Absalom for my sake"* (2 Sam. 18:5). David's forces won this battle decisively, but his beloved Absalom was slain. David mourned his son, weeping plaintively and crying out, *"My son Absalom! My son, my son Absalom! If only I had died instead of you, Absalom, my son, my son!"* (2 Sam. 19:1). David saw Absalom not as a traitor or sinful man, but as his son whom he would treasure beyond life itself. Truly, a figure of God the father! Are we not also called to maintain compassionate communication even with those beloved who betray us?

Having reigned forty years, David died in 962 BCE. It's difficult to imagine a life of greater emotional extremes than David's. He displayed spiritual and psychological shortcomings, but also exhibited outstanding forgiveness, courage, and humility. His greatness consisted of his ability to remain a man of the soil and the community despite his high office.

By the time of Jesus, ten centuries later, the Israelites had forgotten David's failings and had idealized him and his heritage. One wonders how closely Jesus in his own life tried replicating David's finest virtue. "Son of David, save!" "Jesus, Son of David," and many other laudable references to David marked the cry of the people toward Jesus. Further, Matthew and Luke made certain in their infancy narratives that Jesus was known as the Son of David by placing his birth in Bethlehem, David's village. We can't be certain Jesus was physically of David's lineage, but Christians certainly placed Jesus in his spiritual tradition, and Jesus accepted it. That means, as disciples of Jesus, we also derive from the spiritual loins of David. You are a spiritual son or daughter of David!

David, like you, we often cover up our many failings with lies, and we plunge, thereby, deeper into sin and emotional distress. However, you demonstrated also great repentance and commitment to Yahweh. Therefore, intercede for us with Him, our common father, to grant us, your spiritual progeny, these same qualities. We pray the Lord may forgive us for the hurts we have inflicted on our family and community members. We ask this through Jesus of Nazareth, your spiritual son and our brother. Amen.

CHAPTER 25

SOLOMON, SON OF WISDOM?

As a boy, I remember my dad saying mischievously of my mother, "She has the wisdom of Solomon." We all knew what he meant, but only years later did I discover Solomon's identity. Was the son of David and king of Israel really that wise, and if so, can his wisdom apply to my living today?

Adonijah, Solomon's half brother, was first in line of succession to the throne of David, but he realized Solomon, son of Bathsheba, would present fierce competition. He therefore enrolled Joab, commander of the army, Abiathar, chief priest, and others to his cause. But, immediately upon David's death, Solomon arranged his own anointing as king by Nathan the prophet. Adonijah, moving boldly, asked Bathsheba to request Solomon's approval to his marrying Abishag, David's nurse in his last days. He was subtly seeking greater support to his claim to the throne. Solomon recognized the threat and abruptly executed Adonijah, Joab, and then exiled Abiathar. Already, we see Solomon as shrewd, decisive, and cruel. Can such a man become fertile soil for the growth of wisdom; what does this say of our own possibility?

Solomon broke down the old tribal boundaries that David respected by creating twelve new administrative districts, thus providing his bureaucracy with unimpeded authority and greater taxing ability. He conducted an ambitious construction program of government buildings, including his own palace and that of his Egyptian princess-wife, whose father gave Solomon, as dowry, the city of Gezer. Speaking of wives, Solomon enjoyed seven hundred foreign wives despite Yahweh forbidding intermarriage. Solomon used these marriages to harvest political and economic gain from the wives' nations. To keep his ladies satisfied, Solomon respected their worship of foreign gods and even built shrines for them in Judea and Jerusalem. Nevertheless, sadly, the author of 1 Kings 11:4 writes, *"His wives had turned his heart to strange gods."* We have already seen the great test for Israel as being whether the people could maintain their covenant of commitment to Yahweh, or worship their own man-made or natural gods of the nations (syncretism). Strange, but this still remains our test today. What weird gods some of us worship—money, power, health, church, and so many others—while Abba's offer of covenant waits.

Solomon's greatest building achievement was the temple constructed on a ridge purchased by David. It was huge for that era, about 105 feet by 35 feet and about 52 feet high. This elaborate temple was richly adorned and took seven years to build. Solomon leveled the luxuriant, verdant cedar forests of Lebanon and forced northern slave laborers to haul the lumber overland through the Phoenician port city of Tyre in order to complete the magnificent temple. He was then able to centralize worship and gain huge revenue from temple sacrifices. Whatever Solomon did was done shrewdly to build his empire. Such efforts brought power, wealth, and a cosmopolitan flare to his kingdom, but did all this serve Yahweh, or the king's self-serving political will? Today, we ask the same question of our own leaders.

Solomon's wisdom stemmed apparently from three sources: his reputed judicial skill in determining which of two women was a child's true mother (1 Kings 3:16–27); his answering the difficult questions posed by the Queen of Sheba (1 Kings 10:1–3); and his outrageous wealth (1 Kings 10:14–29).

I wonder if your grandmother was as wise as mine when she taught me the ageless adage: actions speak louder than words. We look, therefore, at the legacy of action Solomon left his people and us. We draw on what follows, from the work of Bernhard Anderson.[1] Solomon's forced labor for all these buildings was brutally oppressive. Thirty thousand Israelites were dispatched to the northern labor camps in Lebanon every third month to fell and transport its huge cedars. Eighty thousand toiled in the quarries, and seventy thousand as carriers of heavy burdens.

Revolutionary fury and resentment boiled over in the north, led by Jeroboam, whom Solomon sought to kill. Jeroboam fled to Egypt, and fortunately for him, Solomon died in 922 BCE. Jeroboam returned to the north and led a successful rebellion in which ten of the twelve tribes participated. Israel would never again see its kingdom united under one king. Monarchy had failed for the united kingdom.

Again, the pivotal question is, did Solomon's wisdom derive from a sense of serving Yahweh or self? Does this choice not apply to each of us? Although his behavior seemed to reap bitter fruit, the answer for him and us is "a mixed bag." Even the biblical authors seem unsure of their judgment of Solomon. Before condemning him, however, let's examine our own "mixed bag": yes, like Solomon, what strange gods we create for worship.

We ask you to eliminate all extraneous sensation and withdraw within yourself. Picture Solomon seated on his golden royal chair in a richly adorned throne room of polished cedar. What does all this reveal about the soul of King Solomon? Picture now Christ the King, bloodied and broken on a cross of rough wood. What does this say of his heart? Contrast their motivations, lifestyles, and their true worth. Finally, in whose court do you serve, or sadly, is it a "mixed bag"?

CHAPTER 26

ELIJAH, A MAN OF CONSCIENCE

Swing low, sweet Chariot, coming for to carry me home," sang the African American slaves desperate for justice, at least in the next life, for they knew they weren't about to get it here. Many of them realized their song of poignancy celebrated the Lord's "rapturing" the prophet Elijah in a fiery chariot of ascent into heaven.

Jews, at the time of Jesus, also revered Elijah as one of their greatest. Recall Jesus asking, *"Who do people say that the Son of Man is?"* (Matt. 16:13). His disciples responded, *"Some say John the Baptist, others Elijah, still others Jeremiah or one of the prophets"* (v. 14). Today, many of us might also question, "Who is Elijah? I've never heard of him, nor do I care." The truth is, he remains one of God's greatest prophets (an official ambassador), and his message carries precious meaning for us. The stories of Elijah are told mainly in 1 Kings 17–21, and while they do not carry total historicity, no one can deny the power of their wisdom.

King Ahab of Israel, the northern kingdom, ruled from 869 to 850 BCE. He had married Jezebel, a Phoenician princess from Tyre, and in order to please her, he erected throughout Israel shrines to her foreign gods. Elijah, the prophet of the Lord, was furious and declared a terrible drought. Ahab dispatched in vengeance his soldiers to murder Elijah, who fled east of the Jordan, outside Israel. Elijah, in the third year of drought, arranged to meet Ahab and offered him "a deal." Ahab would invite all Israel to assemble on Mt. Carmel with the 850 false prophets of Jezebel. These prophets would prepare for sacrifice a bowl and place it on the altar, but start no fire. They would call on their gods to ignite the fire. Then, continued Elijah, I will call on the Lord. The god who answers with fire is the true God of Israel. Ahab agreed.

Atop Mt. Carmel, everyone gathered, eagerly awaiting the challenge, certain the nation would prevail over this terrorist, Elijah. Jezebel's prophets called on Baal, their god of weather, from morning to noon shouting, *"Answer us, Baal!' But there was no sound"* (1 Kings 18:26). Elijah taunted them and Baal: *"Perhaps he is asleep and must be awakened"* (1 Kings 18:27). The prophets shouted to Baal louder and slashed themselves with swords and spears until they were bloody, but still, not even one burning ember. Distraught and fearful, they now awaited Elijah, their archenemy; their insolent mood had changed.

Elijah prepared his bowl on the altar. He ordered four huge jars of water and emptied them three different times over the bowl and the altar to increase the difficulty. Elijah then paused to pray, *"Answer me, LORD! Answer me, that this people may know that you, LORD, are God and that you have brought them back to their senses"* (1 Kings 18:37). With that, the fire of the Lord descended to consume the offering, the altar, the water, and all its surroundings. The people shouted, *"The LORD is God!"* (1 Kings 18:39), and they slit the throats of Jezebel's prophets—of course, in the name of the Lord. Whereupon, Elijah informed Ahab a great saving rain was "on the way; leave the mountain at once." Ahab mounted his chariot in the midst of a torrential downpour. Imagine the scene: Elijah running with joyous abandon down the mountain, followed by the muddied careening chariots of Ahab and his retinue.

Wait a moment, Elijah! Don't "count your chickens" quite yet. This story has not ended. The enraged and vindictive Jezebel sent a messenger to Elijah, saying, "By all the gods, I shall do to you what was done to my prophets!" Terrified, Elijah fled south, through desert lands infested with Jezebel's spies and bounty hunters, even to Horeb (Mt. Sinai) about 250 desert miles to the south. There he barricaded himself in a cave.

Then, Lord asked him the same question he asks of all who live in fear: *"Why are you here, Elijah?"* Elijah answered, *"The Israelites have forsaken your covenant...and put your prophets to the sword. I alone am left, and they seek to take my life"* (1 Kings 19:9–10). Elijah, in his loneliness and terror, had given up. Have you, like Elijah, ever "hit bottom"?

Ignoring Elijah's protests, the Lord ordered him outside his cave of apparent safety (his comfort zone). Elijah experienced a mighty wind (confusion), then an earthquake (terror), and then fire (emotionalism), but the Lord was not in any of these. Elijah then heard a tiny whispering voice that told him to return through the desert to do the constructive work of the Lord. Elijah had heard his conscience, the voice of God, and realized that if he truly had faith in the Lord, he would follow it with courage.

The Lord is asking you, like Elijah, to follow his whisper, your true conscience, and forsake your fears and depression. Step out from your cave (your comfort zone) of desperation in your desert. Journey with trust in the Lord! If appropriate, seek professional help. Consider your value, not from your own failings, but through the eyes of your God of love. Reflect on what's best for the Christ in you, and choose your path out of the desert.

Blessed Elijah, you at times exalted excessively in your success, and so have I. You sunk at times into bitter depression, and so have I. You balked at leaving your comfort zones, and so have I. Despite these perils in your life, you remained, in the end, faithful to the voice of the Lord God. With your example and the Lord's presence in me, I also promise to listen, hear, and follow the whispers of the Lord and depart my deserts of despair. Amen.

CHAPTER 27

AH, FOR A JEREMIAH TODAY!

If courage measures the person, then surely Jeremiah stands tall among people. He spoke difficult words of Yahweh to a difficult audience in most difficult times. What a shame his lifestory, one of the most courageous ever lived, lays unread in pages rarely opened! Jeremiah, a very human representative of God, complained and wept over his role but remained always faithful to Yahweh's word within. A telling lesson for us today!

Jeremiah heard in 626 BCE the call of the Lord God to represent him with Judah and its kings, both in their domestic and international relationships. Jeremiah protested to Yahweh but finally accepted in conscience this prophetic role. He had no idea what pain, intrigue, and desperation lay ahead. We also make many decisions without knowledge of the pain or joy they will bring to ourselves and others. We do know this: the Lord is calling each of us to be his prophet representing his wisdom to a society bereft.

Josiah ruled in Judah and was instituting a series of religious reforms when in 621 BCE, a great book was found accidentally in a storeroom in the temple. It would come to be known as Deuteronomy. Huldah, a female prophet accompanied by Jeremiah, advised Josiah to heed this new book. Accordingly, Josiah terminated child sacrifice, idolatry, and sacred prostitution. This great reforming effort was cut short when Josiah was captured and executed by the Egyptians in the Battle of Megiddo in 609 BCE. The Egyptians placed Jehoiakim, son of Josiah, on the Judean throne. He proved to be a cruel despot—very unlike his father. Life for Jeremiah would never again be the same.

Jeremiah dictated his oracles to his secretary Baruch, including the Lord's warning that unless Judah practiced justice and true worship, a great empire, Babylonia, would devour it. Jeremiah proclaimed this message in the temple, but King Jehoiakim responded by forming an alliance, not with Yahweh, but with Egypt, Babylon's bitter enemy. A scroll from Jeremiah was brought to Jehoiakim, who then played out a most dramatic scene. He lounged before the great royal hearth in his winter home. As the columns were read to him, the king sliced them off with his knife and fed them to the flames until the entire scroll was consumed (Jer. 36). Can you feel his royal arrogance?

Jeremiah published a new scroll that warned of impending doom. Accused of treason, he and Baruch fled into hiding. Who are really the traitors, then and now? This new scroll has evolved to form the heart of the current book of Jeremiah. Midst this pathos and pain, Jeremiah dreamed of Yahweh providing a new covenant (Jer. 31:31–34). His vision would endure as the most well-known portion of the legacy of Jeremiah. This new covenant would derive from Yahweh's initiative, and he would never rescind it. Further, its provisions would not be written on the stones of Sinai, but on the hearts of the people of Yahweh. Jeremiah saw this new covenant as a renewal, a deepening, and a re-energizing of the Covenant of Sinai. How mysteriously profound that the covenant, visualized by Jeremiah, finds its fulfillment in the hearts of you who seek truth and love courageously!

Jehoiakim set up idols even in the temple and supported child sacrifice. He promoted slavery by the aristocrats while thinking his nation safe under Egyptian protection. As Jeremiah witnessed Judah's infidelity to Yahweh, his heart broke and he cried out from Gilead, a region across the Jordan famous for its healing balms, *"My grief is incurable, / my heart within me is faint. / ... / Is there no balm in Gilead, / no physician there?"* (Jer. 8:18, 22).

Babylonia defeated Egypt decisively at the famous Battle of Carchemish in 605 BCE, and Jeremiah saw his opening to warn King Jehoiakim again of Babylonian power. He added that unless Judah followed Yahweh, Yahweh would cause the king to die a miserable death and *"The burial of an ass shall he* [Jehoiakim] *be given, / dragged forth and cast out"* (Jer. 22:19). Jehoiakim was furious, and Jeremiah ran for his life. He poured out his heart to Yahweh, and questioned his own call, which seemed to have cost him everything. *"You duped me, O LORD, and I let myself be duped; / ...Cursed be the day / on which I was born! / ...The word of the LORD has brought me / derision and reproach all the day. / I say to myself, I will not mention him* [Yahweh], */ ...But then it becomes like fire burning in my heart, / ...I grow weary of holding it in, / I can not endure it"* (Jer. 20:7a, 14a, 8b, 9). Jeremiah did not want to speak necessarily against national policy, but knowing it was the word of Yahweh, he felt a compelling passion to proclaim its truth. Ah, for a Jeremiah today! Let each of us search his or her heart!

Jehoiakim died in 598 BCE, and his son assumed the throne. Nebuchadrezzar of Babylonia sensed weakness in Jerusalem, and struck. Jerusalem fell to him; its temple was looted. Zedekiah,

Josiah's youngest son, was placed on the throne in 597 BCE, and Nebuchadrezzar withdrew. The stage was set for a most historic and dramatic event in the national life of Judah.

Zedekiah was a king but not a leader. He was easily swayed by his prophetic advisors, chiefly Hananiah, who still counseled allegiance with Egypt against Babylon. Jeremiah preached avidly and courageously for submission to Babylon. *"Thus says the* LORD, *the God of Israel....I will hand over Zedekiah, king of Judah, and his ministers and the people in this city who survive pestilence, sword, and famine, into the hand of Nebuchadnezzar....He shall strike them with the edge of the sword, without quarter, without pity or mercy....I am giving you a choice between life and death. Whoever remains in this city shall die"* (Jer. 21:4, 7, 8b–9). Jeremiah, the prophet of Yahweh, appeared now as a traitor to the nation and to the troops. Sound familiar? What courage was yours, Jeremiah!

The Babylonians did not disappoint. They surrounded the city on all sides. Food supplies and water vanished. Thievery, starvation, and disease spread through the city. Jeremiah was seized and beaten for destroying the nation's morale, but Zedekiah summoned him secretly to speak words from Yahweh. Jeremiah once again warned him to submit to Nebuchadrezzar, and pointed out the deception of the words of Hananiah and the others. He begged the king to return to true worship and just living.

Hananiah intervened, calling Jeremiah a traitor, ordering his seizure, and petitioning Zedekiah for Jeremiah's death. Zedekiah responded pathetically to Hananiah, *"He is in your power"* (Jer. 38:5). Whereupon, Hananiah and his allies lowered Jeremiah into the mud of an empty cistern. However, once more, Zedekiah summoned him in secret. Picture Jeremiah, black with mud of desperation, pleading with the king to surrender. Zedekiah, however, remained frozen in fear. They would never meet again.

The Babylonians breached the city wall in July 587 BCE. They pillaged and burned Jerusalem to the ground, and removed the leaders and princes of the city to Babylon. Finally, they captured Zedekiah as he fled to the East. They forced him to witness the execution of his own son, then blinded him and led him in chains across the desert to Babylon. The Babylonians freed the heartbroken Jeremiah, who accompanied many of the remaining people to Egypt where he finally met his beloved Yahweh.

What a rare breed of a man, and how a Jeremiah is needed today! One wonders what would be the destiny of a prominent American supporting an end to all armed conflict and possession of nuclear weapons. Would an empty cistern lie in his or her future? Imagine him or her supporting the diversion of billions of dollars to an army, not of soldiers, but of educators, physicians, and training personnel. Imagine their departure to teach the building of irrigation systems, health clinics, and schools throughout a starving world; they, without weapons or ulterior motives. Finally, picture the acceptance by desperate nations of our humanitarian efforts, to the consternation of our enemies, thereby saving the image of America abroad and national pride at home. Such men and women might be called traitorous, idealistic, or damn fools, but their future would rest secure in the house of the Lord.

Such persons would represent the dream of Jeremiah, but where are such men and women? Could they be reading these words at this moment? Could a few, even one, decide to take up the challenge of the Word of the Lord as another Jeremiah?

Jeremiah, you felt the call of the Lord. It was insistent, compelling, and by accepting it, you were doomed to rejection, threats, and death. But, in the end, the Lord saved you, and your life resonates through the centuries as a model for us. Pray that those who learn of you may courageously follow your path to greatness and eternal reward. Amen.

CHAPTER 28

EZEKIEL, A PROPHET AMONG US

What a shame! A man whose message of wisdom applies so aptly to our current sociopolitical condition is unknown to nearly all except scripture scholars. Certainly, part of the reason rises from his visionary experiences that, if understood literally, defy reason, but his underlying profound messages abound with divine wisdom.

Ezekiel appears to have been among the several thousand captives whom Nebuchadrezzar exported from Jerusalem to Babylon in 598 BCE. He dated his prophetic call from Yahweh to a vision he experienced on July 31, 593 BCE. He described a huge firestorm approaching from the north (Yahweh's symbolic home) with Yahweh riding atop a glorious chariot. Four living, winged quasi-human figures (suggestive of Assyrian cherubim and the two cherubim that guarded the Ark of the Covenant) supported the chariot. This vision demonstrated not only the transcendent glory of Yahweh, but also his presence to his people even in the enemy's stronghold.

Ezekiel was awestruck and collapsed as a voice exclaimed, *"Son of man, I am sending you to the Israelites...they and their fathers have revolted against me to this very day...say to them: Thus says the LORD God! And whether they heed or resist—for they are a rebellious house— they shall know that a prophet has been among them. But, as for you, son of man, fear neither them nor their words when they contradict you and reject you...but open your mouth and eat what I shall give you. It was then I saw a hand stretched out to me, in which was a written scroll"* (Ezek. 2:3, 4, 5, 8–9).

This vision provided Ezekiel the fundament for his entire prophetic career. The reference to the Son of Man emphasizes his mere humanity as opposed to his envisioned majesty of God. Jesus himself would later choose this title indicating his own true humanity and his knowledge and affection for the historic Ezekiel. Yahweh, in this vision, is surely telling Ezekiel to consume passionately his Word by making it the central theme of his life. Can anyone doubt the Lord desires similar dedication from us to his Word? This surely means we are being called to witness to this word of truth in our lives by our words and especially our lifestyle. The Lord is directing us to have no fear of the hostility or contradiction that will surely confront us. Further, whether they, the people in your life, heed you or not, at least they'll know a prophet walked in their midst.

To convey Yahweh's message, Ezekiel expands on an allegory employed by Hosea and Jeremiah: namely, that Israel lived as a wanton harlot. She betrayed her Lord from the beginning and "ran off" with any idol she could find. Consider the courage this message demanded of Ezekiel. Who of us has such courage? We who would profess the wisdom of Abba and live his Words can surely expect similar derision in our relationships. *"Hard of face and obstinate of heart are they to whom I am sending you"* (2:4). Our societal problem today, however, is not hostility to God's Word, but worse: that so few manifest the tiniest bit of interest.

Ezekiel describes in chapter 24 the death of his beloved wife, but even this carries a message. Yahweh tells Ezekiel to avoid all signs of mourning to symbolize to the people the imminent death of Jerusalem, and their not having the consolation of community grief when it would happen because of their deportation and hardness of heart. Still, they dismissed blithely his message.

Finally, it happened! Jerusalem was sacked and leveled in 587 BCE. The people fell into a collective shock, and Ezekiel responded to their desperation with his well-known Vision of the Dry Bones in chapter 37. Ezekiel sees a vast valley littered with dry human bones. The bones, directed by the Word of Yahweh, come together, take on flesh, assume new life, and form a vast army. Jerusalem shall rise again! Is this a foretaste of the central event of the Christian Testament and of our lives as well?

Ezekiel portrays in chapter 34 the Good Shepherd who himself will shepherd Israel to rich pastures. Once again, Ezekiel is pointing to Israel's need to follow Yahweh and all he stands for. Yahweh says, "Do this, and my people will dwell in their homeland, secure from nations and in peace." Later, Jesus would apply this image to himself and to his disciples as well. Therefore, we must ask ourselves the question: Am I a good shepherd of service to the people in my life?

Following Jeremiah's new covenant, Ezekiel writes of the Lord God saying, *"I will give you a new heart and place a new spirit within you, taking from your bodies your stony hearts....I will put my spirit within you....[T]he neighboring nations that remain shall know that I the LORD, have rebuilt what was destroyed and replanted what was desolate"* (36:26, 27a, 36).

Ezekiel dreams of a new people, filled with God's spirit of goodness, returning to their Lord and their home. He doesn't stop there, however. Ezekiel describes water (so precious in these desert lands and symbolic of God's Spirit) flowing out from beneath the altar of the temple in all directions. Quickly, the water rises to ankle depth, then knee-deep; its flow gains power and becomes hip-deep. Finally, surging torrents form a river that can only be crossed by swimming. Everywhere the river flows, trees, fish, and every kind of creature gain life. It's the Spirit of God reaching out with life to a parched people! Israel has gained new life, the life of Yahweh himself.

Could the Spirit of God be clamoring through Ezekiel across the centuries to us and our nations, "Put away your war machines, your moneyed obsessions, and make the world's steppes, deserts, and cities teem with life and goodness"? Could our hearts of stone soften toward the starving, the disenfranchised, and even those we label enemy? Could one or more who are reading these lines commit to overcoming runaway nationalism and to promoting justice everywhere? On the other hand, perhaps we shall continue to live our bloated lifestyle while others die of thirst and starvation. As for Ezekiel, whether we hear or heed his message today, at least we'll know a prophet has been among us.

Ezekiel, you were a great prophet of the Lord. Pray for us that your dreams and images stir us to a fundamental searing decision: that we might seek to understand your visions as Abba's challenging call to us, centuries later, to become good shepherds reaching out with the Spirit of the Lord. May your visionary waters give life to all whom we touch; if they refuse and insist on dying, at least they will know prophetic disciples have witnessed in their presence. Amen.

CHAPTER 29

"HERE I AM: SEND ME!" (ISAIAH 6:8)

I t's been said that you can tell something of a person's character from the books he or she reads. One wonders what were the favorite books of Jesus of Nazareth? Judging from his quotes in the New Testament, Jesus had four: Psalms, Daniel, Deuteronomy, and especially Isaiah. Therefore, it's imperative for anyone of the Judaic/ Christian Tradition to uncover the prophetic wisdom Jesus found in the book of Isaiah.

Who is Isaiah, this teacher of our hero, Jesus? What was his message then, and how can we learn from him today? We pray this chapter will cast at least a sliver of light on him and his unparalleled message.

Isaiah hailed from Jerusalem and there exercised his ministry from 742 to about 687 BCE. Little is known about the man, but the book of Isaiah ranks as a masterpiece in message and imagery. Because of historical, literary, and thematic content, scholars are relatively certain Isaiah consists of at least three separate books:

chapter 1–39, ascribed in part to Isaiah himself; Deutero (2nd) Isaiah, chapters 40–55, written anonymously during the Babylonian exile 587–532 BCE; and Trito (3rd) Isaiah, composed after the rebuilding of the temple in 515 BCE. Lawrence Boadt states, "His [Isaiah's] words contained that rare mix of ethical insight, realistic warning of disaster, and long-range hopefulness that mark his as the most profound vision of the Hebrew Testament."[1] We cannot hope to cover adequately this masterpiece, but we can reflect on several central themes and invite you to search the depths of this literary jewel.

1st Isaiah (1–39):

Yahweh speaks, *"Sons have I raised and reared, / but they have disowned me! / An ox knows its owner, / and an ass, its master's manger; / But Israel does not know, / my people has not understood"* (1:2–3). This image of the ox, the ass, and the manger is commonly related to the nativity scene, but actually, they refer to the divine pathos arising from the intense heartbreak of the Lord. Israel does not understand Yahweh's message and rejects or ignores his role in their midst. Severely troubled by Israel's blindness, the remaining book of Isaiah comprises, in general, his response.

Isaiah describes his call by the Lord in 742 BCE, chapter 6, wherein a seraphim touches a fiery ember to his lips to purge him of evil so that he can prophesy. *"Then I heard the voice of the Lord saying, 'Whom shall I send? Who will go for us?' 'Here I am;' I said; 'send me!'"* (v. 8). Because a prophet is God's official messenger, you by being anointed at baptism as king, prophet, and priest have also been officially sent. Do you have the courage to respond to Christ in commitment as did Isaiah?

Ahaz, king of Judah, trembled at this time in fear of an enemy coalition that surrounded Judah. In chapter 7, the Lord told Isaiah to inform Ahaz to ask for a miraculous sign from the Lord to prove he, the Lord, would save Judah. The Lord added, *"Unless your faith is firm, / you shall not be firm"* (v. 9).

Planning rather to trust an alliance with Assyria, Ahaz answers hypocritically, *"I will not ask! I will not tempt the LORD!"* (v.12). Whereupon, the Lord responds in anger, through Isaiah, that he would give Ahaz a sign anyway: *"The virgin shall be with child, and bear a son, and shall name him Immanuel"* (v.14).

We know that the early translators of the Bible and many church fathers use this quote as evidence of Mary's virginal conception of Jesus. Actually, the cited verses give evidence of Ahaz's refusal to trust the Word of the Lord. The insistence of Yahweh's providing the sign proves his persistent support of us despite our lack of trust in him in the face of horrendous challenge.

Isaiah envisions the astounding messianic peace of Immanuel's presence: *"The wolf shall be a guest of the lamb; / ... / The calf and young lion shall browse together, / with a little child to guide them / ... / The baby shall play by the cobra's den, / and the child lay his hand on the adder's lair. / There shall be no harm or ruin on all my holy mountain; / for the earth shall be filled with knowledge of the LORD"* (11:6, 8–9). This graphic theme of the Lord's promise of surpassing peace penetrates every sinew of Isaiah, and he revels in its wonder. Is there anyone who refuses to sow these pastures of peace?

2nd Isaiah (40–55):

Isaiah authors herein four passages of poetic brilliance known as the four Servant Songs. These speak of a person or people of mystery who will commit fully to Yahweh's service. Jesus treasured these Servant Songs and seemed to pattern his life on their message. Truly, they rank among the most important verses in the entire Hebrew Testament. These citations from 2nd Isaiah are as follows:

Isaiah 42:1–4: The first Servant Song speaks of a person committing himself to the service of earthy and transcendent justice not in an aggressive manner but in quiet peace.

Isaiah 49:1–6: The Lord accepts in the second song his servant's pledge and broadens his or her influence beyond Israel to "the ends of the earth."

Isaiah 50:4–9: Next, the servant understands she or he will suffer, but still will never abandon this sacred calling.

Isaiah 52:13—53:12: Finally, a cruel and egregious death is promised, but this servant shall keep invincibly her or his commitment to the end, and the Lord will provide just reward to his beloved.

Jesus poured over these Isaian passages that summon one to the heights of humanity, and he embraced their supreme challenge. He thus became the center-point of a turning world, the fulcrum of the cyclical wheel of history, the only person to whom we, whether disciple or not, must affirm that, here walked one of us who could not be compromised; who, with spirit fulfilled, became one with the transcendent. This marks the ultimate ideal for you and me!

3rd Isaiah (56–66):

Surpassing justice drives the servant who realizes he or she is anointed by the Lord to be witness to the injustices inherent in human living and seeks to correct them. All restraint, all shackles are abolished—the servant has one and only one pursuit, to comfort all in justice. Isaiah seized this as a divine mission that shall bear fruit and will impact all nations: *"I am about to create new heavens / and a new earth; / The things of the past shall not be remembered"* (65:17).

The Lord asked for his servant to help him: *"What kind of house can you build for me; / ...This is the one who I approve: / the lowly and afflicted man who trembles at my word"* (66:1–2).

The Lord is still calling through Isaiah to each of us to become that servant by co-creating with him. Etty Hillesum, the young girl martyred in a Nazi death camp, responded to this poetic dream with her life and words: "One day we shall be building a whole new world. Against every new outrage and every fresh horror we shall put up one more piece of love and goodness."[2] Then she went to her death, but, like Jesus, her dreams live on. Listen to the voices of Christ and his innocent martyrs echoing through the halls of time, calling each of us with Jesus to become committed servants of our sisters and brothers and, because of that service, to live forever in love.

Isaiah, servant of the Lord, how privileged we are to drink in the beauty of your inspired poetic wisdom. Even Jesus became your student. Help us not only to explore your message but, like Jesus, to live it as Yahweh's fully dedicated servants. Pray we may make the courageous decision to explore your wisdom more deeply and resolve to become thereby true servants of the Lord. Amen.

CHAPTER 30

JERUSALEM: TRAGEDY AND TRIUMPH

Whether the promise of physically visiting the city is realistic or not, "Next year, Jerusalem," remains the cry of the faithful Jew in the diaspora to this day. Jerusalem certainly refers to the city of that name in Israel, but it means even more to the faithful Jew. Jerusalem remains forever his or her spiritual home. Every Jew feels a soulful reverence for that city. Its history, its people, its presence and promise summon him or her, as a bema to all Jews. Muslims and Christians also reverence deeply this city as sacred. Jerusalem is never far from any biblical page; we visit now, spiritually, the "Old City."

According to Genesis 14, over eighteen hundred years before Christ, Abram's nephew, Lot, was living in Sodom and was taken captive by a coalition of tribal chieftains. Abram was informed and journeyed to defeat the coalition in battle. Returning home, he passed through Salem, the city of peace. Melchizedek, its chieftain and priest, offered him the staples of life, bread and wine, and a joyous blessing of peace. The city would become known as Jerusalem, and bread and wine still play a vital role in Christian ministerial and spiritual life. However, as in all our lives, Jerusalem's future would take many turns of both tragedy and triumph.

Jerusalem encompassed originally an eleven-acre rectangular area on a plateau of two ridges separated by the Tyropoeon Valley. The southern section of the eastern ridge became known as Ophel (the City of David) and was the original place of settlement. Because of its site atop the hill, it was easily defended and considered impregnable. Thus, Jerusalem became a stronghold of the Jebusites, a powerful desert tribe of the hill country in Canaan who controlled the site until 1000 BCE.

At that time, David, intent on seizing the city, ordered his army commander, Joab, and volunteers to scale silently by night the nearly vertical shaft through the hill from the Spring of Gihon outside the wall to the Pool of Siloam inside. Imagine the terror of these men as they climbed upward in total darkness into the city of the hostile Jebusites. This terror reminds one of our fears as we climb through our dark tunnels of pain and rejection into the light of our heavenly city. Once inside, they opened the gates (2 Sam. 5, 6–12), and David's army charged through to overrun the city. Later, David wisely made this small town (population about fifteen hundred) his capital city, for it lay unaligned between the northern tribes of Israel and those of the south, and was therefore accepted by both. Jerusalem's capture symbolizes our spiritual breaching the heights of our own heavenly city from our murky depths below.

David purchased the adjacent threshing floor on Mt. Moriah and added it to the city. Eventually, this threshing floor became the seat of the great temple to be constructed for Yahweh. Solomon, David's son, built the temple and royal buildings atop Moriah and surrounding Jerusalem. Upon Solomon's death, Israel split into two kingdoms, with Israel becoming the northern kingdom and Judah the southern, with Jerusalem as its capital.

Centuries later in the summer of 588 BCE, Nebuchadrezzar, king of the Babylonians, surrounded Jerusalem, and the city suffered its most disastrous catastrophe. One could hardly grasp the horrific terror within it, which we discussed more fully in chapter 27. Suffice to say, at this time, the Babylonians leveled the temple, destroyed the city, and carried off its leading citizens. The poet author of Lamentations weeps and mourns, *"How the Lord in his wrath has detested his daughter Zion...(2:1). He withheld the support of his right hand when the enemy approached...(2:3b). The babies cried for food, but there is no one to provide. Those accustomed to fancy food perish in the streets...(4:4b–5a). The joy of our hearts has ceased; our dance has turned into mourning...(5:15). O' Lord, lead us back to you that we may be restored"* (5:21). May we of the twenty-first century who suffer terrible tragedy, whether self-inflicted or not, relate to the faith of this poet who addresses the pain and prays to rise from the ashes and return to the Lord. When the exiles from Jerusalem were allowed to return in 537 BCE, the city began its resurgence from disaster. The temple was completed in 515 BCE and its walls thereafter. How fascinating to observe that the life of this city follows human life in its cycle of ups and downs.

The Greek period began with Alexander the Great conquering Jerusalem in 332 BCE, but reached its low point in 168 BCE when Antiochus Epiphanes placed the Abomination of Desolation, a statue of Zeus, in the heart of the temple of Yahweh. He constructed gymnasia in the city, offending Jewish morality because of the nudity of its athletes. Antiochus built fortified Greek garrisons and destroyed much of the remaining city. All this was reversed by Maccabeus and his seven sons, who waged a successful guerrilla war against the northern invaders in 167 BCE. We take special note of the repeated historic reversals of Jerusalem to demonstrate such reversals in our lives. Rejection, depression, and death seem at times to overwhelm, but can, with our insight and courage, lead to our own rising from ashes.

The most pivotal chapter in the history of Jerusalem was about to begin. Herod started the expansion and reconstruction of a massive temple in 19 BCE. Its construction was not completed until 64 CE. The temple, occupying over thirty acres, consisted of a series of massive courtyards and spectacular porticoes. The Jews believed its central building housed Yahweh, and before it stood a colossal altar of sacrifice. It's no wonder the disciples of Jesus were astonished when one day, Jesus exclaimed, *"You see all these buildings? Amen, I say to you, there will not be left a stone upon another stone that will not be thrown down"* (Matt. 24:1–2).

Deeply aware of its poignant history of tragedy and joy, Jesus loved Jerusalem deeply. He sensed the oncoming political and military vise by which it would soon be squeezed, and he grieved soulfully at its future. One can feel his dire sorrow as Jesus intones this dirge: *"Jerusalem, Jerusalem, you who kill the prophets and stone those sent to you, how many times I yearned to gather your children together as a hen gathers her young under her wings, but you were unwilling! Behold, your house will be abandoned, desolate"* (Matt. 23:37–38). Jerusalem and the temple were sacked and burned to the ground by the Romans in 70 CE. Jerusalem has not regained such glory to this very day.

Jesus exclaimed in Matthew 23:39, *"I tell you, you will not see me again until you say, blessed is he who comes in the name of the Lord."* Could Jesus have meant by this that Jerusalem can endlessly play politics or seek military power, but it will never experience lasting peace until it accepts what the Lord stands for: compassion, forgiveness, and love.

Certainly, we can apply this history of glory and tragedy to all our nations, cities, and even each of us. You and I relate every day to all kinds of people: friendly, hostile; black, brown, yellow, white, Muslim, Christian, Jewish, or other. Jesus is surely calling us to accept each other in his name as his brother or sister. To live this way eliminates our seeking to overpower or compete with others but does empower us to enter the heavenly Jerusalem, where we will surely experience peace.

Lord, the joy of returning home reflects our joy in searching for our heavenly Jerusalem. Help us understand that, like the physical Jerusalem, we must first endure the sacking and destruction of our own egoism, and then our rising from it.

You, Jerusalem, have modeled for us this lesson most pointedly. You have suffered and risen many times from apparent "final solutions," and still you endure. Grant that we may learn from you never to lose hope in ourselves or in our brothers and sisters so that we can rise from our present earthly city to the glory of an eternal Jerusalem. Amen.

A TRANSITION

HEBREW TESTAMENT—CHRISTIAN TESTAMENT
PEOPLE OF COVENANT—PEOPLE OF FAITH

Each of us has affection for his or her home. What about Jesus?
According to Matthew, Jesus called Nazareth his home: *"He
went and dwelt in a town called Nazareth, so that what had been spoken through the prophets might be fulfilled"* (Matt. 2:23). However,
no prophet, nor even the entire Hebrew Testament, ever mentions
Nazareth even once. How then can Matthew state that Jesus' residing there was spoken through the prophets, and does this mean we
Christians have been wrong for centuries in calling Jesus a Nazarene? This text, among many others, certainly raises the question,
"Does the Christian Testament relate to the Hebrew Testament, and
if so, how?" Many Christians and Jews never relate to the "Other
Testament." Unfortunately, this contributes to their estrangement
when actually the Hebrew and Christian Testaments could reflect a
bonding between these seekers.

In general, there are three possibilities in the relationship of the
testaments: first, the authors of the Hebrew Testament wrote with

147

the Christian Testament in mind; second, there is no relationship whatsoever; and third, there is some other less-extreme relationship.

First, did the authors of the Hebrew Testament write to point to the Christian Testament? Let's return to Matthew's statement that seems to say the prophets wrote to establish Jesus being a Nazarene. As we have observed, historically this is patently false. Note, however, that *neser* (meaning in Hebrew "a bud") is used by Isaiah to describe a descendant of Jesse of the house of David. Further, *nazir* refers in the Hebrew Testament to one consecrated especially to God; for example, Samson. Matthew, when referring to Jesus of Nazareth, could be stating that Jesus is *neser* and *nazir*; that is, he derives from the house of David and was specially consecrated to God. Incidentally, did Jesus really grow up in Nazareth? Perhaps, but it was not spoken of by the prophets. When the prophets make references within the scripture, they are not referring consciously to events or to a certain person (i.e., Jesus) who might come centuries later. They are referring to events and characters of their own era, period.

Second, does a relationship exist between the two testaments? Absolutely, for a multitude of textual references confirm it. The Christian Testament authors are nearly all Jews who knew the Hebrew Testament very well. They refer to it often, especially Matthew, who writes to draw Judeans into the Way (Christianity). John Shelby Spong, formerly Episcopal Bishop of Newark, writes, "It is impossible, in my opinion, to understand these Christian Scriptures without a profound knowledge of that Jewish past."[1] Pope John Paul II writes similarly, "To deprive Christ of his relationship with the Hebrew Testament is to detach him from his roots and [empty] his mystery of every meaning."[2]

Third, what *does* characterize this relationship between the Hebrew and Christian scriptures? Fred Holmgren writes, "In numerous passages from the Hebrew Testament, the Christian believer can find Jesus present...not because the author of these texts had him in mind, but because what happened earlier was analogous to what happened to (Jesus),"[3] and early Christians rejoiced in discovering and highlighting these perceived analogies. For example, *"He took a cup, gave thanks, and said,... 'This cup is the new covenant in my blood, which will be shed for you'"* (Luke 22:17, 20b). Informed Christians see in this as fulfilling, through the blood of Christ, the Hebrew Covenant that was ratified by sprinkling the blood of bulls first on the altar, then on the people (Exod. 24).

Just as an infant's understanding grows as he or she matures, likewise, a Christian's understanding of God's revelation grows from his or her ever-increasing knowledge of the Hebrew and Christian Testaments, and from Jesus the Christ emerging from theses pages. The Word of God remains fully present in both testaments, but is more clearly visible for Christians in the Christian Testament chiefly because of the direct presence of Jesus, who alone among humans has lived that Divine Word (Hebrew and Christian scriptures) fully. Thus, both testaments are of singular importance to the Christian! We can describe the relationship between the Hebrew and Christian Testaments as one of interdependence: you can't have one without the other.

Jesus accomplishes his singular life by living as a Jew. He studied the Hebrew Testament and practiced Judaism in its surpassing spiritual truth, not as the priests and Pharisees understood it, in a mere legal or literal way. So, as we explore in the Christian Testament who Jesus is, we are at the same time discovering the best of what Judaism is, and what that stands for. Norbert Lohfink and Duane Christensen, write that Jesus' heart is "entirely one with Torah" and that "we see a fulfillment of the promise of the 'new covenant,'" in his heart.[4] We understand that Jesus lived his human life as freely as we do and was never constrained to fulfill Hebrew Testament prophecy. If he did fulfill such prophecies, it was done without his intent and was so interpreted by his contemporaries and early disciples.

As we open the pages of the Christian Testament, we gain the opportunity not only to view directly the life of Christ but also the life of an ideal Hebrew. Addressing a group of Belgian pilgrims on September 6, 1938, Pius XI asserted, "Spiritually we are all Semites."[5] It's no wonder that, as Christians, we view Jews as our unique brothers and sisters, and pledge a certain singular allegiance to them. May we always promote their faith and their right to live it without equivocation until the day we are all one in the bosom of Adonai.

The Hebrew Testament speaks of circumcision as the sign and seal of the Jewish covenant with God. *"Circumcise the flesh of your foreskin, and that shall be the mark of the covenant between you and me"* (Gen. 17:11). Circumcision denotes, therefore, early in Hebraic history, the *sine qua non* (the essential physical requirement) for the male Jew that he would follow the law as his participation in the covenant.

Surely, this applied to Jesus and his disciples, yet Jesus never spoke of circumcision. He emphasized continually faith as the fundamental essential for his followers: *"You have faith in God; have faith also in me"* (John 14:1). Did Jesus reject keeping the law and circumcision as its sign? Not according to the Christian Testament. Rather, the faith Jesus demands supersedes covenant and circumcision.

When Jesus speaks of faith, he is not referring to belief in a certain doctrine, morality, organization, or people. Karl Rahner describes faith for the Christian as Jesus intended it: "Faith is man's comprehensive 'yes' to God revealing himself as man's savior in Christ."[6]

Paul, the Jew who had followed the law, writes, *"I have lived my life as a Pharisee, the strictest party of our religion"* (Acts 26:5). He continues, *"We consider that a person is justified by faith apart from works of the law....God is one and will justify the circumcised on the basis of faith and the uncircumcised through faith"* (Rom. 3:28, 30). Faith in Christ becomes the hallmark of the Christian Testament and is necessary for understanding the person and message of Jesus the Christ. Faith demands your entire being give assent not to ideas about Abba but to Abba and Christ themselves, and then to live your life accordingly.

The demands of faith far outweigh merely following Judaic or church laws. Faith requires that we accept the answers of Jesus to the fundamental questions that have challenged all mankind: Abba, life, death, resurrection, spirit, evil, and eternity. Do you accept the views of Jesus, and are you willing to risk your life for them? Viewed in this challenging way, we should not be surprised that many Christians live their entire lives without ever professing an in-depth act of faith.

Because of this supreme challenge, many doubt. Let not your doubts disturb, for if one does not doubt, one cannot believe. A God who can be totally proven can't be believed. Can we not now understand that faith is a lifelong journey fraught with danger but that carries rewards that are beyond belief before and after death? Are you a person of faith?

Implant within my heart, Oh God, the fiery zeal of a Jeremiah, the conviction of a Ruth or Rebecca, and the zest of a Francis of Assisi.

Stir my slumbering soul, that it might sing a song of passion and devotion, drunk with dancing joy and desire for you, my divine and loving Friend.

May my heart be as hot as the heart of Moses for all your children burdened by slavery, for all who feel oppression's steely heel or suffer rejection in an alien land.

May I, like your son Jesus, be consumed with zeal for you, Divine Beloved, for life, for justice, and for peace; for all that I know in faith.

Fill me with zeal, O God.[7] *Amen.*

CHAPTER 31

THE FOUR EVANGELISTS: WHY CAN'T THEY AGREE?

M any great women and men have had numerous biographies written about them. This is true of Jesus of Nazareth, but the four gospels are not among them. These authors never intended their works to be biographic; rather, each wrote uniquely to educate and inspire his particular community to embrace Jesus. Further, they wrote forty to seventy years after his death and were not able to listen to Jesus and transfer immediately his speech to their writing. Thus, each evangelist heard different stories about Jesus, selected those he desired, and wrote them in his own style to fit his own purpose. This colors our interpretation of their writings; for example, references to the fires of punishment occur most often in Matthew because he writes primarily to Hebrews who are familiar with the tales of unquenchable fires in Gehenna. This might cast doubt for some readers as to the reality of fire in hell. Also, is it because John writes a highly theological gospel dealing with abstract subjects such as light, love, and life, that he alone tells the story of Jesus raising

Lazarus? Does John intend this Lazarus story to be historical or to convey a message or both? We can also observe their disagreements in their widely varying versions of the birth, death, and resurrection of Jesus. With this in mind, we see the necessity and wisdom of piercing beneath the authors' words (in contradistinction to fundamentalism) to discover the meaning each author intends to impart.

Are you familiar with the phrase, "He left his mark"? It applies most fittingly to Mark's gospel. His was the first written gospel (about 70 CE) and influenced substantially the others, especially Matthew and Luke. Because these three are similar, we call them the synoptics (meaning, "with one eye"). As we enter their world of the gospels, be aware of their following significant distinctions.

The salient characteristics of Mark are three:

- The kingdom is not a geographical area, a regal empire, or even a set of teachings, but Jesus himself. *"Jesus came to Galilee proclaiming the gospel of God: 'This is the time of fulfillment. The kingdom of God is at hand'"* (Mark 1:14–15).

- Earthy and realistic: *"When his relatives heard of this they set out to seize him, for they said, 'He is out of his mind'"* (Mark 3:21).

- Mark's Jesus is largely a tragic figure: rejected, attacked, and executed.

Mark's gospel "tells it like it is," and is treasured, therefore, by those who revere especially the historic, active Jesus. Finally, because it was the first gospel written, many consider this gospel the most important book ever written. It is frequently recommended as a starting place for beginners and those who wish to walk with Jesus as he really was.

Matthew or Luke could have been the next gospel written, probably in the eighties. Matthew's gospel was aimed primarily at drawing the Jews into the "Way," the earliest reference to Christianity. Therefore, it features a genealogy of Jesus beginning with Abraham, the father of the Jews. Also, his infancy narrative has magi (non-Jewish astrologers) coming to worship the Jewish baby, whom they proclaim as king of the Jews.

Matthew's text contains five great discourses, each concluding with "when Jesus finished these words" beginning in 7:28. These discourses are known as the Sermon on the Mount (5:3—7:27); the missionary discourse (10:5–42); the parable discourse (13:3–52); the discourse on life in his kingdom (18:1–35); and the eschatological discourse (24:4–25, 26). Each discourse has its own theme and is preceded by a narrative section. One who is aware of this organization can better understand each discourse and apply it to his or her life with greater clarity and impact.

When speaking of Matthew, we recall *"I say to you, you are Peter, and upon this rock I will build my church"* (16:18), which the Roman Catholic Church designates as its foundation text. Still today, these words are emblazoned above the high altar of St. Peter's basilica. However, the word *church* appears in no other gospel, and otherwise only once in Matthew, chapter 18:17, wherein it refers to a local community. Reflect on whether Jesus envisioned in 16:18 a centralized, severely hierarchical church. If not, imagine what shape his "church" would assume today.

Luke writes in two parts, with his gospel as volume 1 and the Acts of the Apostles as volume 2. He writes with literary Hellenistic skill, a quasi-history of the "Way." He begins with the birth of Jesus, continues with his mission, death, and resurrection, and completes his effort with the spread of the "Way" through Israel, its environs, and even to Rome. Accordingly, Luke, in contrast to

Matthew, is writing to Gentile Christians and literally, through the centuries, to us. His message has several emphases: First, he accepts the imminent second coming of the Son of Man (12:38), for which we are still waiting unless understood spiritually. However, Luke stresses more importantly the daily living of Christians; for example, his Sermon on the Plain (6:20–23), which is his version of Matthew's Sermon on the Mount. Second, Luke includes women in the Christian calling more than any other evangelist (for example, 8:2–3). Third, Luke emphasizes the power of God's Spirit for Christly living (4:18).

Luke devotes much of his gospel to Jesus' one journey to Jerusalem, 9:51—19:44 (traditionally 19:27). This reminds perceiving Christian readers that they also journey just once through their lifetime in the footsteps of Jesus to their death and resurrection in Christ. Finally, Luke adds one curious discrepancy: he concludes his gospel (volume 1) with the ascension of Jesus on the same day as his resurrection (24:50–53). However, he begins volume 2 (The Acts of the Apostles) by stating Jesus appeared to them forty days later, then ascended (Acts 1:3). Could it be the author forgot what he had written, or was mistaken? Not hardly. Rather, the forty-day reference symbolizes a long period of trial as discussed in chapter 15. In reality, Luke is saying that each of us has forty days (our lifetime) to absorb and live his life and teachings; who knows how many, if any, of his or her forty days remain?

Only the eagle can stare directly at the sun and not be blinded. This could be why the eagle represents John's gospel; after all, this gospel does focus on the transcendent God. However, at the same time, the gospel views God not only as transcendent, but also as present in the person of Jesus. He is the incarnate (enfleshed) Son of God, the Messiah, in whom we can safely place our trust. This theme plays consistently beneath every story and discourse of the gospel.

Immediately in the prologue, the author ignores the mundane nativity of Jesus, which Matthew and Luke narrate. Rather, he proclaims the bursting forth of God in and through the Word. This Word carries two fundamental meanings: First, the platonic notion of God's wisdom encompassing his patterns and ideas of this world. Second, the Hebrew notion of *dabhar* ("word") refers to a creative agent expressing its effective, self-revealing reality; for example, *"God said, 'Let there be light,' and there was light"* (Gen. 1:3). God's Word was effective (accomplishing exactly its goal), thereby revealing a dimension of himself, in this case, God as spiritual light. In a sense, don't we also manifest God's Word? For we are also portals of God's wisdom and light, and designed to be his effective agents.

Christians have come to identify this incarnate Word with God the Son and view the Son (the second person of the Trinity) taking on humanity in the form of Jesus. Therefore, Jesus becomes the Son of God on earth. This gospel helped to generate deep and prolonged discussion on the nature of the Nazarene until finally, the Council of Nicea defined in 325 CE the divinity of Jesus, and the Council of Chalcedon in 451, the full humanity of Jesus. This carries powerful meaning for us: the certain assurance that his is the authentic life for us to live. As we have seen, John writes of Jesus as being light and life. Thomas Browne comments insightfully in the seventeenth century, "Life itself is but a shadow of eternity…and light, but the shadow of God."[1]

John's gospel records seven so-called miracle stories, but they carry far deeper meaning. As examples, after the wine (symbolizing Judaism in the Hebrew Testament) runs out at the Cana wedding feast, Jesus changes water into superior wine (symbolizing the spiritual body of Christ in whom we participate). Jesus raises Lazarus to life (resuscitation to this life) to symbolize his and our approaching resurrection into eternal life.

Profound discourses also characterize this gospel. Jesus discusses with Nicodemus, a Pharisee in chapter 3, his and our calling to a spiritual life. He insists in chapter 6 that he is truly present in bread from heaven and proves his truth by challenging in chapter 8 anyone to accuse him of sin.

John compiles Jesus' greatest discourse in chapters 14–17. Therein, Jesus exclaims his only commandment: not to pray, do penance, or even to believe certain doctrines, but to love as he has loved. One wonders why our churches don't more profoundly and effectively prioritize his one commandment. He will send an advocate to us, however, (a Paraclete) to energize the powers of our love. Finally, he prays this mutual love will make us one; incredibly even as he and Abba are one.

Jesus proves the purity of his love when he endures his passion and death. He dies in abject human defeat and still trusts and loves his Abba, himself, and his followers. What a challenge it is for us to love as he loved! His resurrection is proclaimed by a woman from Magdala whose physical journey to the tomb of resurrection symbolizes her victorious spiritual journey. We are also called to rise with him from our cross, and that call echoes through the centuries of ages and locations to where today you are being called at this moment to rise from your Magdala.

Wherever you dwell, whoever you are, all of us will agree these four gospels continue to impact Western society more than any other written manuscripts in human history. For us who believe in their divine inspiration, the Gospels take on supreme dignity and value. We ask you, therefore, to participate in a possible life-changing enthronement. Arrange a place of honor in your home for the Bible. Whether you live alone or with others, take it in hand every day and read a brief passage. Then, discuss it for ten minutes, or if alone, pray over this passage. Most importantly, try to live its message that day. Martin Luther exclaimed, "The Bible lives; it speaks to me. It has feet, and runs after me. It has hands, and it seizes me"![2] How fortunate and sacred, those who are so seized!

Loving Spirit of Abba, because we believe you inspired the sacred biblical authors, we promise to increase our commitment to learn and drink in your wisdom expressed therein. May we become women and men of your Word not only by understanding but especially by living your inspired wisdom. Amen.

CHAPTER 32

HEROD TO CHRIST:
THE GREAT DIVIDE

W hat fools these mortals be,"[1] writes Seneca, a Roman first-century philosopher, and how apropos of Herod, who had everything, only to discover he had nothing: a telling lesson from Herod to those of us who worship "upward mobility"!

He was born in 73 BCE, the son of Antipater, an Arab Idumean (Edom lay southeast of Israel), and was hated by the Jews. Antipater (meaning against the father) possessed great wealth and political "savvy," both of which he passed on to Herod, the eldest of his four sons. Antipater appointed Herod governor of Galilee in 47, but six years later, when the Parthians invaded, Herod fled to Rome. There, he solidified his relationship with Marc Antony, whom he would support in Rome's political maneuverings. Later, despite Cleopatra's convincing Antony to grant her many of Herod's lands, Herod remained loyal to Marc Antony, who became his patron. After Marc Antony suffered his final defeat at Actium in 31 BCE, Herod decided to "throw the dice" by admitting to Octavian, Antony's conqueror (later Emperor Augustus), that he had "backed" Antony. He begged at the same time for mercy. Octavian recognized Herod's self-serving honesty and confirmed him as king of the Jews. Herod reigned for thirty-three years. He built huge fortresses, splendid cities, especially Caesarea (named for Caesar), but his most ambitious project was the mammoth temple occupying over thirty acres in Jerusalem. Herod had fortune, talent, and power, and remains as a symbol of all this world has to offer to many of us capitalists who suffer similar seductions. Oh Herod, what could have been, if only you had sought the truth!

Herod suffered a deep shadow in his character to which eventually he succumbed. He trusted no one; even family bonds meant nothing to Herod, who executed three sons and numerous others. Caesar himself was heard to say, "I would rather be a fattened pig than one of Herod's sons." Although Herod had once loved his wife, Mariame, he became insanely jealous of her and eventually murdered her, his two sons, brother, grandfather, and mother. Truly, Herod was a tortured man. Some say he was manic-depressive; all would agree to his extreme paranoia. This was the Herod who, Matthew writes, slaughtered the male babies in Bethlehem. There is no other historical evidence of this, but certainly he was capable of such.

Josephus, the Jewish historian, writes of Herod's final tragedy. Herod was dying in his palace at Jericho. In despair, but without success, this man who had it all attempted suicide. Later, realizing death was imminent, and the Jews would rejoice at it, he locked the Jewish leadership in the Jericho stadium. He ordered them to be murdered at his death, hoping to preclude Jewish celebrations. Afterward, these final orders were ignored. A funeral procession of several hundred courtiers and slaves with banners and incense wound its way from Jericho to the Herodium fortress over twenty miles away. Herod's body was dressed in royal purple, bedecked in gold and jewels, and carried on a golden bier. The body was buried in garish splendor atop the Herodium Mount, and so this man of "tyranny and depression" met his creator with only empty baubles to recommend him. He teaches us, in his dreadful death, not to live for the futility of earthly power even in our prosaic relationships. Despite whatever power we believe we possess, finally we are rendered powerless.

Herod divided his property among his three remaining sons: Philip received the far north, Archelaus, his favorite son (whom Rome deposed in 6 CE), inherited Judea and Samaria, and Antipas, Galilee. Antipas was he whom Jesus called "that fox": the one who murdered the Baptist. Pilate, the Roman Procurator, disliked Antipas, but during Jesus' trial referred him to Antipas as a courtesy. This led to resolving their prior hostility. Even in death, Jesus the peacemaker was healing. He calls us to the same role in our lives.

The malevolence in this family begins, as far as we know, with Antipater. Herod learned this lesson from him and, through his example, passed it to his three sons. It's easy to criticize the Herodian family, but what of our own? We may not inherit the egregious patterns of the Herods, but every family has its shadow, whether mental disease, hostility, alcoholism, estrangement, or whatever. Are you and I healers, dividers, or mere bystanders in our familial dysfunction?

Herod remains an evil figure in human history and Jesus, the greatest. Most would agree to these two characterizations, but consider whether it's not true that Herod still lives today, that some portion of him and Jesus lives in the heart of each of us. This is not to say you and I are Herods, but it is true that we strike out against others and ourselves, whether violently, orally, or conceptually. The spirit of Jesus living in us stands for our commitment to compassion, courage, and peace-making. Truly, our life becomes, with the magi, a journey from Herod to Christ.

Lord Jesus, there were only two kings in Israel at the time of your birth, you and Herod. Herod embodies jealousy, greed, and power; you, innocence and passion for life and truth. Help us in our daily relationships to choose you and all you stand for. Save us from our Herodian pathology. Like the magi, help us return to our eternal home, not by following the path leading to Herod, but on another leading to you. Amen.

CHAPTER 33

MERRY CHRISTMAS!

It's just one week until Christmas. I must address the cards; buy and send three more presents; decorate the tree; and plan Christmas dinner! There's little time, less money, and more anxiety. This is a crazy Christmas!" It's been said John Masefield, England's poet laureate of the early twentieth century, commented that the jingle of the cash register sadly silenced "O Come, O Come Emanuel." Unfortunately, that jingle has, for many of us, become a bustling, compulsive cacophony.

One sure solution for this trivialization of Christmas is to return to the nativity of Jesus in its genuine, profound meaning. Since medieval days, we Christians have settled for the homey stable and the cutesy crèche. This dimension of the nativity carries with it great charm, especially for the young, but the understanding adult is entitled to an in-depth explanation of this momentous event.

Our classical Christian Tradition maintains the Son of God took on humanity at the nativity. By assuming this personhood,

Jesus bridges the gap between God and humanity. Therefore, we humans are now able to see God in human form and can more easily lead a godly life. This has formed the foundation of most Christian spirituality and has great value.

However, this stable vignette overlooks the fundamental theme of Christianity that is notably absent from contemporary Christian spirituality. The great Karl Rahner stated this theme succinctly: "Divinity has taken on humanity so that humanity can take on divinity."[1] Rahner suggests that God sent his only begotten child to earth so that all of us might assume divinity by adoption. Angelus Selesius writes poetically, "If, in your heart, you make a manger for his birth, then God will, once again, become a child on earth."[2] Rahner and Selesius are suggesting an expansive incarnation whereby God takes flesh, not only in Jesus, but also in each of us.

Accordingly, Christ is calling us not only to follow him but to be him, to be a Christ. The Second Vatican Council stated, "The church rightly looks to her who gave birth to Christ...so that he (Christ) could be born, and grow in the hearts of the faithful."[3] Therefore, our identity is Christ. Jesus lived as a Christ by teaching, healing, and loving fully, even to his death. This is also your calling and mine, and it all began at that first Christmas when Jesus was born as the cornerstone of divinized mankind. If you and I realized and lived this identity, consider the magnificent possibilities for our world. Could Jesus have intended this by proclaiming, *"I [you] am the light of the world"* (John 8:12)? You might be thinking, "How idealistic; how impractical!" Not so! Abba is calling each of us commoners to live in his light. God is not impractical but is spiritual.

My mother was such a beacon. Seven years before her death, she contracted peripheral neuritis, in which excruciating pain began in the extremities and eventually encased her entire body;

the pain became unbearable. She complained, "What good am I; I can't even get out of bed anymore; why doesn't God take me?" However, it wasn't long before she realized her Christly calling. She could still read the newspaper every morning, and she noticed the crises other people were enduring. She followed up by sending a daily letter, praying, or phoning one of those in need of encouragement and comfort. One day, she read of Willie, a power-forward for a local basketball team who was suffering from depression. She sent an immediate note to Willie saying, "You're a six foot ten black man, and I, a four foot eleven white woman who no longer can get out of bed. I want you to know how much joy you have given me." He wrote back, "Dear Mrs. Carroll, I have always played just for the money; I never knew anyone actually cared. With all my heart, I thank you." She was a beacon, shining brightly each day until her death: she was, and is, another Christ.

It's no wonder Pope Paul VI quotes Augustine in his encyclical, *Ecclesiam Suam*: "Let us rejoice, and give thanks that we have become not only Christian, but Christ. Do you understand the grace of God our head? Stand in admiration, rejoice, we have become Christ."[4]

Because of the centrality and powerful spiritual impact of this extraordinary truth, we suggest you promote in your church community a dedication of all Christmas services to this identification with Christ. What could be more fitting than to center our focus on this foundational Christian calling and its demands. Finally, with this in mind, your pastor might lead the community in a Christmas renewal of their baptismal vows.

Henri LeSaux sums up the real meaning of the Christmas Nativity: "The joy of Christmas is not only the crèche; the crèche is just a sign. The true crèche is: Jesus, born in us, and, being born in us, makes us unto himself."[5]

And so whatever today's date might be, we wish you in its amazingly divine meaning, "Merry Christmas!" You are born anew this day as another Christ.

Joyous Lord, you were born to bring heavenly life to earthly life that we might lead your spiritual life in our human life. Help us make your incarnation live anew in each of us. Grant that Christmas may assume its Christian significance again, but this time in its incarnate wisdom that has us reach out as a Christ to all whom we touch. Amen.

CHAPTER 34

THE COLORFUL VISITORS

If the birth of Jesus was so extraordinary, then why didn't John or Mark even mention it? Again, if it was so miraculous, why did Matthew and Luke disagree on the details? Matthew writes of the Magi, and Luke of the shepherds. Neither even notes the existence of the other set of visitors, as if they didn't exist. Could it be these two evangelists were using the stories of these visitors to symbolize deeper messages, and if so, what are these messages?

Luke initially mentions the shepherds in chapter 2, verse 8 with the angel of the Lord appearing to them. Why shepherds? Why not priests or Pharisees, who followed the law so meticulously? Shepherds lived on the hillsides beyond the control of the temple priests. They dwelt on the lowest rung of Israel's socioeconomic ladder. In a word, they were lowly sinners, and Luke had the audacity to describe God appearing to these social rejects through angels, and then they were given the privilege of visiting the Lord. Surely, this is the gospels' first suggestion of Jesus' coming not so much for the wealthy, the holy, or "legal eagles," but for the ordinary and the sinner. Therefore, you and I, as sinners, were spiritually present through these shepherds at the nativity of our lifelong search for the savior and all he represents.

Appearing to the shepherds, the angels burst into praise with the keynote address of the New Testament: *"Glory to God in the highest / and on earth peace to those on whom his favor rests"* (Luke 2:14). This hymn of ecstatic joy represents heaven's pent-up passion for God's great breakthrough into human consciousness. All creation exalts!

The angels sing of peace, not the forced peace of the "political or military machine," or the mere absence of hostility. This is a transcendent, new kind of peace for which this baby would eventually give his life. This peace rises not from the external but from our human depths because it springs from the Christ dwelling within each of us. It is indestructible unless we ourselves destroy it. Finally, your peace in Christ embraces ideally all as with the original shepherds who *"made known the message that had been told them about this child"* (Luke 2:17). From Jesus' beginning to the end in his shalom ("peace") of the Risen Christ, Abba tries to catch us up in this message of the Prince of Peace.

This peace-promise is directed to "all on whom his favor rests." Does this mean God selects certain ones whom he favors? No, it's just the opposite. His favor (grace) rests on all. The pivotal question is, who of us shepherds is open to this peace; who will dismiss his or her own agenda to choose to live in Christian peace? Becoming passionate for such sublime peace will cause your relatives and friends to detect a new serenity flowing from you. Surely, they would wonder; and *"all who heard it were amazed by what had been told them by the shepherds"* (Luke 2:18).

However, others visit the newborn Christ, for the author of Matthew describes three magi coming from the East. Magi were considered to be royal advisers with expertise in astrology and dream interpretation. If literally true, they would have come hundreds of miles through the desert following a star. In ancient times, people believed that any royal birth would signal the appearance of a new star. Perhaps, Matthew was actually intending to identify Jesus as royal. Possibly, Matthew is referring to Numbers 24:17, wherein the author speaks of future victory for Israel: *"I see him, though not now; / I behold him, though not near: / a star shall advance from Jacob, / and a staff shall rise from Israel."* One certain dimension of this story is that you and I are called to follow a star through our deserts, and that star is the Jewish Jesus, the Christ.

The real key to this passage lays, however, in the three gifts the magi bring to the baby Jesus. Gold is a gift fit for a king; incense reminds a first–century Judean of priesthood, and myrrh was an aromatic gum used to embalm the dead. So we realize this mythic tale is telling us with literary elegance, this baby will become a king and priest, and will accomplish it by his death. In this story of crucial spiritual significance, the fourth gift carries most importance. This is your gift, and it's your life. Are you willing to commit to this baby?

The authors did not intend it, but if we combine the messages of the shepherds and the magi, a clear theme emerges. The magi tell us Jesus is our king and priest to whom we give allegiance. The shepherds add that such fidelity gives us deep abiding peace, the peace Jesus would enjoy. This message (combining the Jewish shepherds and Gentile magi) extends the story to all people. God, through his angels and magi, invites every one of us to the person of Christ, not only on his day of birth, but through every day of our lives.

You, shepherds and magi, first visitors to the blessed Babe, give us the courage to withdraw, as you did, from our daily activity to visit daily with the newborn Prince of Peace. Jesus, just as you were born historically, now you are born spiritually within me. I promise I shall grow into a new person by visiting you daily within my spirit. Accordingly, I shall now select one activity that I perform daily and arrange to set aside, in some way therein, my own self-interest to reflect consciously on this spiritual gift I will present to my Lord. Amen.

CHAPTER 35

JOHN, MENTOR AND BAPTIZER

W ho does this wild man claim to be? We're already Jews—
why is he baptizing us? Some say he is talking repentance.
For us? We're already the chosen people!"

These questions and others are "driving us crazy" as we plod the
road centuries ago from Jerusalem to the Jordan to see and hear a
man of mystery called John. The walk is long, dusty, and hot, but
when we arrive, we can't believe our eyes or ears. There's the river, and
in it, a man with water above his knees. His face is weather-beaten
by wind and sun; his frame is gaunt, clothed in scant loincloth; and
his words pierce like sharpened arrows. No wonder shouts from the
crowd arise: "Who is he?" "He looks like a desert man!" "Could he
be another Elijah?"

His message is the most astounding of all, *"Repent, for the kingdom of heaven is at hand!"* (Matt. 3:2). Repent for what? We're Jews,
and we have nothing for which to repent.

John continues, *"You brood of vipers!...Produce good fruit as evidence of your repentance. And do not presume to say to yourselves, 'We have Abraham as our father.' For I tell you, God can raise up children to Abraham from these stones"* (vv. 7–9).

By challenging the Jews in such fiery language, John proves his courage and conviction. He brings deeper insight to the Jews; namely, that who we are has no meaning compared to what we are. If he were living today, would his message remain the same? We who claim with our lips Jesus as our Lord have at times judged ourselves closer to God than others and have in his name even condemned others for not being one of us: other denominations, non-Christians, sinners, gays, alcoholics, foreigners, and illegals. Do you suppose John would exclaim to us, *"You brood of vipers!...Even now the ax lies at the root of the trees. Therefore every tree that does not bear good fruit will be cut down and thrown into the fire....He will clear his threshing floor and gather his wheat into his barn, but the chaff he will burn with unquenchable fire"* (vv. 7, 10, 12).

Many miles away in Galilee, Jesus heard of John and his message, and decided he must learn more about this man. He would not visit the affluent priests in the temple, but rather, the river rebel. Following his long journey, Jesus discovered finally a man with whom he could agree. Priestly status, wealth, and religious sacrifice were not Yahweh's priorities. John understood that, and to all who didn't, he called for repentance. Baptism was its symbol, and the Day of the Lord was quickly approaching. It not surprising that John Meier, an expert on Christ, describes John as the "mentor" of Jesus. Meier writes, "By submitting to his message and baptism, Jesus became the disciple, the pupil, the student of this rabbi called John."[1] Some disciples of Jesus might object to the apparent leadership of John with regard to Jesus. All of us must surely remember that Jesus was fully human and therefore grew spiritually just as we do, and his growth was nurtured in the milk of humanity as is ours.

The pivotal test for a great teacher remains how profoundly she or he can live that teaching. By that standard, John proved his greatness. Eventually, Jesus expanded John's message with his own, and though some of John's disciples left to accompany Jesus, there is no hint of John ever resenting this.

John courageously continued his own mission with determination, even to his beheading. He learned that King Herod had married Herodias, the wife of his brother Philip, and felt compelled to denounce publicly this sin. (What a lesson in courage for today's preachers and disciples alike.) Herodias was furious and convinced Herod to imprison John, probably in the dungeon Machaereus far out in the desert.

John's visitors told him of the surpassing teachings and work of Jesus, his soul friend; so, John sent messengers to Jesus to question his possible messiahship, for John had expected the Messiah to appear in fiery judgment. Jesus answered with quotes from Isaiah spotlighting his compassion and sensitivity. He then advised the messengers to tell John, *"Blessed is the one who takes no offense at me"* (Matt. 11:6). Then speaking to the crowd, Jesus praised his beloved mentor even more: *"Why did you go out? To see a prophet? Yes, I tell you, and more than a prophet. This is the one about whom it is written: / 'Behold, I am sending my messenger ahead of you; / he will prepare your way before you.' / Amen, I say to you, among those born of women there has been none greater than John the Baptist"* (11:9–11).

We picture John, alone and friendless, in a dark, dirt-floor cell waiting the beheading he knew was coming. After his messengers reported back, John realized his former disciple, Jesus, was now mentoring him because of his superior message, and that he was the one. Further, John understood he had successfully introduced the Messiah. His life was finished, but he believed his beloved Jews would overcome their blindness in some unknown, mysterious way because of Jesus, the Messiah, the man he was privileged to mentor. John then heard the clattering approach of soldiers' boots and swords in scabbards. He would never know that as he prepared the way for Jesus in his life, he would do the same in his death.

John's disciples collected the remains and buried them. They told Jesus what had happened, and Matthew wrote poignantly, *"When Jesus heard of it, he withdrew in a boat to a deserted place by himself"* (14:13).

John, you were truly a great human being, a prophet, and loyal Jew, committed to bringing your people to Yahweh. You gave your life in that effort, so this very moment you and Jesus, your old friend, live together again. Please, help each of us to live your role; that is, to introduce the Christ in us to the people in our lives. As you gave your life in this effort, help us to give ours in the cause of Christ: to become a John. Amen.

CHAPTER 36

WILL YOU MARRY ME?

I recall attending years ago an outdoor wedding reception at a lake in the countryside. Suddenly, the wine ran out. Near panic set in as the wedding party and guests realized there was no place within ten miles to purchase a "happy" replacement. Yes, I can certainly relate to the need for Jesus changing water into wine at the reception described by John. This action of Jesus carries, however, far more wisdom and importance than merely stoking the conviviality of a wedding reception.

John begins, *"On the third day there was a wedding in Cana"* (2:1). If you review carefully John's first chapter, you will notice it's really the fifth or sixth day. It's not that John can't count; rather, he is tipping us off to a deeper symbolic meaning embedded in the story. The number three meant to the Hebrews, not only a numerical reference, but also "carrying divine intervention." Remember, for example, the three days of Jesus' redemptive act on Calvary. John's gospel breathes the air of high, even mystical theology, and so, the events in his gospel resonate with deeper meaning.

In the text, John implies the mother of Jesus was chiefly invited; Jesus and his disciples were an afterthought. Thus, when the wine ran short, his mother, being in the inner circle, was immediately informed. Accustomed to obtaining help from her son, she informed Jesus. Note that in Hebraic history, the grape, the vine, and wine were symbolic of Judaism; John is portraying Judaic effectiveness as running out.

Jesus responded, *"Woman, how does your concern affect me? My hour has not yet come"* (2:4). How could Jesus respond so insensitively to his mother by calling her "woman"? Actually, this reaction registers as a supreme compliment. Adam and the first woman, Eve, were associated in the fall of mankind, so it was fitting that the Son of Man and "woman" be joined in the redemption of mankind at the "coming out party" of Jesus. To support this, the term "My hour" always refers in John's gospel to Jesus' act of redemption. Both genders play, therefore, an active and just role in our fall and redemption. Our churches ought to consider carefully the wishes of their founder by implementing the equality of genders preached by John and lived by Jesus.

Mary said to the waiters, and says to us, *"Do whatever he tells you"* (2:5). Because I believe Jesus is my savior, I have been trying to follow her instruction throughout my life. How fitting for my redemption and yours to begin at a wedding celebration, the supreme sign of human commitment, symbolizing the spiritual wedding of Christ with each of us.

Jesus told the server to fill six huge jars with water, totaling about one hundred fifty gallons. These were genuine purification jars used in Judaic ritual, suggesting again that, according to John, official Judaism has been superseded. Notice also, the hugely excessive volume of wine for approximately fifty guest residents of the village. John wrote frequently in terms of excess, as if to remind us that the whole idea of redemption is beyond all reasonable calculation. For some, sadly, this excess is "too good to be true," and so they refuse to acknowledge the largesse of Abba.

Jesus then ordered the servants to take some water to the steward for tasting. The steward remarked, *"Everyone serves good wine first,... but you have kept the good wine until now"* (2:10). John is suggesting through this deeply meaningful story that, in his opinion, the wine of Christ (symbolic of the Kingdom of God) supersedes Judaism. His hour has indeed come and ours also, insofar as we live in the Kingdom. Spiritually, each of us, regardless of gender, stands as the bride of Christ in the wedding at Cana.

We must comment on John's broad brush toward "the Jews" that has aroused such rancor between Jews and Christians through the centuries. John errs, by today's more enlightened standards, in blaming the "Jews" for the murder of Jesus (John 19:7b et al.). Thank God, the Vatican II documents spoke so forthrightly in rejecting all forms of insult toward God's first chosen people. "Neither all Jews at that time or Jews today, can be charged with the crimes committed during his passion.... The Jews should not be spoken of as rejected or cursed as if this followed from holy Scripture.... [The church] deplores all hatreds, persecutions, and displays of anti-Semitism leveled at any time or from any source against the Jews."[1]

You and I, his disciples, are being called by this story to share in continuing this celebration of love. He associates, not only the woman, but each of us in the ongoing momentous struggle to transform vengeance into forgiveness, violence into peace, apathy and hate into passionate love: water into wine.

The wedding still remains as the greatest promise and celebration of human love. This story, however, thrusts us beyond time, space, and human distinctions to invite all people to a "oneing" with Christ our lover. The Christ represents the ultimate truth and goodness each of us can become and express. Jesus, alone among humans, has achieved total identity as Christ. He, therefore, shows us the path, safeguards our progress, and becomes our reward. You have the certainty of faith that he will remain loyal to you, drawing you forever to himself. Will you promise that you shall likewise dedicate yourself to him by teaching, healing, and loving others, and thereby sealing your mystical marriage to him and them?

Lord, we ask you to draw together today's Jews and Christians in a great evolutionary embrace. Help us to smash our walls of division so we may realize that true greatness will arise from us when our families unite in spiritual marriage and thereby become one. Amen.

CHAPTER 37

"BEHOLD THE MAN!"
(JOHN 19:5)

Christians agree Jesus stands as the central character in the Bible; some would say, its only character. However, many Christians have little knowledge of what Jesus stands for, and many actually promote, in his name, the opposite of that for which he gave his life. Such Christians support war, capital punishment, and greed, justifying such stands in terms of patriotism, justice, or capitalism, respectfully. Some wallow in loneliness, depression, and boredom, not realizing Jesus has addressed all of these woes successfully. Indeed, his life and views provide the foundation for humanity's addressing today's political, and relational challenges. As Christians and even as human beings, we are certainly called at least to acknowledge these solutions from Jesus, of whom Mark Link writes, "Down the corridors of time, has traveled a man whose life and spirit have changed men's lives and shaped the course of history as no other man has ever done."[1]

We Christians generally accept the divinity of Jesus as defined in 325 CE by the Council of Nicea, but generally ignore the full, genuine humanity of Jesus as defined in 451 CE by the Council of Chalcedon. This has proven disastrous because few of us can now relate to Jesus as a real human being calling us to a personal and social love revolution. Wolfhart Pannenberg, the renowned German Protestant theologian, writes insightfully, "You must inquire first into the historical Jesus, and find therein, his divinity."[2] In other words, Jesus can lead us because he suffered from his own psychological and physical baggage. Despite that, he faced his terrible terrors with faith, courage, and compassion for others, even his persecutors. Bereft of knowing and embracing this humanity of Jesus, the world grows violent, and the church, tepid. Tragically, we view Jesus as being able to call upon his divinity at any time for "miracles" to ease him through his challenges. This minimizes his "humanness" and renders his pain as mere theatre. Thus, Jesus becomes distant from our condition and experience. My embattled life and yours cry out for the challenge and solace that the human Jesus can provide when he's understood; therefore, this chapter implores each of us to ponder Jesus "humanly, daily, and decisively."

Because Jesus was fully human, he was not immune to human limitations. He did not enjoy full knowledge of circumstances, events, or even himself. Mark records Jesus saying to his disciples concerning the last days, *"Of that day or hour, no one knows, neither the angels in heaven, nor the Son, but only the Father"* (13:32). Rather, he blended his parents' instruction, the Hebrew Testament, the example of his peers, his own experience, and especially his prayer life to develop the loftiest teachings ever taught. As we wrestle with our limitations, we can draw from similar sources and from him to overcome our challenges, which radically were the same as his. Yes, even his referring to himself as Son of Man unites him with us, who are also sons and daughters of man.

He made some horrendous mistakes. Luke describes Jesus praying all night to select the right men to comprise the twelve. The next morning he chose them, including *"Judas Iscariot, who became a traitor"* (Luke 6:16). Later, he would have to admit of his selection, *"It would be better for that man if he had never been born"* (Mark 14:21). Jesus became furious in the temple: *"He made a whip out of cords and drove them all out of the temple area, with the sheep and oxen, and spilled the coins of the money-changers and overturned their tables,"* (John 2:15). He became lonely and discouraged: *"My soul is sorrowful even to death"* (Mark 14:34). Jesus was terribly tempted, and could have "given up" in Gethsemane: *"My Father, if it is possible, let this cup pass from me; yet not as I will, but as you will"* (Matt. 26:39).

Worst of all, he was alone in his moment of desperation. Perhaps, you have experienced such loneliness. Jesus steeled himself against this agony, but was forced by ignorant people steeped in cruelty to continue on their path of apparent destruction. However, in the end, his torture and death introduced his greatest achievement.

Realizing deeply his humanity causes us to wonder at his secret. How could he, a human being like ourselves, live so heroically when people jeered, others insulted him, his friends abandoned him, and all refused to believe in him? We will explore in a future chapter the supreme importance of his Abba experience while acknowledging now that Jesus lived intimately as one with his father. This was his overarching anchor. He even explained in John 10:30, *"The Father and I are one,"* and calls each of us to this union. Because he is the face of Abba on earth, he is really calling us to himself. In the light of this, one would think we, his disciples, would through prayer, study, and determination, focus acutely our attention on him. However, few of his disciples devote even ten minutes a day to reading or studying his revolutionary life. We Christians seem too busy. The poet Ron Seitz writes insightfully, "Can you think of a greater tragedy or worse loss or sin than our not understanding the real message and person of Jesus?"[3]

His message, in brief: whatever pain you endure, nothing, not even death, can prevent you, his disciple, from striving to love as he loved. To gain an ever-increasing understanding of this spiritual master is our ongoing desperate need, privilege, and reward. It's time to waken from our "Gethsemane sleep" and rebel against the seductive culture of a pagan society, and with courage commit ourselves to Jesus in our daily experiences and relationships. This decision could well prove to be the difference between our life and death.

Lord Jesus, I pledge to seek ever-growing knowledge and intimacy with you. I shall begin each day by communing with you through your Word. Then, in your presence, I will choose for today one specific act of love for a specific person. Please, grant me the courage to make this my chief objective every day, and thereby, grow in greater intimacy with you and our Abba. Amen.

CHAPTER 38

PRAYER: EMBRACING THE DIVINE

I can clearly remember sitting as a child of four or five years on the lap of my wonderful grandfather. The flesh of his neck sagged beneath his chin, and I would stroke it with utter affection and trust. This adult can still feel the warmth and strength of Grandpa's chest as I rest gloriously my head upon it. Those moments of formative love still color, as they did then, my daily activity and illustrate the definition of prayer: a Godly way of living punctuated by moments of exquisite impact.

A troubled divorcee once questioned me, "In prayer, how do I know I am communing with God and not just with myself?" I responded, "You'll know by whether and how your interaction impacts your daily lifestyle." Effective prayer assumes the pray-er is experiencing intimately the presence of the Lord, and this experience touches her or his daily living.

In contrast, the late Rev. Gene Walsh, a noted American expert on communal prayer (liturgy) often joked, "The most common characteristics of church liturgy is that it's dull and boring. It puts me to sleep, and when I look around it's putting everyone else to sleep."[1] Walsh maintained that one causal component of such dullness was the endless reading of words from books of prayers. He prayed that prayer and liturgy would become soul-stirring. One wonders whether this bland prayer (private or communal) is feeding the passionless apathy gripping our churches today.

The Bible often describes Jesus as praying, but can you imagine his pulling out a Book of Common Prayer to read to Abba? Rather, Jesus reached to the core of his soul to commune with his beloved, divine Daddy. Surely, there is room for printed prayer in the prayer and liturgy of Christians, but we baptized children of Abba are called to pray primarily as Jesus prayed: from the depths of his heart.

St. John Damascene described in the eighth century such prayer not as communication or reading, but "as the elevation of the soul into God."[2] Genuine prayer remains an experience of the whole person, particularly from our core.

Prayer has three basic stages: meditation, affection, and contemplation, all of which are preceded by placing oneself in the presence of Abba, Jesus, or the Holy Spirit. When applied to the Bible, the entire exercise is called Lectio Divina "a divine reading":

Meditation: We read the Bible deliberately until a word, phrase, or event catches our attention; for example, we are drawn to the words of Jesus, *"I thirst"* (John 19:28). We stop reading, for we have in focus the subject matter of our prayer.

Affection: We then wrestle with this passage by asking, "Who's thirsty; for what or whom does he thirst; why does he thirst; is he still thirsting?" Do you thirst for him?

Contemplation: For those who have experienced meaningful prayer, only a moment in silence is needed to carry the pray-er into a unitive presence with his or her Lord. Abba is calling all his children, including you, to a contemplative lifestyle, thereby validating the truth of our prayer.

Notice we have not mentioned the prayer of petition that consumes the prayer of many. This raises a legitimate and explosive question: Does God change his mind because of our petitions, or do we change because of our residing in his presence? Surely, it's the latter. Thus, Jesus proclaims, *"Everyone who asks, receives; and the one who seeks, finds; and to the one who knocks, the door will be opened....*[and] *how much more will your heavenly Father give good things to those who ask him"* (Matt. 7:8, 11).

Whatever I ask of Abba, whether health, success, or even salvation, Abba gives me more, something greater: divine intimacy, even oneness. In true prayer, we dwell with and in him, and are thereby transformed into him through our loving intimacy and our challenging acceptance. We become the arterial pulse of the heart of God, love itself. Such transformation is profoundly more precious than whatever the object of our request and proves the truth of the words of Jesus quoted from Matthew 7.

Therefore, one could question, why not just enter into God's presence without ever seeking any gift? Jesus would likely respond that we are the children of Abba, who, by nature, seek sustenance from their mommy and daddy with needy and trusting dependence. What could be more appropriate in our relationship to Abba?

At the same time, remember the powerful warmth of the words of Pope John Paul I, September 17, 1978: "God is Father; even more, God is Mommy to us." We can ill afford to continue deleting from Abba (its root is *Ab* which is non-gender) the excelling qualities of the female, such as compassion, sensitivity, and courage in suffering. Whispering our needs to our creating-parent affects our touching the Divine and affects our subsequent transformation.

When Jesus was asked by his disciples to teach them to pray, he responded with the Our Father. This bedrock of Christian prayer is of the community but still finds its foundation in the intimate presence of Abba. So, in praying together, we remain focused on our presence in Abba and his presence in our community. Viewed this way, one can understand that in genuine prayer, we enter the anteroom of heaven itself, the inner chamber of Abba.

May all who read these words join hearts at this moment in the presence of Abba, our Mommy and Daddy. Regardless of our separation in time and space, let each of us now from our depths pray for each other, co-searchers of the biblical wisdom of Abba. Listen for Christ's certain response until the day it finds completion in the heart of Abba. Amen.

CHAPTER 39

HIS SECRET PASSION

W hat are you looking for?" asked Jesus of the two disciples who were curiously following him (John 1:38). That's a question he is asking you at this very moment: what's the foremost objective in your life? Many would say, "I've never thought about it," or "I don't have a central passion driving me to one goal." If you ask Jesus that question, he would, according to sacred scripture, respond with one clear and worthy goal. Our primary objective in this chapter is to identify that goal and "fire" us, as his disciples, to seek it.

Jesus remains a man of mystery. Why would he wash, as a slave, the feet of his disciples, even of Judas? What empowered him to look into the eyes of violent men pounding nails into him and pray, *"Father, forgive them"* (Luke 23:34). It's easy to say, "he's divine," but that ignores his true and full humanity. Rather, as theologian Roger Haight writes, "God's presence to Jesus must be regarded as a presence within his humanity. By this, I mean that the divine in Jesus does not appear over and above Jesus being a human being."[1]

Unfortunately, many find it difficult to acknowledge Jesus as human, but rather, insist on viewing him as overwhelmingly divine, thereby diminishing his "humanness" and our relating to him as a brother. Please refer to chapter 37.

As any believing person would, Jesus prayed before major decisions. He did not ordinarily read prayers from a book, as noted in chapter 38, but realized deeply and intimately Yahweh's presence within himself and all others. He developed an endearing and genuine familial relationship with Yahweh such that he began referring to Yahweh as Abba: Daddy, or Mommy. This was not a mere spoken title; it expressed the ultra closeness he experienced with Abba. Further, this filial intimacy gave birth to a surpassing trust in the ultimate goodness of Abba and his universe by which Jesus found this intimation of Abba even in pain, rejection, and death. Jesus used his every human experience (whether uplifting or degrading) to express his gratitude, love, and joy for his life and his solidarity with Abba. This union formed the absolute foundation for all his wisdom and courage. It's not surprising Jesus would exclaim to us as his disciples, *"Your hearts will rejoice, and no one will take your joy away from you"* (John 16:22).

Scripture scholars insist on describing this explosive driving force of Jesus as being his "Abba experience." Theologian Elizabeth Johnson writes, "Jesus' Abba experience is the heart of the matter, the dynamism behind his preaching the reign of God and his behavior. God, Abba, was the passion of his life."[2] Sadly, this passion remains unrecognized to most of his followers today, who slumber in spiritual apathy.

If Jesus was anything, he was a faithful Jew. Accordingly, he followed the commandments, especially the first two: total love of Abba and all his beloved. Jesus knew the Hebrew Testament "like the back of his hand" and was deeply familiar with the spiritual infidelity of his Jewish forefathers through the centuries. Because of this, Jesus marveled at the continuing unbelievable loyalty Abba manifested for his beloved Israel. Yes, Abba was the love of his life.

Jesus did not view Abba merely as someone "up there." Rather, he saw Abba as the abiding spirit of impassioned love within and everywhere. As he affirmed his love for Abba, he also asserted his love for all Abba's beloved. The journey of Jesus could indeed be described as one from Yahweh to Abba.

As Jesus deepened his understanding of his Abba, he eliminated all barriers between himself and Abba's other children. He embraced lepers, the disabled, enemies of Israel, and sinners of all kinds. He excluded no one, not even Judas. We personally, and our churches, must ask ourselves, "Do we, in the name of Jesus, exclude any of Abba's children in the name of law, doctrine, or morality? Are we trying to narrow his vision of universal love and close his wide-open arms?"

Furthermore, as noted in chapter 6, Jesus did not relate to Abba in its exclusive, masculine connotation to the negation of the feminine. Jesus lives and breathes the finest feminine virtues as they derive from Abba; namely, spiritual birthing, compassion, and wisdom. Jesus succeeded, not so much because of his leadership, astounding strengths of character, or even his charisma, but because of his intimate oneness with his beloved Abba. *"The Father and I are one"* (John 10:30). This he accomplished, even if it took a cross to prove it.

So few of us acknowledge his commitment to Abba, and even fewer practice it in their own lives! As a result, most of us live without passion, and our lives ebb away beneath the curse of mediocrity. Let us hear and respond, as did Jesus, to the cry of Isaiah: *"Awake, Awake! / Arise, O Jerusalem, / … / Awake, awake! / Put on your strength, O Zion"* (Isa. 51:17; 52:1).

Eliminate from your consciousness all that is present except Abba (your Daddy and Mommy), your ultimate beloved. What do you say to your spiritual parent who thirsts to become the central passion of your life? Could you promise to "come away for a little while" each morning in preparation for loving that day's experiences (whatever they may be) as gifts from Abba? Can you begin to live more deeply in your life this central passion and solidarity with Abba that Jesus lived in his? Carpe diem!

CHAPTER 40

MARY, HIS FIRST DISCIPLE

When I was a little boy and playing outdoors, I would hear her call, "Norm! Norm! Dinner is ready!" Ah! They who feed life to others are they who are most alive! She and I have a special bond that neither years nor death can erase. Such bonding is surely not exclusively ours; hopefully, you profit also from similar golden memories. Karl Jung, the master psychiatrist, declares the mother relationship to be our strongest archetype or universal human pattern.

Jesus and his mother were no exception. We see this in the dark night of his soul in Gethsemane just before he was seized by six hundred soldiers (the cohort). He whimpered from the depths of his soul, *"Abba,…[t]ake this cup away from me, but not what I will but what you will"* (Mark 14:36). How could Jesus have acquired such courage? Clearly, from his mother's belief system experienced during his youth. Note the stark similarity of her words: *"I am the hand-maid of the Lord. May it be done to me according to your word"* (Luke

1:38). This confirms the poetic genius of Gerard Manley Hopkins: "Through her, we may see him, made sweeter, not made dim."[1]

Just as many Christians experience difficulty in accepting the full humanity of Jesus, many are also reluctant to view Mary in her real humanity. They tend to see her as the perfect, blameless mother who suffered heroically, who died (maybe not), and was taken to heaven where she wears a blue mantle. As appealing as such a person might be, Mary's greatness actually arises, not from some idyllic transcendency or semblance of divinity, but from her humanity, and how her faith grew despite the monumental challenges she faced.

Keeping in mind her most important role of mothering and subsequent nurturing of Jesus' psyche (providing a strong female anima), we trace this growth in her faith from her most prominent biblical appearances.

Luke describes in chapter 1 of his gospel a mythic story of the angel Gabriel appearing to Mary with the message of her approaching conception and her bearing a son. This story tends to gloss over her remarkable courage. She learns she will conceive during her year of betrothal (Matt. 1:18 and Luke 1:27), which Jewish law considered sin, punishable by stoning to death. She and Joseph were so tormented by this that Joseph decided to divorce her (Matt. 1:19). Imagine the stress these two endured! Matthew 1:23 and Luke 1:27 both refer to her virginity, which has received much theological attention, but her faith and courage stand pre-eminently in the suffering she endured because of dire threats to her marriage, her life, and the life of her baby to be. Luke writes of Mary and Joseph finding their twelve-year-old in the temple where he had been lost. The boy Jesus responds to them, *"Did you not know that I must be in my Father's house?"* (Luke 2:49). *"But they did not understand what he said to them"* (2:50). Thus, Luke is questioning whether Mary knows the extraordinary nature of her son. This calls into serious question a literal interpretation of what Luke wrote in Gabriel's annunciation to Mary (1:26–35). She returned with Jesus to Nazareth and continued mothering her boy while keeping *"all these things in her heart"* (2:51). Her faith born in dark uncertainty was beginning to mature.

Mary appears also with the family in Mark 3:20–21, which we probe in our next chapter. Therein, her faith is severely challenged, for it must have seemed to her that her boy was compromising the traditional Judaism the family revered and practiced so avidly (refer to chapter 41). However, in her next appearance, she stands courageously at the foot of the cross, which indicates a tremendous transformation has taken place in her soul. This dramatic change signals hopefully a singular journey in each of us.

As noted, John places Mary at the cross atop Calvary (John 19:26, 27). She, like us, had experienced doubt in him and his career. This became a source of horrific pain for this loving and loyal mother who, it seems, finally resolved her doubt by observing his unconquered faith and spirit even on a cross. John writes of Jesus exclaiming as he died, *"'Woman, behold, your son.' Then he said to the disciple, 'Behold, your mother'"* (John 19:26–27). Mary, an elderly woman of gray, watched with broken spirit the death of her son. She had observed his career of acclaim, and now his crucifying end. During these days, Mary pondered so many questions: What does his crucifixion mean? Is he really a devil as the priests say? Do I know my son? All I really know is that I believe in his goodness. I believe in my son Yeshua.

According to Jesus, she entered now into an intimate, saving, spiritual relationship with his disciples as represented by John. In other words, she became spiritually your mother; and you, her child. This "woman" who grew in faith and courage throughout her life, now calls us to follow her on the same path. John writes that he "*took her into his home*" (John 19:27). Will you take her into your spiritual heart and, like Jesus, learn at her knee? Surely she is repeating to you the same message she delivered years ago: "*Do whatever he tells you*" (John 2:5).

Mother of Jesus, my mother, you taught your child goodness, acceptance, and growth in faith. He was deeply indebted to you. You teach us the same lesson, and we are also in debt to you. Grant that we may live out your lesson of faith until the day you and your son welcome us into your home forever. We ask this through your beloved child, Jesus. Amen.

CHAPTER 41

THE CHALLENGE
OF FAMILY LIVING

Don't you ever disobey me again," shouted his father. "You can't tell me what to do!" retorted the seventeen-year-old, Daniel, and his mother didn't know whose side to take. Psychologists describe dysfunctional, troubled, and relatively happy families, but no perfect family, for such doesn't exist. Because Jesus, Mary, Joseph, James, and the other family members named by Mark 6:3 constituted a human family, relative dysfunction also tainted their relationships.

Years later, it's very possible Jesus, an artisan, became the family bread winner (Mark 6:3). If so, we can understand the familial resistance he must have encountered when informing them of his plan to depart in order to spread the Kingdom of Yahweh as he understood it.

Mark tells an astonishing story in his third chapter. Jesus had been working signs and preaching in Galilee from his new residence in Capernaum, probably the home of Peter. One day, because of his notoriety, a great crowd gathered inside and around the house such that he and his disciples couldn't even eat. His mother and family came from Nazareth, about twenty miles, *"to seize him, for they said, 'He is out of his mind'"* (Mark 3:21). Despite their witnessing his growth from child to teen to manhood, and dialogues concerning his passionate and radical religious beliefs, they had apparently little or no sympathy for him and his grand ambition. This episode surely reeks of long-standing disagreement. Behold in Jesus a man with powerful charisma who teaches and gains the favor of multitudes but is rejected by his own family. How his heart must have broken! Who of us has not experienced brokenness from his or her own family? This is one more example of why we can relate so intimately to the human Jesus.

Later, Jesus returned to Nazareth and visited the synagogue on the Sabbath. He read Isaiah 61 before a huge crowd. This is a prophetic messianic citation that includes the words, *"The Spirit of the Lord is upon me"* (Luke 4:18). Jesus seemed to be claiming a prophetic calling. Returning to his seat, Jesus cried out to them, *"Today this scripture passage is fulfilled in your hearing"* (Luke 4:21). They were amazed at what he was claiming. Afterward, outside, the crowd recalling his local, ordinary upbringing, seized him. They complained, "Who do you think you are?" "You're just one of us!" They were furious, and without any mentioned defense by his family, dragged him to a nearby cliff to slay the imposter for his grandiosity. Somehow he managed to escape. Later, he exclaimed, "No prophet is accepted in his own native place." Jesus: rejected again by those he loves! How true it is that they, whom we love, are the ones who can really hurt us. Have you experienced such familial rejection, and how have you reacted?

One day, as he was preaching, a woman called out, *"Blessed is the womb that carried you and the breasts at which you nursed"* (Luke

11:27). We may be sure this woman was a mother. She was praising Jesus in the way she knew best. He replied, *"Rather, blessed are those who hear the word of God and observe it"* (Luke 11:28).

Jesus was not denigrating the physical relationship of mother and son; rather, he was elevating the spiritual role of his disciples to a level beyond this most fundamental human relationship of mother and child. He preserves intimate family bonds but prioritizes the bonds of discipleship even above those of family.

One perceives clearly Jesus as a dreamer. He dreamt of Yahweh as a parent figure, Abba, and by extension all Israel, and finally humanity, as his family. We can't dismiss this as hyperbole because of his many other similar references, e.g., John 17:21, Luke 9:61–2, John 15:12. The scriptures reveal Jesus in a kind of oldest child role in a family circle with Abba as parent and all of us as his beloved brothers and sisters.

Mark revisits the same scene of the overcrowded house. His family arrived and was unable to enter. They sent a messenger to him who explained to Jesus, *"Your mother and your brothers* [and your sisters] *are outside asking for you"* (3:32). Then, his amazing response was, *"Who are my mother and* [my] *brothers?"* (v. 33). Looking at those seated in the circle, he responded, *"Here are my mother and my brothers.* [For] *whoever does the will of God is my brother and sister and mother"* (3:34–35). Yes, you who follow the designs of Abba are closer to Jesus than Mary in her physical relationship as his mother.

Jesus is calling us, regardless of our politics, race, sexual persuasion, moral status, religion, or its absence, to be brother or sister to him. Again, he is not diminishing physical family ties of blood or law, but founding a universal spiritual family. Family ties, in the mind of Jesus, are not to be denigrated but elevated to symbolize the divine family, which will suffer no dysfunction and will endure forever, and to which you are invited. By breaking down the walls of the world, whether physical, psychological, religious, or national, Jesus births his own beloved transcendent family and invites your membership. Whether your name is Patrick, Indira, Ali, or Hideki, Christ desires all of us to embrace Abba as we know him or her.

We invite you to consider who in your family has proven most hostile to you. Place yourself with Christ in this person's presence. Listen to Jesus counseling you in the dynamics of this relationship. Reflect, resolve, and heal.

CHAPTER 42

THE _____ OF ABBA

Consider the following question: What word or phrase summarizes the assembly Jesus gathered and the truth he taught them? If you respond with the word church, recall carefully that Jesus used that word just twice and in only one gospel. He verbalized the phrase we seek 115 times in all four gospels. Unfortunately, because we have pedestalized the church so excessively, Jesus' vision of Abba and his family has nearly vanished from Christian consciousness. The phrase Jesus used was "the Kingdom of Abba," and it is largely ignored. The word translated as kingdom resonates with sexism, but because of its commonality, we will tolerate it. If you are Christian, do you consider yourself first a member of a church or the kingdom? Many would respond, "church"; however, Jesus gives priority to the kingdom. This raises many questions: What is the kingdom? Am I in the kingdom? What are the truths of the kingdom, and what is the role of the church?

Paul declares what the kingdom is and is not: *"The kingdom is not a matter of food or drink, but of righteousness, peace, and joy in the holy Spirit"* (Rom. 14:17). When we think of the usual kingdom, we picture a ruler; an opulent palace; food and court retinue; peasants on the outside, nobles on the inside; and soldiers to maintain the status. This has nothing to do with the kingdom Jesus preached. He is referring to a spiritual kingdom that begins with himself: *"This is the time of fulfillment. The kingdom of God is at hand"* (Mark 1:15). John Paul II writes, "The kingdom of God is not a concept, doctrine, or program…(but) a person with the face and name of Jesus of Nazareth, the image of the invisible God."[1] By this, John Paul means the life of Jesus is the life to be lived by those in the kingdom. Christ becomes our model and identity in the kingdom. We are called to live a virtuous life and especially to transform our whole being into that of a Christ in our corner of the world. How, then, can some Christians support unchristian policies and practices such as war, abortion, capital punishment, homophobia, sexism, and elitism? As an example, a virtuous Christian might subscribe to capital punishment in a thoughtless spirit of retribution. However, for a Christian who identifies with the innocent, imprisoned Christ who died at the hands of the state, capital punishment becomes sinfully absurd. Such a Christian practices virtue on a higher level, on the mountaintop with Christ. Living his lifestyle demands a dramatic transformation. We have now touched the heart and soul of biblical wisdom: identifying with Christ, which earns one membership in the Kingdom of Abba.

Take note of the biblical teaching of Jesus, with its absence of doctrines and laws. We do not wish to minimize their importance, for religious truth must always be protected, explored, and understood more thoroughly. Jesus, however, dug deeper by asking his followers to climb Calvary and then experience resurrection with him. How do we do that? We refer you to our next chapter, "The Constitution of God's Kingdom."

Now is the time to respond to that second question: "Am I in the kingdom?" The answer is not black or white. It admits of progress and regress on our continuing journey to Christ. James Finley wrote graphically of this: "Life is essentially a journey in which one sets out to quench thirst, not simply to know that a God exists but to drink directly from God's own life to which man is bonded in the depths of his being."[2] Thomas Merton identifies Christ in God so that when one seeks Christ, one is already successful in life despite his or her inability to achieve it. This seeking represents your membership card in the Kingdom of Abba.

We stated earlier that Christ is the kingdom. That's true but incomplete, for that would leave you out. The Kingdom of Abba exists firstly and fully in the person of Jesus and continues in your person insofar as your person is fulfilled in all its possibilities. If you cease your search for Christ, to that degree, his kingdom is aborted in you. Therefore, when we pray "Thy kingdom come," we are not praying for the descent of a conquering Christ, but as de Chardin explains, "The Risen Christ, the center and peak of creation...will appear as a charge that has been exploding in the heart of mankind." [3] In the final analysis, the kingdom of God is present in Christ and in you insofar as you participate in him.

What then is the role of church? Is it arbitrary? The church answers in its own Vatican II document on Church, paragraph 5: "The church has the mission of proclaiming and establishing among all peoples, the kingdom of Christ."[4] In other words, I belong to a church insofar as that church leads me to the kingdom.

Church participation bonds every one of us in a magnificent effort to establish ever more deeply and universally this kingdom. Andrew Harvey writes, "Only a vast army of...beings who have consciously chosen the path of Christ...can effect the changes that are needed in every arena of life if the planet is to be saved."[5]

Therefore, join or deepen your commitment to a particular church, mosque, or synagogue, not because it's perfect, or because of what it promises, but because it intensifies your service of Abba and his or her creation, especially of your sisters and brothers. This comprises our greatest worship of the Risen Christ. Pursuant thereto, The Congregation of the Doctrine of the Faith, (Joseph Ratzinger, Prefect, currently Pope Benedict XVI) authored "The Lord is the goal of human history...the center of mankind, the joy of all hearts and the fulfillment of all aspirations."[6] This constitutes the role of every house of worship and the true standard by which we judge that house.

Place yourself in the presence of Christ. Hold his hand and join him in meditative prayer as he leads you in his prayer, "Our Father who art in heaven, hallowed be your name. Thy kingdom come, thy will be done, on earth as it is in heaven..."

Lord, insofar as our religious houses lead us to you, they succeed. Give us the wisdom to gauge them according to that standard and no other. May we support them insofar as they lead us to love of your earth and your mankind. Amen.

CHAPTER 43

THE CONSTITUTION OF GOD'S KINGDOM

The U.S. Constitution and how it is interpreted remains always in the spotlight. Indeed, we have a huge segment of our judiciary that spends most of its time debating and interpreting the constitution. Most Christians, however, are unable to even name or locate the constitution of God's Kingdom: the Beatitudes. If Matthew 25 tells us whom we are called to serve, the Beatitudes describe how we are to serve them and our reward for that service.

Both Matthew and Luke give us similar but differing versions of the Beatitudes in chapters 5 and 6 respectively. Matthew's Beatitudes are part of the Sermon on the Mount; Luke's, the Sermon on the Plain. But where given and in what form is of less importance than the message of the Beatitudes. We notice each of the eight Beatitudes begins with the word *blessed*. Jesus is not "big on commands"; he prefers the term *blessed* (*makarios* in New Testament Greek, meaning "how joyous"). Jesus is really telling us how joyous we shall be by living the charter of his kingdom. Incidentally, Jesus avoids establishing laws and rules even in this, his most "telling" homily. Would that our churches "take a clue" from him!

Some say these Beatitudes present an impossible challenge to modern living, but they were equally formidable in the days of Jesus. Truly, they prove we have in him a radical revolutionary who is calling us to live his same radical life. We shall comment on Matthew's version from his fifth chapter.

"Blessed are the poor in spirit, / for theirs is the kingdom of heaven" (v. 3). The Greek word *penes* ("peasant-poor") is not used; *ptochos* ("desperately poor") is used. Jesus is saying they who have nothing are more likely to live desperately for Abba. "Oh, Lord, I need you desperately; please help me!" is prayed by one who is needy rather than one who believes he is self-sufficient in his wealth. Who of us is desperately poor? Karl Barth, the influential Protestant theologian, lamented that God is identified with success. He called this the greatest obstacle to true religion.[1] Nevertheless, some religionists, many of them in the media, preach that material success is the standard of God's approval. How unbiblical, misleading, and tragic, for one who does not enjoy such benefits could easily believe God has abandoned him or her. Truly, by such a standard, God would have forsaken even the crucified Jesus, his own son.

"Blessed are they who mourn, / for they will be comforted" (v. 4). To observe the sins of apathy, greed, power, and addiction in this world gives deep cause for grief. To find these in my own soul gives even greater cause. They who mourn the presence of such evils, and rise from them, will be comforted by the great consoler.

"Blessed are the meek, / for they will inherit the land" (v. 5). What a shame for us to have corrupted the meaning of the word *meek*, especially by us males! Today, to be meek connotes weakness. Biblically, meekness denotes being considerate and gracious. Why can't we males, and to some extent females in a different way, realize that meekness denotes courage while "machoism" connotes timidity. The "macho" person covers his poor self-esteem with loud bravado while the truly meek has no need for such deception. To inherit the land is taken from Psalm 37:11 wherein it meant the Promised Land. Here, it refers to the kingdom of Abba where the meek shall reside. Jesus, the most courageous of all humans, was truly meek. Are you?

"Blessed are they who hunger and thirst for righteousness, / for they will be satisfied" (v. 6). Food and especially water are, even to this day, treasured in Israel. When we want water, we simply turn a knob, but searing thirst never left many residents of Israel. Jesus uses this powerful need for water and food to symbolize the need for righteousness among the blessed. What is righteousness? God's saving action. Yes, blessed are they who so yearn in desperation for salvation from Abba that they change their lifestyle. They will be satisfied.

"Blessed are the merciful, / for they will be shown mercy" (v. 7). The Hebrews used the word *chesedh* for mercy. It does not refer to transient healing, or even an act of mercy, but rather to a habitual way of living with compassion. Chesedh places us inside the oppressed by experiencing his or her emptiness and pain, and our consequent reaching out to help. Christ dwells in us, experiences our spiritual emptiness, and reaches out to us with chesedh.

"Blessed are the clean of heart, / for they will see God" (v. 8). Ritual cleanliness was critically important to the Jew. Before entering the temple, and before every course of every meal, one washed, and in a certain fastidious manner. Violating these rules and very many others comprised, in their parlance, impurity or sin. Jesus, however, rejected the shallowness of the rules of legality and defined cleanliness spiritually in terms of freedom from evil.

The Jews believed anyone who saw Yahweh would die. But Jesus, with great courage, called on his followers to see Abba spiritually, and live. One can imagine the hostile reaction of the Jews to this beatitude.

"Blessed are the peacemakers, / for they will be called children of God" (v. 9). We all desire and love peace, both personal and communal. Despite this, peace remains an elusive dream politically and personally. Jesus directs this beatitude to those who work for the dream of peace. This includes those of us who work for peace in our personal relationships. Jesus calls these also children of Abba. Have you and I ever performed such work? There are certainly more than enough people who work for the military establishment. Surely, it's time to take seriously the words of Jesus, "Blessed are the peacemakers"!

"Blessed are they who are persecuted for the sake of righteousness, / for theirs is the kingdom of heaven" (v. 10). Our spiritual ancestors were hounded to their death by the Romans for refusing to proclaim publicly "Caesar is Lord." Their tortures were gruesome, but still they professed, "Jesus is Lord." Their faith promised them the invincible spiritual joy of dying for Christ and a heavenly destiny.

Polycarp was the eighty-six-year-old bishop of the City of Smyrna about the year 170 CE. Emperor Marcus Aurelius ordered all his subjects to proclaim Caesar as Lord. Soldiers came to Polycarp, but he refused their order. He was then taken to a public arena. This venerable bishop then demonstrated true episcopal leadership so desperately needed today. Before thousands, the proconsul ordered him to reject Christ for Caesar and the status, power, and wealth he represented. Polycarp responded, "Fourscore and six years have I served him, and he hath never done me an injury. How then can I blaspheme my King and Savior?"[2] They then burned him at the stake. Polycarp is a bishop among bishops, for he lived and died for the most fundamental doctrine of Christ: to love Abba and shepherd his people.

Some years ago, I was assigned the task of preparing a series of Lenten talks entitled "How to Live the Beatitudes." After some thought, I realized one could not live fully the beatitudes because they describe in words what Jesus, and he alone, lived fully. This explains why Christianity remains always a journey and not an attainment, why I am being saved and not saved. However, with God's grace, we remain consistently en route to living his life of beatitude. I remember believing some years ago that the Christian is called to live exclusively a life of love; that is, he or she need only love, and that was enough. Considering, however, the beatitudes and the multiple facets of life they encompass, we realize there is more to life than love. Love remains the foundation to a healthy and human Christian life, but those other virtues that flow from it impact mightily its healthy and balanced manifestation. Only Jesus has led a fully balanced life of all virtue: courage and compassion, self-esteem and humility. Could this be the proof of his divinity and the evidence of our participation in it?

Lord Jesus, you alone have lived the beatitudes fully and in balance. Help us to bond with you in deep communion so that you may live in us. You are the way to our living a beatitudinal life. No event or pain could separate you from Abba in whose joy you constantly dwelt, and you call us to that same joy. "Come, you who are blessed by my Father. Inherit the kingdom prepared for you from the foundation of the world" (Matt. 25:34). You promise that this is the destiny of those who strive to live by your constitution, the beatitudes of your kingdom, Amen.

CHAPTER 44

SHALOM ALEICHEM!

It was August 27, 1928, and the dreams of Aristide Briand, foreign minister of France, and Frank Kellogg, American Secretary of State, were finally being realized. They had, with representatives of sixty other nations, signed a peace pact outlawing war for all time. Through the ages, they and others had dreamed this impossible dream: Names such as Isaiah, Siddhartha Gautama (the original Buddha), Aristophanes, Muhammad, Francis of Assisi, Mahatma Gandhi, Martin Luther King Jr., and many others come to mind. They were heroes of mankind despite their inability to convince people of power to sacrifice their imperialist dreams rooted in violence.

René Girard, a French anthropologist, explains his theory of "why." Violence lies in the very heart of human nature as a result of its mimetic quality; namely, that human nature has an inexplicable desire to imitate the violence it observes. This explains the "copycat" crimes that police fear in the wake of a startlingly criminal public act, and the ongoing violence every generation experiences. Therefore, according to Girard, when Jesus exclaimed, "Blessed are the peacemakers," he was seeking to save humanity from its own shadowy self. Jesus becomes thereby the ultimate revolutionary, and he not only spoke it but also lived and died for it. Jesus never retaliated for the violence inflicted on him, but absorbed it, and thereby ended it. An outstanding example occurred when Jesus was dragged before Herod. The soldiers, Herod, and the priests cursed, abused, and mocked him. Jesus did not respond (Luke 23:9). Their venom could not penetrate or motivate him. Behold the man! Deep in your heart, are you willing to follow him?

Girard dissects another component of human nature: the scapegoat. He finds that when confronted by another, we tend to project our own failings on our supposed assailant, and then denigrate him for our shortcomings. The high priest presents an ideal example by calling Jesus a blasphemer (one who insults Yahweh), but he became the blasphemer of Yahweh by hating and not loving as Yahweh commanded. Jesus, the Son of Man, represents the ultimate scapegoat, for they heap on him every possible abuse because he called on them to live the letter and the spirit of the law. They not only refused, but justified themselves by following only the letter of the law. Today's fundamentalists walk comfortably in their sandals. Jesus remarks to a fundamentalist of his day, *"You are a teacher of Israel and you do not understand this?"* (John 3:10).

Jesus, our scapegoat, teaches us a precious lesson: be aware of the scapegoat you have selected, for he or she may be reflecting back your own shadowy sin. Today, we the United States, possessor of more nuclear weapons than any nation on earth, initiated our war in Iraq over their possible possession of nuclear weapons, and threatened more war against Iran for its progress in developing nuclear energy. We claim we are trustworthy and they are not—the scapegoat artist must always justify his or her behavior. We must never forget Jesus takes the role not of the aggressor but of the scapegoat, and becomes thereby the world's champion for peace.

Jesus counsels us also to make peace with that person who stands as the most offensive to us: he or she who has hurt us the deepest. He even models this for us in the person of Judas. Jesus had chosen him as his treasurer in preference to Levi, the tax collector, who was better qualified. Betrayed and disappointed, Jesus knelt heartbroken at the foot of Judas and washed his feet with hope for his spiritual cleansing, but *"it was night"* (John 13:30).

The peace Jesus advocated did not reflect a mere absence of violence, a toothy smile, or mere "positive thinking." Rather, his peace rose from the roots of his being, from his indestructible union with Abba, who is pure peace. He would allow no person or event to destroy this union, and would overcome for himself and for us the worst of our enemies, death, and its child, fear. He and we now have nothing to fear. Shalom Aleichem!

If we, as Christians, really seek peace, we can't just bemoan its absence, but must work for its achievement both in our own relationships and nationally. I am reminded of Mary Keighley, a widow from my home parish who spent many summers working for peace in Central America, sometimes on her own and other times with peace organizations such as Pax Christi or the War Resisters League. She heard, and responded to, hallowed echoes from the mountain top. *"Blessed are the peacemakers, / for they will be called children of God"* (Matt. 5:9).

We can't all be a Mary Keighley helping in a foreign country, but we can devote ourselves to peace in our relationships and support those national leaders who truly seek peace. So, in the favored greeting of the Risen Christ, I wish you, with all my heart, Shalom aleichem (deep and selfless peace).

Father of Peace, we have often warred interpersonally and internationally in the name of defending you or seeking peace. Help us to realize that whenever we employ violence, we are, in effect, destroying peace; and by attacking peace, we disavow you, the author and sustainer of peace. Grant that we may work tirelessly even to our death to model, teach, and promote peace even as did Jesus, your peacemaker and our hero. Amen.

CHAPTER 45

EVIL: OUR STEPPING STONE TO SUCCESS

To introduce this most vexing of all human problems, recall the worst injustice you have ever suffered, or perhaps what you are now enduring. Bring to mind your soul-searing emotional onslaught and heartbreak. For me, the death of two newly born children and my wife's consequent struggles qualify eminently. I'm certain your tales of trial carry as much or more grief.

The world's greatest philosophers, theologians, and sages of every age have sought, without success, the answer to the problem of evil. How many millions have "given up" on God and religion because of this apparently insoluble question: how can a God of love perpetrate or allow horrific evil to be inflicted on innocent human beings? The absence of an acceptable answer has become an additional evil in itself. Even Pope Benedict XVI when visiting the death camp at Auschwitz in May, 2006, pleaded, "In a place like this, words fail: in the end, there can be only a dread silence which itself is a heartfelt cry to God: 'Why Lord, did you remain silent? How could you tolerate all this?'"[1]

Listen to a similar crushing lament from a nine-year-old girl of Kashmir who survived somehow the Pakistan earthquake of October 2005. Forty thousand perished in that quake, and her classmates were among them. Afterward, she begged to return to see the former site of her school. She viewed the bodies of her friends still being removed, and in tears, cried out, "Oh God, how could you have done this to us children?" Humankind faces such heartless and desperate torment, and apparently at the will of God!

Because the Bible deals with humanity in all its desperate experiences, many stories therein beg for an answer to this same ageless question. Despite all this questioning, only one person has ever responded successfully, and that person is Jesus of Nazareth. If he had accomplished nothing else, his answer would rank him truly as the savior of humanity. Curiously, even those who profess faith in Jesus don't seem to realize his surpassing solution, or its wisdom. However, we are getting ahead of ourselves. Let's consider first the classical answers to this timeless problem of evil.

The first answer is really a non-answer. Many say God doesn't cause this evil. He just allows it. This is patently a "cop-out," for it assumes that the evil exists outside his control. That's not possible for our sovereign Lord in whom *"We live and move and have our being"* (Acts 17:28). Further, even if God only allowed evil, he could still be charged with permitting needless human tragedy, which is hardly acceptable to our God of perfect love.

The Hebrew Testament makes a better attempt to solve the problem of evil in the fabled literary masterpiece known as the book of Job. Job is a wealthy tribal chieftain, sorely tested by Satan, an angel of God. Job quickly lost his children, health, all his property and fell into deep depression. He anguished, *"My soul ebbs away from me; / days of affliction have overtaken me. / ... / My blackened skin falls away from me; / the heat scorches my very frame. / My harp is turned to mourning, / and my reed pipe to sounds of weeping"* (30:16, 27, 30, 31). Those of us who have experienced agony or deep depression can especially relate to Job's melancholy.

Three wealthy friends arrived and placed the blame for Job's degradation on his sin, for surely Yahweh is just and requites to man only what is fair. Job denied evildoing, but Bildad, one of his so-called friends, responded, *"How can a man be just in God's sight, / or how can any woman's child be innocent?/ ... / How much less man, who is but a maggot, / the son of man, who is only a worm?"* (25:4–6).

Job repeated vehemently that he had not sinned and finally asked Yahweh the reason for the evil inflicted on him. Yahweh answered Job pointedly, *"Where were you when I founded the earth? (38:4) Who determined its size; do you know? (38:5a) Have you entered into the sources of the sea? (38:16a) Have the gates of death been shown to you? (38:17) Have you comprehended the breadth of the earth?"* (38:18).

A humbled Job reflected on the greatness of Yahweh and responded, *"I am of little account; what can I answer you? / I put my hand over my mouth. / Though I have spoken once, I will not do so again"* (40:4–5). The message of the book of Job, therefore, expresses the truth that not one of us has any right to complain or question Yahweh in any way or to any degree. He resides in a dimension of which we have no comprehension. However, this does not truly answer the question; it merely silences the questioner.

Jesus accepts the theme of Job, but surpasses it by providing his masterful challenging solution to this problem of all human problems. Most would agree Jesus suffers the horrors of hell inflicted without justification by his own religious leaders. He loves these brothers (priests, Pharisees, Sadducees) so deeply he forgives them, and even opens his arms to them. In other words, he views evil and the pain it generates (no matter how egregiously) as an extraordinary opportunity for loving. In a sense, his pain provides Jesus and each of us the chance to prove that our love is completely genuine and fully indestructible. Nothing and no one can diminish his love, which he models for us. Henri Nouwen writes, "The deep truth is that our human suffering need not be an obstacle to the joy and peace we so desire, but can become, instead, the means to it."[2]

As for his part, Abba wills for us only the very best. And the very best for us means our participating in Abba in all his manifestations: love, forgiveness, compassion, trust, etc. Nothing else has value except insofar as it serves, in some way, this heart of the divine. Financial gains, long life, pleasing relationships have worth only as we use them to promote Abba's universal pulse of divine love. This principle rings true through all the vagaries of everyone's life. Indeed, the more tragic the circumstance, the greater the opportunity for one to promote this overarching singular essential. Barbara Reid declares, "He must reside at the center of the cross,"[3] and we might add, to reign over all pain. Terminal illness, poverty, abuse, and all supposed tragedies provide for the victims (who incidentally have no rights beyond those given by God) the chance to share more effectively in the divine nature of selfless, genuine love—the summit of human living. We insist these events are evil because we view them only through the lens of human experience. We tend to ignore their transcendent divine dimension from which viewpoint they provide the supreme opportunity to realize our life objective. There is no greater value or role for any human being. It's no wonder James Mohler entitled his book *The Sacrament of Suffering*. Mother Teresa writes, "Sorrow, suffering…is but a kiss of Jesus—a sign that you have come so close to Jesus that he can kiss you—I think this is the most beautiful definition of suffering."[4]

I am surely not dismissing the grief and terror of a broken heart, for I have experienced such anguish. Neither do I advise that pain of itself has value, because it doesn't. Paul states that evil and even death lose their sting. Actually, they serve our singular ultimate life objective; namely, solidarity with our God of love. We call this *resurrection*.

A distinct and final question remains as to whether we have the depth of faith and courage to interpret injustice perpetrated on ourselves, our beloved, or our community as an opportunity to lead us to love, to Abba. If so, we have solved in our own lives, as Jesus did in his, the problem of evil, and it can be said of you as of Jesus, no pain could diminish her or his love, and all pain served it. Thomas Merton writes, "Love is my true identity....Love is my true character; love is my name."[5] My dear friend, insofar as you accept and live this, your true identity, you create and become a dynamic pulsation from the heart of God..

Lord Jesus, we humans have suffered since the beginning from apparent evil. Indeed death, one of its children, has reigned over us. You, however, have embodied in your words and deeds love as more powerful than all evil; and in resurrection, it rises and conquers even death.

Lord, you have therefore answered the problem of evil for humankind and freed us from its shackles. You have transformed evil into a mere means by which we can achieve greater love that provides transcendent human success. No one, in human history, has given us such insight. Now we have nothing to fear, for evil lies now "at our service." On behalf of all humanity, we kneel before you in total gratitude and promise to use your insight to propel us ever more securely into the arms of our beloved Abba, where we shall love with you in the absence of evil, for ever and ever. Amen.

CHAPTER 46

SEEDS OF THE FINAL CONSPIRACY

Wherever there's human relationship, there's conflict. Surely you've experienced the impact of conflict in your life. We can sometimes anticipate conflict, and at other times it's inexplicable and therefore more difficult to accept. I have a deacon friend who whether he preached, celebrated liturgy, or counseled, was criticized severely for years by a confrere, and he never knew the actual reason. He planned to ask his antagonist, but the man died prematurely, and now he will never know.

Jesus suffered from hostility and didn't always know the deeper reasons. Mark begins his gospel (chapters 2 and 3) with five such stories of conflict. They conclude with the frightening chapter 3, verse 6: "The Pharisees...began to plot with the Herodians against him, discussing how to destroy him."

Jesus innocently believed people would be open to truth, but realized eventually that the truth of a message is often irrelevant when it threatens people's "comfort zones" whether psychological, spiritual, or physical. One of these conflict stories describes the call of Levi (Mark 2:13–17). Levi was a tax collector in the service of Herod Antipas. As such, he had to provide Herod with a fixed amount of tax from the people; however, he could collect as much as he could extort from the taxpayers and pocket the overage. No wonder these publicans were despised by the people; nor allowed to serve in any judicial proceedings, or even set foot in the synagogue. Summarily, the Jews believed they were "God-forsaken" sinners.

Amazingly, Jesus, the Jew, sought out Levi to be in his inner company, and Levi accepted. We are not told the reason. Perhaps Levi may have just wished to gain better repute among the people. Anyway, Jesus visited Levi for supper in his house. Mark notes, *"Many tax collectors and sinners sat with Jesus and his disciples"* (2:15). Mark writes that some scribes and Pharisees saw he was eating with such sinners and tax collectors and asked, "Why?" Jesus responded, *"I did not come to call the righteous but sinners"* (2:17). How grateful we should be that he came for the likes of Levi and each of us. This scene is truly amazing. It may be likened to a Christian having supper with felons and prostitutes. Recall that sharing supper at that time signified a giving of oneself to the other; as if to say, you are welcome in my family and in my heart. Is he still welcome in your soul with these ideals?

Jesus is sending them and us a powerful message; namely, that he and his disciples must be open to all peoples, even notorious sinners. Ask yourself, "Does your Christian Church reach out to such as these, or does it assume an elitist arrogant attitude by prioritizing its own theology or rules over certain human beings? I recall in the 2004 general election a few bishops denied Eucharist to candidates who didn't agree with them on certain moral questions. One wonders whether they have reflected on Mark's second chapter. How would Jesus respond to a Christian church or Christian who acts in such a way? On a personal level, deep in your soul, what is your opinion of people of different religions, no religion, or of a different sexual persuasion, nationality, race, gender, or socioeconomic level? Do you or I have the right to make ungodly judgments about God's people, and even condemn them to hell? If Jesus accepted all, even the worst of sinners, what justifies us or our churches rejecting anyone in his name?

The scribes and Pharisees with closed minds disagreed with his openness. If our minds are closed, does this not place us in alignment with them against Jesus despite proclaiming our Christian discipleship? Jesus heard the scribes and Pharisees, and said, *"Those who are well do not need a physician, but the sick do"* (Mark 2:17). He was referring directly to these religious leaders and to those of us who are similarly sick. If we don't recognize our illness, how can we overcome it by responding to Jesus' call to give ourselves fully to all our brothers and sisters?

Would you join in the following open declaration? "Thank God, I know I am sick! Thank God, I know I am biased and judgmental! Thank God, I know I languish in apathy! Thank God, I know I need a physician! Thank God, his name is Jesus, and like Levi, thank God, I am his patient." Amen.

CHAPTER 47

JESUS CHALLENGES
CAPITALISM

Perhaps, you have heard the other version of the Golden Rule: "He who has the gold, rules." Originally, money served as a means of exchange; for example, I will give you a shekel for a sack of beans or barley. There was little thought of taking financial advantage of another or storing money for a rainy day. Eventually, folks realized that more money would exchange for more or better goods, and that led to saving money. Centuries later and torturously, capitalism evolved. It measures monetary worth as its standard of success. This can't be the standard for disciples of the biblical Christ. Pope John Paul II points this out in his *Catholic Social Ethics*: "The church is aware that the bourgeois mentality and capitalism as a whole, with its materialistic spirit, acutely contradict the gospel."[1] This necessitates our reflection on this timely and highly charged subject.

Psychologists agree today's unrestrained seeking of wealth symbolizes our search for and exercise of power. This rings true for individuals or any group whether corporate, church, or nation.

Most of us seek justifiably a secure standard of living for ourselves and family. That is one thing; boundless accumulation of excessive money is another. We'll now sketch briefly the evolving biblical attitude toward endless affluence and how it applies to us today.

The author of Ecclesiastes writes probably in the third century BCE, *"The covetous man is never satisfied with money, and the lover of wealth reaps no fruit from it; so this too is vanity"* (5:9). We have seen his words proven true in many lives of capitalists whether on Wall Street, Hollywood and Vine, or even Main Street, USA. They seek continuously more money although they possess already more than enough. Before condemning anyone, however, we should be searching our own hearts by comparing our attitudes and use of money in relation to what Jesus in the New Testament recommends.

Mark describes Jesus setting out on a journey when a rich man runs up to him. The man's journey would prove far lengthier than he had ever dreamed. He asked Jesus what he might do for eternal life (Mark 10:17ff.). Jesus listed the commandments and then added, *"Go sell what you have, and give to* [the] *poor…then come, follow me"* (v.21). Because he lacked the courage to give up his money, the man departed sadly. Do monetary attachments cause us also to walk away from Jesus? Matthew quotes Jesus "upping the ante" by saying, *"It is easier for a camel to pass through the eye of a needle than for one who is rich to enter the kingdom of God"* (19:24). I have heard media preachers, perhaps wealthy themselves, asserting a gate existed in Jerusalem that was difficult for a camel to squeeze through. "No way!" There is no historical or archeological evidence of any such gate. We must take Jesus at his word despite its searing impact. We are so ingrained with the struggle for upward mobility that detachment from riches is devastating to our cultural psyche.

Jesus elevates detachment from materialistic values by proclaiming as his first beatitude (chapter 43) the following: *"Blessed*

are the poor in spirit, / for theirs is the kingdom of heaven" (Matt.
5:3). Jesus promises eternal riches to those who are detached from
temporal riches. If we had any doubt as to the value of forsaking
excessive wealth, Jesus destroys it. Dorothy Day exclaims, "We have
not yet loved our neighbor…to the extent of laying down our life
for him. And our life very often means our money, money that we
have sweated for; it means our bread, our daily living, our rent, our
clothes. We haven't shown ourselves ready to lay down our life."[2]

Having stressed the importance of detachment, Jesus provides
us a conclusive example. Luke in 21:1–4 depicts Jesus sitting near
the treasury in the Temple. Some wealthy people contribute ostenta-
tiously large amounts. Then, a poor widow entered to give two cents,
and all laughed her to scorn. Jesus exclaimed, *"Amen, I say to you, this
poor widow put in more than all the other contributors to the treasury.
For they have all contributed from their surplus wealth, but she, from
her poverty, has contributed all she had, her whole livelihood"* (Mark
12:43–44). The physical fact is this widow had given clearly not as
much; Jesus was wrong when judging from a monetary standpoint.
As usual, however, Jesus is gazing through a spiritual lens. In his eyes,
she had given from her heart, and this is what earned his praise. Jesus
had journeyed from asserting the great difficulty of a rich person's
entering the kingdom to praising a poor widow giving from her need.
Have you or I given even once in our lifetime from our need?

Finally, Jesus teaches the ultimate lesson on poverty, not with
words but with his own flesh. He suffers and dies in abject desti-
tution, and thereby models for us total detachment. He has only
himself to give, and he does precisely that. So, he dies, not consumed with "toys" or estate, but with love for Abba and humanity.
His bloodied eyes see no lasting value in money and property.

Most of us agree with Jesus in our minds, but frequently our
actions don't follow. As capitalists, we must remain on guard against

the insidious sin of attachment to money and using money in frivolous ways while others starve. What is your attitude toward money? Has it changed since reading this chapter? Are you willing to allow biblical wisdom to impact your attitude toward wealth? Finally and most importantly, will you increase your giving for the cause of the Risen Christ? To join you, I dedicate any gain from this volume to his cause as found in the At Risk Children's Foundation. The foundation manages somehow to devote 100 percent of contributions to Haitian orphans born with HIV, our little brothers and sisters in Christ. To seek information, visit www.atriskchildren.org.

> "Oh ever understanding lover,
> I have grown up in a world
> which is addicted to [financial] success,
> which places halos on those
> who achieve fame and fortune.
> Free me, I pray, from this addiction....
>
> Fix my heart firmly only upon the work at hand
> and not upon the final product,
> whether it be victory or defeat.
> Let my delight be only in the task before me,
> for to you, my God,
> I dedicate the fruits of all my acts."[3]

CHAPTER 48

JOHN 5 AND JOHN 9: A STARK CONTRAST!

J esus heals the sick, stills the waters, and raises the dead. Many view such "miracles" of Jesus as God intervening in physical human affairs in a supernatural way and then withdrawing until his next intervention. Two such signs in John 5 and 9 demonstrate a far deeper meaning to the wonders Jesus worked.

HEALING THE PARALYTIC, John 5:1–18

Just north of the temple site in Jerusalem, archaeologists have uncovered a five-sided pool believed to be the Bethesda Pool that attracted the attention of Jesus in John's fifth chapter. The pool was sizeable and halved by a central bisecting wall. A spring at the bottom supplied its water to the pool and would erupt at indeterminate times. The Jews believed the first one to enter the pool after the eruption would be cured of his ailment. Accordingly, the sick and disabled (females are noticeably absent) lay on all sides of the pool in large numbers awaiting their chance. Because they were ill, they were believed to be sinners and therefore not allowed entrance to the Temple. Further, no priest or Levite, who was ritually clean, would ever visit this pool for fear of his contamination.

In contrast, Jesus desired to be with the sinful sick and attended the pool even on a Sabbath. Midst the groaning of the sick and the despicable fetid scents of their wounds and excretions, he spotted a man who has been crippled for thirty-eight years. Jesus asked him, *"Do you want to be well?"* (5:6). It sounds like a needless and foolish question, but don't we search at times in our illnesses for secondary gain? For example, if I plead illness, I may receive sympathy, or if I don't wish to get well, I need not sacrifice my alcohol or cigarettes. Jesus' query was a masterful diagnostic line of inquiry for therapists. Each of us who is sickly (and who isn't) would do well to ask him or herself this question, and answer in honesty of heart.

The man responded, *"Sir, I have no one to put me into the pool when the water is stirred up; while I am on my way, someone else gets down there before me"* (5:7). After thirty-eight years? Could he have been conning Jesus, and did Jesus "buy into it"? Despite knowing that healing was forbidden on the Sabbath, Jesus exclaimed with compassion, *"'Rise, take up your mat, and walk.' Immediately, the man became well, took up his mat, and walked"* (5:8–9).

The Jewish leadership, hearing of this healing on the Sabbath, summoned the man and asked him, accusingly, who did it. The man responded he didn't know. Later, Jesus found the man, and they conversed. Whereupon, amazingly, the man betrayed Jesus by telling the Jews that Jesus was the one who made him well. *"Therefore, the Jews began to persecute Jesus because he did this on a sabbath"* (5:16).

Why would this man, who was healed by Jesus, turn him in? Probably out of fear, or to curry favor with the authorities. The man and the temple leaders were both prioritizing the letter of the Sabbath law. Many of us still live that way: love of law trumping the law of love and compassion that Jesus followed.

This man may have been healed physically, but he would not permit his own spiritual healing. Did he want to get well? Not really; not fully. He remained in the same spiritual place as before the physical healing. Are we like him, seeking mere physical relief for our debilities, or do we wish to be well even in our spiritual depths? Jesus healed the man courageously in violation of the Sabbath law. This constituted legal sin. For Jesus, however, another more important dimension prevailed beyond the law: namely the person's total health over and above any law. This man refused, and Jesus was disappointed, but he still seeks our total healing and awaits our response.

THE MAN BORN BLIND: John 9:1–41.

As Jesus walked outside the Temple on the Sabbath, he noticed a blind man begging at an entrance gate. He had undoubtedly conversed with him because John wrote that Jesus presumed to spit on the ground, make a kind of clay, smear it on his eyes, and tell him, *"'Go wash in the Pool of Siloam'* (which means "sent"). *So he went and washed, and came back able to see"* (9:7). His friends, shocked, asked the man, *"How were your eyes opened?"* (9:10). He said a man called Jesus did it.

They then brought him to the Pharisees, unlike the cripple who sought out the authorities in order to inform them. They wished to know who dared to work on the Sabbath. He responded in truth that it was Jesus the prophet. Notice he now called Jesus not a man but a prophet (9:17). The Pharisees then asked his parents, who fearfully referred them back to their son. Again, they asked the man about Jesus. This time, he called Jesus a man of God (9:33), whereupon they threw him out of the Temple. Jesus found him and asked him whether he believed in the Son of Man. The man responded, *"'I do believe, Lord,' and he worshipped him"* (9:38). The man now called Jesus not a man, or prophet, or man of God, but the Lord to be worshipped. This man traveled the journey of faith in Christ to which each of us is called.

The crippled man was physically healed, but refused to draw closer to Jesus in faith. The blind man was also physically healed, but he set out on a spiritual journey to Christ that had four stages: man, prophet, man of God, and Lord. Spiritual healing is more difficult, even for Jesus, because we are free to refuse it. We can choose to live with closed or fear-filled minds. But Jesus, trusting Abba, always seeks spiritual healing.

What of our response to the miraculous in our life? The Lord provides daily spiritual healing gratuitously to us. Do we refuse the gift and reject Jesus by remaining spiritually crippled, or do we use his spiritual gift en route to him with eyes that recognize the life of Jesus as the life to be lived?

We invite you to a spiritual exercise. Move close to a mirror. Look deeply into your eyes and ask yourself whether you see with these eyes only the physicality in life, or are you willing to see the spiritual meaning of yourself and of the events of your day? Jesus did not come primarily to teach us dogmas, principles, or laws, but to open our eyes that we might see into our souls and address honestly our most devastating spiritual illness. Jesus is asking us this moment, "Do you want to get well?" Are you willing to try to change in some way our society, to take up your mat, and walk? Is you mind closed? Are you the cripple or the blind man?

Lord Jesus, the crippled man accepted selfishly your gift of physical healing but would not accept your spiritual healing. The blind man was willing to journey spiritually to you in faith. We ask you to cure our spiritual blindness by helping us to acknowledge our own blindness by committing ourselves to you no matter the cost to self. For us, this decision is momentous and costly, but with the blind man, we exclaim, "We do believe, Lord, and we shall live that vision." Amen.

CHAPTER 49

YOU CAN WALK ON WATER!

Max is a close friend whom I would trust with my life. He professes to be an atheist, but in my opinion, that man can "walk on water." His goodness and honesty lay beyond question. I have many times suggested he could reach for the heavens, and do it with a divine companion, but he responds only to what he can see, hear, and touch. Still, I believe he is walking unknowingly in the footsteps of Christ, atop the water. The three synoptic evangelists, Matthew, Mark, and Luke, describe Jesus walking on water, but what does this mean, and how does it impact each of us, including Max?

Recall the first two verses of Genesis wherein the author pictures a mighty wind (the Spirit) hovering over the waters of chaos and disorder. Remember also the story of Genesis 7 (chapter 10) in which the author depicts water as the source of Noah's death-dealing trial. Then, the waters of the Sea of Reeds block the Hebrews' escape from Egypt. The psalmist sums up this meaning of water as extreme distress, crying out, *"Save me, God, / for the waters have reached my neck. / I have sunk into the mire of the deep, / ... the flood overwhelms me"* (Ps. 69:2–3).

Matthew recalls all this water of distress in a startling story from his fourteenth chapter. The disciples were crossing the Sea of Galilee in a boat. It was the fourth watch of the night (between three and six a.m.) when suddenly a violent storm descended upon them. Waves were crashing over the boat as they rowed desperately for the distant shore in fear of their lives. There's not one of us who has not experienced such moments of panic. We humans endure at times savage pain: divorce, the death of a beloved, financial ruin, terribly twisted relationships, loss of health, and so much more. Perhaps even now, you are being tossed in such a storm. Truly, this story is for each of us.

Then Jesus approached, "walking on the sea." Thinking it was a ghost, they all cried out in terror. The fearsome storm was bad enough, but worse, were they also losing their minds? In such moments, the Lord always seems aloof, even in a different medium as noted here. Then, above the wind, Jesus cried out to them, *"Take courage, it is I; do not be afraid"* (v. 27). Truly, the wise Christian views whatever evil befalls him or her as a spiritual opportunity for his or her human success (chapter 45) today and forever.

Still unsure, Peter called out, *"Lord, if it is you, command me to come to you on the water"* (Matt. 14:28). Jesus met the challenge with one word, *"Come"* (v. 29).

Reassured in faith, Peter left the security of the boat, his comfort zone, and approached Jesus while walking atop the waters of his own fears. Then, as the storm worsened, as it always seems to, Peter lost his focus on Jesus and began to sink.

Peter screamed, shouting for many of us, *"Lord, save me!"* (v. 30). Immediately, Jesus reached out to support him, and guided him back to the security of the boat. Jesus asked Peter and each of us that question of questions, *"Oh you of little faith, why did you doubt?"* (v. 31). Why do we doubt? Because we can't see, hear, or touch him? Yes, indeed, because we process what we sense and begin to believe there is nothing beyond the sensible in which to believe. Then, we lose faith in his presence and begin to sink into our own stormy fears and worries.

After Jesus returned Peter to the boat, *"the wind died down,"* wrote Matthew, verse 32. Our storms will also abate when we recognize we have the supportive attention of him who is greater than all the storms of life, including death. Living with, in, and for Christ empowers us to overcome any and all storms and dwell in his sheltering serenity forever. As for Max, he may not explicitly recognize the presence of Christ, but surely his recognition of goodness and trust reflect implicitly Christ's presence in his life.

Lord Jesus, as we make our way through this life journey, we are battered by many and varied storms from dysfunctional relationships to illness and even death itself. Give us the insight to realize you are always present; the grace to believe in your loving support; and the perseverance to walk atop our stormy waters and rest in your safety now and forever. Amen.

CHAPTER 50

THE CANAANITE TEACHER

How long has it been since you experienced a deeply meaning-ful lesson that truly impacted your living? Life is constantly teaching us precious lessons, but are we learning them? Once we stop learning, we cease to grow. Because Jesus was fully human, this lesson applies also to him physically, mentally, and spiritually.

Jesus, a homegrown Jew, rarely traveled outside Israel. On one of those occasions, he experienced an amazing learning encounter for him and us. Jesus visited Tyre, an island city, joined to the main-land by a causeway. It lay about fifteen miles northwest of Galilee. A Canaanite woman cried out, *"Have pity on me, Lord, Son of David! My daughter is tormented by a demon"* (Matt. 15:22). The audacity of this woman calling out to Jesus! She had already three strikes against her. First, she was a woman without any right to initiate a con-versation with a Jewish man in public. Second, she was a despised Canaanite, the old and bitter enemy of the Hebrews. Third, her daughter being ill would indicate for many that she, the mother, was a sinner and had passed this sin on to her daughter. Take notice: the desperate, whatever their nationality, are the ones attracted to Jesus. Most of us cry out to God only when events boil beyond our control; otherwise we seem quite satisfied without his presence. Our ungodly affluence could explain our ungodly indifference.

This woman was not only bold, she was also clever. She called Jesus, *"Lord, Son of David"* (Matt. 15:22), a complimentary Hebrew phrase. She was obviously trying to ingratiate herself with Jesus, but he refused to speak to her. That's not the Jesus we have come to know! After all, isn't he always gentle and caring, especially toward women? Yes, but he's also a Jew, and that takes precedence, as we shall soon see.

The disciples were also disturbed with the woman: *"Send her away, for she keeps calling out after us"* (Matt. 15:23). The mother, however, would not quit. Rejected by Jesus and his disciples, she continued her plea. Jesus finally spoke to her, but it was not pleasant, *"I was sent only to the lost sheep of the house of Israel"* (Matt. 15:24).

Again, she felt the sting of rejection; only this time, it was from his lips. Furthermore, she could do nothing to correct his narrow-mindedness. She was only a woman, a Canaanite, while he was a Jewish male, a chosen one. She represents those who find themselves in minority status or who are disabled or deeply troubled; that means all of us in one way or another.

Despite facing the impossible, the woman refused to give up. It was almost like she would die first; she was desperate and became personal by pleading, *"Lord, help me"* (Matt. 15:25).

Jesus thought like a Jew and spoke like a Jew. Derisively he exclaimed, *"It is not right to take the food of the children and throw it to the dogs"* (Matt. 15:26). Jesus used the word *kyon* in New Testament Greek, meaning a scavenger, a dog of the streets. This was a Jewish phrase of utter contempt for Gentiles like her. We have so pedestalized Jesus that we forget, "He worked with human hands, thought with a human mind; he acted by human choice and loved with a human heart....He has truly been made one of us, like to us in all things except sin" as the fathers of Vatican II declared. [1]

However, this foreign lady was not only bold and clever; she was also determined. She fell to her knees, looked up directly into his eyes, and responded, *"Please, Lord, for even the dogs eat the scraps that fall from the table of their masters"* (Matt. 15:27). The Greek word she employed was not *kyon* but *kunaria*, meaning a house pet. She was actually saying humbly to Jesus, *"Yes, I'm a dog, but an affectionate pet, one that receives scraps from the table."* She had overcome the heart of Jesus, and he blurted out, *"'O woman, great is your faith! Let it be done for you as you wish.' And her daughter was healed from that hour"* (Matt. 15:28). As I write these words, I question my own desperation and faith, and how they "stack up" with that of this unknown and otherwise forgotten woman. What of your faith?

The healing of the daughter was hardly significant; it occupied only the last sentence. This story focuses sharply on the exchange between Jesus and the woman and the lessons taught. What were the lessons? Matthew suggests we must broaden our vision to include people who are supposed to be inferior, alien, or our enemy, and that we must never quit on our journey in faith to the Lord.

The unique and amazing surprise of this tale arises when we ask, "Who is the teacher, and who is the student?" The answers? Of course, Jesus is the student who is awed by this woman's faith and determination. She teaches him that faith is not limited to Jews, and he must therefore broaden the scope of his mission. He must have always remembered this lady with great affection. His greatness derives in this story from his selfless willingness to learn and grow from a sinful foreign woman. It's no wonder theologian Michael Cooke writes, "He (Jesus) learns from her."[2] She is the teacher, and we learn a startling truth that Jesus grows not only physically but spiritually as well. Like Jesus, are you willing to learn from others: disabled, aliens, enemies, children, and sinners, even from this unnamed Canaanite woman?

Lord Jesus, by your own learning from the lady at Tyre, you teach us to learn from each other. I must admit we learn, not so much from what others speak or write, but from what others are. We learned in this unique story from you and from her that whatever our age or condition, growth is our model, our teacher, and our standard for success. To fail to grow is to fail. I thank you, Lord Son of David, for this lesson of biblical wisdom from a nameless woman of long ago, and from you who continued to grow in every way until your last breath. Amen.

CHAPTER 51

A WOMAN EN ROUTE
FROM MAGDALA

We know how to locate a particular biblical text; for example, John 14:3 means John's fourteenth chapter, third verse. However, the biblical authors had no such advantage, and writing without the benefit of these numerical references, they composed an uninterrupted text.

Stephen Langton, Cardinal Archbishop of Canterbury in the early thirteenth century, deserves credit for the Bible's division into chapters. Then, Robert Estienne, a sixteenth-century Parisian printer, introduced that division into the verses of our present renditions. The fact of the biblical author continuing his thought and writing without knowledge of any interruption often provides fascinating insight into the meaning of the text.

One such connection may well occur in the final section of Luke 7 and the first three verses of chapter 8. Luke describes in chapter 7, a distraught woman. Desperately seeking forgiveness from Jesus, she barged into a male power-domain: dinner in the courtyard of a Pharisee and his male guests. She, a woman, was forbidden on both counts under pain of sin to invade such chauvinistic confines. Her heart pounding in fear, she inched along the wall toward Jesus. He was reclining at a low table in the center of the courtyard, leaning on his left forearm as was customary with his forelegs folded behind him. She approached Jesus from the rear. Would he accept her? Would he or others "throw her out"? Her fateful hour had come. She wept, perhaps in fear, certainly in repentance; and lowered herself to his feet. The men watched in condemning judgment to see whether she would dare touch him, which would, for a sinful woman, constitute even greater sin, and communicate her sin to him. The men were now ridiculing her. Perhaps, she would flee from the courtyard in disgrace.

Trembling, casting aside all restraint and with trust in the kindness of Jesus, she leaned forward to wash his feet with her tears. She dried them with her free-flowing hair (another sin), kissed them, and anointed them with expensive ointment. The host Pharisee frowned and condemned the woman for touching Jesus, and Jesus for allowing it. Jesus, however, bent to the woman in tears, and looking deeply into her soul, said, *"Your sins are forgiven.... Your faith has saved you; go in peace"* (Luke 7:48, 50). The heart of the lady leaped in joy, and her tears glistened with gratitude. She decided, then and there, to follow this caring and sensitive man. There is no faith as deep as that of one who rises from "hitting bottom."

Continuing his story, Luke wrote in 8:2, *"Accompanying him were...some women who had been cured of evil spirits and infirmities, Mary, called Magdalene, from whom seven demons had gone out, Joanna, the wife of Herod's steward Chuza, Susanna, and many others who provided for them out of their resources."*

Could this prominent mention of Mary Magdalene immediately after this story of a sinful woman anointing Jesus be merely by chance? Not hardly. Note also this woman worshipped at his feet, and Mary Magdalene worshipped at his feet in Matthew 28:9 and by inference in John 20:17. These citations present a strong case for the woman of chapter 7 being Mary from Magdala. We don't know whether the word "demons" (Luke 8:2) designates her moral, psychological, or physical status or a combination thereof; all would qualify in the Hebrew mind as sin. We do know she had been in frightening distress of some kind, and Jesus freed her. Elizabeth Schüssler Fiorenza writes, "Rather than speculate on how ill she had been, we would choose the better part by focusing on how completely (indicated by the number seven) she had experienced the liberating power of the realm of God."[1] Are you distressed? Do you have the faith and courage to come to Christ and trust in his forgiveness?

Her moment of triumph comes when all four evangelists place her among the first at the tomb of the resurrection. Mary of Magdala represents a tale of spiritual "rags to riches." It wasn't only Jesus who rose that resurrection morning. When she encountered the risen Jesus, she must have recalled the moment of their first meeting. The history of these two is a spiritual love story that has no equal. A recent best-selling fictional book and movie, *The Da Vinci Code*, has seized the attention of the public by portraying their relationship as physical marriage. Admittedly, Dan Brown, the author, writes cleverly, but why can't the public give similar attention to the true story of Mary's spiritual marriage and her triumph?

Other than her appearance with Mary the mother of Jesus at the cross, Magdalene is always mentioned first in the listings of the women who followed Jesus. Mary also represents all women whom Jesus has called from the bondage of patriarchy to that of equal prominence among his male followers. Chauvinistic male disciples in our churches have much to learn from the example of their founder in his relationship with women.

Expanding our vision broadly and rising above mere physical gender, Mary stands collectively for the People of God, male and female. Jesus calls each of us from his or her own Magdala (the land of shadow) to the brightness of the Easter morning sun of resurrection. How fortunate you and I are to have Magdalene as our exemplar, advisor, and companion on our lifelong journey to resurrection, at which she will surely be present. May we have, with her, the courage to embrace in our hearts the feet of Jesus the Christ in repentance and gratitude and hear him, as she did, call us by name to himself.

Reflect on the Magdala from which you are coming, not geographically but spiritually. Your reading this book surely suggests you are also journeying toward the tomb of resurrection. One remembers those poetic lines of an anonymous black slave author:

O'Lord, I ain't what I wanna be; O'Lord, I ain't what I otta be; O'Lord, I ain't what I'm gonna be; but thank you Lord, I ain't what I usta be!

Saint Mary, help me on my journey from my Magdala until the day you greet me at my resurrection and introduce me to our beloved Lord.

CHAPTER 52

A TALE OF TWO SISTERS

It's always surprising to note the vast differences between peers in the same family. My wife has a twin sister, but even they are clearly distinguished, physically, psychologically, and spiritually.

The stories of Martha and Mary, two sisters, highlight the differences between the two women and the way Jesus interacted with each. The sisters appear probably on three occasions. First, Luke 10:38–42. Therein, they act as hostesses for Jesus. Second, John 11:1–44, the raising of Lazarus, to which we shall refer in a later chapter. Third, John 12:1–8, the anointing of Jesus.

Luke introduces the first story with the connective phrase, *"As they continued their journey"* (v. 38). Our thoughtful readers will recognize that a meaningful event in the spiritual journey of Jesus and his disciples (including us) is about to occur.

They entered the village of Bethany. Martha, the extroverted leader of the two, ran outside to welcome Jesus. Later, Mary sat at his feet listening to his words, a position typical of a pensive disciple. Martha, intent on serving Jesus, complained almost imperiously to him about Mary's lack of help in the kitchen. One suspects Martha had noticed similar neglect by Mary on other occasions. Martha expected Jesus to act on her suggestion. However, Jesus uttered those famous words, *"Martha, Martha, you are anxious and worried about many things. There is need of only one thing. Mary has chosen the better part"* (vs. 41–42). His wisdom is directed not only to Martha, but to each of us. So we ask ourselves, "What is my one thing today?" Jesus advises that unless this chief concern includes deepening our personal relationship to him, you and I are "spinning our wheels." Martha was busy with mundane tasks for Jesus; Mary centered on Jesus himself ("the one thing"). Both are necessary, and both are complementary to the other. Commitment to Christ does not mean abandoning our daily necessary tasks, but completing them with the motivation, behavior, and generosity of Jesus, our guest. To lead this "Christly" life, we must "sit daily at his feet, listening to him speak"; this is a transforming component essential in our journeying to Christ.

The second story, the raising of Lazarus, merits it own chapter, 66. However, we can now state that this tale confirms the characteristics of extroversion and introversion of Martha and Mary respectfully. The story also demonstrates Jesus' love for both sisters as he draws them through the physical to the spiritual.

The third and final appearance of the sisters occurs again in their home in Bethany where they lived with Lazarus their brother. Once again, Martha was preparing dinner for Jesus and his disciples while Mary rested at his feet, this time anointing the feet with nard, a scented perfume worth a year of labor. Mary's devotion seems boundless. Who of us would spend so lavishly? If you respond, "I would," then ask yourself whether you are today spending such time and effort in the cause of Christ.

She then dried his feet with her hair. Even today in the mid-East, free-flowing hair for a female constitutes sin, and thereby subjects her to insult and innuendo. Mary's personal devotion to Jesus seems unlimited, while Judas, the treasurer and thief, by objecting to such expenditure, demonstrated he didn't adequately value Jesus. How well do you know him? Jesus intervened and related her act to anointment for his burial. He was thereby associating her with his great act of impassioned love, the giving of his life for all searchers. Notice Jesus did not prioritize Mary over Martha. Activity in his name (represented by Martha) and commitment to his word (represented by Mary) relate reciprocally. "Now Jesus loved Martha and her sister." John 11:5. Indeed, a bit of Mary and Martha complements our calling in Christ. Both Martha and Mary live hopefully in each of us, regardless of gender. I am privileged to agree with the eminent scripture scholar Barbara Reid, who writes, "It is my hope that this book will help both women and men, particularly those who preach and teach the Scriptures, to do so in a way that will promote a church of equal disciples, where gender differences would no longer determine ministerial roles. This would be today's way of 'choosing the better part.'[1] We are called to prayer and its extension of labor. The more they live authentically in us, the more we can live the life to which Jesus calls.

Meditation: read first through the following, remembering generally its components

1. *Close your eyes; seal off all sound and objects of touch.*

2. *Remove yourself from your body fully and come to the feet of Jesus.*

3. *In silence, experience his presence.*

4. *Listen to nothing else but his words within.*

5. *What is he saying: does he speak of your deepest concern, or his?*

6. *What does he ask of you this day?*

7. *Resolve to respond to his plea.*

8. *Thank Jesus and return to daily life in the spirit of Martha and Mary.*

CHAPTER 53

THE GOOD SAMARITAN
LIVES ON

The Irish and English; the Germans and French; the Indians and the Pakistanis; Christians and Muslims; Catholics and Protestants; blacks and whites: the list of religious, racial, and national antagonists extends to the horizons of history. Some say one or more of these enmities have etched in some way the troubled lines of every war that has ever been fought. One thing is certain: we still suffer from our cultural discriminations, both nationally and personally. Such odious failings are also described in the Bible, and there was none worse than the mutual hatred of Judeans and Samaritans. That's why Jesus' solution to their hostility would prove so instructive if we had the courage to embrace it.

Samaria was part of the kingdom of Israel and lay immediately north of the southern kingdom of Judah. The powerful Assyrians conquered Israel in 722 BCE and deported many of Israel's leading citizens. The Assyrians then transported foreign settlers into Samaria, who intermarried with the remaining Israelites, thereby causing the

Judeans to view their northern neighbors as impure because of their mixed blood. Racism rises again!

Later, in 587, Babylonia defeated Judea, sacked Jerusalem, and like Assyria, killed or exiled its leadership. These Judeans were permitted to return to Jerusalem fifty years later, following which they rebuilt the city, the walls, and finally the temple. The Samaritans offered to help, but the Judeans, citing their impurity, refused them. The angered Samaritans then built their own rival temple atop Mt. Gerizim in Samaria, and their racial and religious hostility deepened.

Then, the incident on the eve of Passover about 8 CE. The Judeans were surely aware of any event that could render the temple impure, thus rendering it unavailable for use at the feast. One possible event would be the presence of dead human bones within the temple precincts. Cancelling the temple rituals would cost the Judeans hundred of thousands of dollars and destroy the nation's central ritual of the year. Thus, they placed guards at the temple night and day. One night before the feast, vandals managed to penetrate one of the massive temple gates, avoid the guards, and spread human bones within the temple. The Judeans, filled with fury, blamed the Samaritans, cancelled the celebration, and their anger and hate stoked the fires of racism that raged at the time of Jesus.

Jesus plunged headlong into this seething cauldron. He told a lawyer one day to love his neighbor. This commandment extended exclusively to other Jews. The lawyer questioned him, *"Who is my neighbor?"* (Luke 10:29). Jesus responded with the famous story of the Good Samaritan, Luke 10:30–37. Some of us have believed this is a nice story that answers artfully the lawyer's query. How shortsighted! Actually, Jesus is sounding a call of revolution against racism and rampant nationalism, thereby endangering himself severely by challenging this dominant cultural icon. After all, the Judeans considered themselves God's chosen people, and the Samaritans,

Yahweh's enemies and theirs. He could have chosen in the story the priest or Levite to be the hero. Instead, Jesus labels the priest and Levite as hierarchical types who don't love their neighbor or inherit eternal life; whereas Jesus honors the hated Samaritan as the hero of his story. Thus, Jesus proves himself a fearless revolutionary in the cause of love of enemy. How the temple leadership must have hated him as they heard Jesus quote the despised Samaritan telling the innkeeper, *"Take care of him. If you spend more than what I have given you, I shall repay you"* (v. 35).

Jesus is addressing each of us to root out her or his sinful biases even toward so-called enemies. What a heaven a world of good Samaritans could construct, and Jesus calls us to form such a world, beginning with ourselves! O Collins provides us the perfect example: "At his own personal cost and risk, he stops to save wounded beings who have been robbed and stripped. In this case, however, love for his neighbors costs much more than possessions, money, and time. Jesus as the good Samaritan will himself be stripped and wounded. He will turn into Jesus the Victimized Traveller, not rescued but left to die on the road."[1] Do you, do I have such courage? Only we can determine that. An anonymous poet writes,

"I sought my God, and my God I could not find.
I sought my soul, and my soul eluded me,
I sought my brother to serve him in his need, and
I found all three, my God, my soul and thee."[2]

Reflect in the presence of Jesus on your feelings concerning that group of people you dislike the most deeply and why: Jews, Catholics, Protestants, blacks, gays, the current national

enemy, or whoever it might be. Jesus has just shared with you
his narration of the Good Samaritan. Listen silently to hear
him say to you, "Go and do likewise" (v. 37).

CHAPTER 54

THE GREATEST
SHORT STORY EVER TOLD

Having explored, albeit summarily, Jesus' intimacy with Abba in chapter 39, Jesus now attempts to tell us what Abba is like. He does this in the parable of the Loving Father. This has been called the greatest short story ever written. No wonder painters, sculptors, and authors have for centuries focused on this masterful tale, to fashion fabulous creative works from it. Its message applies to each of us and to mankind collectively. We shall dwell on the former while remembering the latter.

Traditionally, in those days, the elder son received two-thirds of his father's inheritance; the younger, one-third. But at least, they could have delayed their claim until their father had died. In this case, the younger son demands his share immediately. What of the commandment to love your father and mother? How insulting; but amazingly, his father complies. This is surely a different kind of father.

The young man departs for a Gentile country, thereby turning his back on his heritage, including family, country, and religion;

he then squanders all the money. Ask yourself, "Have I with-drawn from my spiritual, psychological, or even physical home to waste my time on useless or purposeless living?" Finally, the young man has nothing left. Desperate, he finds work tending pigs. One would think this Jewish man could find some work other than tending pigs. Leaving Israel and cavorting with pigs is tantamount to high treason for this Jew. Luke adds the ultimate sin, *"He longed to eat his fill of the pods on which the swine fed"* (v. 16). Luke has painted a picture of the worst sinner his culture could conceive. This man has "hit bottom." Have you ever hit bottom, and have you risen from it?

The younger son finally acknowledges what he has become, and so determines to return home. Psychologists suggest the most difficult step in our journey to wholeness is the first: to look hon-estly at ourselves and admit, "I am an alcoholic or an abuser, lonely, depressed, or self-centered." Once we admit what we are, then we can begin to become what we are not.

His father has been desperately looking daily down the road for his son's return. One day, he sees what he believes is a familiar figure at a distance. "It's my son," cries Abba as he runs to greet each of us on our return home. No reprimand; no insults; not even questions. Abba embraces you in a dance of delight, and kisses you with tears of joy. His love is so genuine and full for you that despite what you have done, or neglected, he still embraces you on the way.

"Quickly bring the finest robe and put it on him [symbol of honor]; *put a ring on his finger* [symbol of authority] *and sandals on his feet* [symbol of membership in the family]*"* (v. 22); finally, the supreme sign of celebration, a feast with the fattened calf for his son. Abba can scarcely contain his joy. You, amazed at his love, begin emerging from your shame and guilt to realize that despite whatever your sins or apathy, you are invited to Abba's ongoing banquet.

Now the older son has been working in the fields. "What's all the excitement?" he asks a servant. When told of his brother's return, he becomes angry and refuses to attend the feast. Why is he angry? He has his two-thirds of the estate. Again, Abba leaves his home to receive this son who then berates him, *"Not once did I disobey your orders; yet you never gave me even a young goat to feast on with my friends"* (v. 29). Giving up one's own ambitions and self-interest for a brother or sister is the final crowning step to greatness. The older son is unable to take that step. He feels falsely his ego has been assaulted because his father honored his brother.

Abba is speaking to us even through this son. He knows only love and so responds to us, *"My son, you are here with me always; everything I have is yours. But now we must celebrate and rejoice, because your brother was dead and has come to life again; he was lost and has been found"* (vs. 31–32). So with arm around your shoulders, he is inviting you to his feast.

These two sons live in each of us. A part of you and me is rebellious and ungovernable. Another part looks good, pious, and loving, but actually has his or her own agenda. Still, Abba never fails to call us to himself and his banquet. Abba loves you this moment and every moment just as you are. His arms are open to engulf and welcome you home. Some might object that the father in this story suggests that we must allow others to continue abusing us. Such behavior is not loving but enabling, a psychological illness, and is not the message of Jesus' parable. Rather, the father is urging us to seek always the spiritual good of another without condition. Tough love, at times, has its place. If our continuing overtures are rejected, we shall nevertheless always maintain open lines of communication, for no person or circumstance can stop the insightful Christian from loving.

Look into a mirror; peer through and beyond your face. Search your soul to discover what you are holding back from Abba. You'll know! Then consider that despite your shadows of shame, you are his/her beloved child whom he awaits with unconditional love. Your entire life is encapsulated in your lifelong response to Abba's invitation to return home to the banquet he has prepared in your honor. As Abba runs to you on the road of your journey, he kisses your cheek in sheer joy, and with his arm around your shoulders, he guides you home. Whisper to him your full gratitude and follow him today into his feast.

CHAPTER 55

SIMON PETER AT THE HELM

In the scriptures, everyone who allows Jesus to touch her or him spiritually is transformed, but none more than Simon Peter. We who search the Bible also seek his transforming touch, so we can also learn from the life of Peter.

Simon was a fisherman who had become a sometime follower of John the Baptist. While sojourning with John, Simon encountered another follower of John, one Jesus from Nazareth. It was entirely natural for Jews at that time, including these disciples of John, to discuss their religious heritage, contemporary Judaism, and their occupiers, the Roman Empire. Simon realized quickly that this Jesus blended tremendous insight into these issues with unique charisma.

Later, Jesus visited Simon in Capernaum and impressed him even more deeply. Jesus taught the townspeople from Simon's boat. One day he suggested Simon and his friends set out into the deep for a catch. Simon, the experienced fisherman who had caught nothing all night, objected to useless fishing during daylight hours, but fascinated with this man, he finally acceded. Thereupon, Simon, his brother Andrew, and his friends James and John caught so many fish, their boats nearly sank. Picture the proud Simon falling to his knees in the bow of his boat before Jesus in awe, exclaiming, *"Depart from me, Lord, for I am a sinful man"* (Luke 5:8).

We see already the character of Simon: self-assured, headstrong, and yet sincere. Years later, after Simon learned to trust, not in himself, but in Jesus the Christ, he would never ask Jesus to leave him, but rather to save him. Each of us is called to this same lesson: truly we are all Simons learning to trust not in self but in Christ.

All listings of the twelve place Simon first, thereby demonstrating his primacy of honor, but this primacy derives chiefly from the famous scene in Matthew 16:13–19. Jesus was trudging along one day with his disciples on the road to Caesarea Philippi, nearly ten miles north of the Sea of Galilee. He asked them, *"Who do people say that the Son of Man is?"* (v. 13). How do you respond to that question, and does your response impact your way of life?

The disciples replied with varied names of prophets. Apparently unsatisfied, Jesus asked, *"But who do you say that I am?"* (v. 15). As usual, Simon spoke up, *"You are the Messiah, the Son of the living God"* (v. 16). Simon had no difficulty speaking for all, and they didn't object to his leadership. To call Jesus the Messiah was a massive declaration. The Jews had been awaiting the Messiah for centuries. Simon was again showing his audacity; except this time, he was correct, and Jesus praised him for it: *"You are Peter, and upon this rock I will build my church"* (v. 18). Jesus had changed Simon's name, which indicated his exercising his authority over him. Jesus was actually initiating the birth of a new person, who would journey and eventually be transfigured from the previous Simon. This new man, Peter, becomes the foundation of the church because he was the first to recognize the true identity of Jesus. We are also called by Jesus to become new persons, and like Peter, begin a new transformed way of life patterned on that of Christ. We are in the same boat with Peter.

We also acknowledge the self-assured attitude of Peter, who had the nerve to rebuke Jesus concerning his future suffering, *"God forbid, Lord! No such thing shall ever happen to you"* (v. 22). Don't you and I also rely on our own knowledge and resources, never realizing how little we understand?

This self-reliance of Peter is most visible at the Lord's Supper. Jesus spoke, *"All of you will have your faith shaken"* (Mark 14:27). Peter responded, *"'Even though all should have their faith shaken, mine will not be...*(v.29). *Even though I should have to die with you, I will not deny you.' And they all spoke similarly"* (v.31).

Ah, the brash cockiness of the self! Years ago, I myself walked in those same cocky sandals with Peter. Now, much older, I am acutely aware of my frailties. Perhaps you have had the same experience. Jesus responds sadly to Peter and us, *"Amen, I say to you, this very night before the cock crows* [3:00 a.m.], *you will deny me three times"* (Matt. 26:34).

That same night, Jesus was "picked up" by the police and taken to Annas, who would reign as the godfather figure of the family that would occupy the lucrative position of high priest for twenty-four years. His palace was separated from that of his high priest son-in-law, Caiaphas (a bit of nepotism here) by a courtyard. Peter was seated in the courtyard when a servant girl accused him of collaborating with Jesus, and Peter denied it. Again, she accused him, now more loudly; Peter denied it again, this time with an oath. Uncomfortable, Peter went to warm himself at the charcoal fire when some bystander said, *"Surely you too are one of them; even your speech gives you away"* (v. 73). Whereupon, Peter cursed and swore *"I do not know the man!"* (v. 74). Immediately, the three o'clock bell tolled, the time of the cock crow! At this very moment, Jesus was being led, bound, across the courtyard. As he passed by the light of the fire, his eyes met those of Peter who, with mask removed and ego crushed, ran out weeping bitterly, tears of remorse, guilt, and cleansing. Have you, like me, peered into his eyes, and fled? Perhaps, some still remain "on the run."

After the resurrection of Jesus, Peter and the disciples were returning from fishing when they saw the Risen Christ on the shore. He had cooked fish and bread on a charcoal fire. This fire resonates with the charcoal fire at which Peter had denied Jesus. Could this be mere coincidence, or is the author of John's gospel referring to the correction of what occurred at the previous charcoal fire? Jesus asked Peter three times if he loves him. Provided the opportunity to reverse his three denials, Peter then affirmed his love for Jesus; however, he did not state that his love was greater than the others. Further, his three responses, for example, *"Lord, you know everything; you know that I love you"* (John 21:17), did not represent the bold, self-assertion of the young Simon. Simon had learned to recognize and acknowledge his fragility, and realized Jesus accepted him even with his shadow. If we are honest, we must also admit that we continue denying Jesus by refusing to give ourselves fully to his cause, but Jesus even understands this, and accepts.

Jesus perceived who this new person, Peter, was and said in effect, Peter, when you were younger you did what you wanted, but the day is approaching when you grow older that you will accept what you don't want (John 21:18): a sign of spiritual wisdom. So, Peter would one day accept crucifixion, only upside down because he knew he was unworthy to die as his Lord had.

This momentous growth of Simon Peter foreshadows the transforming to which his church and we are called. The church has been arrogant at times; so have we. At times, the church denies what Jesus stands for; so do we. The church, however, is transforming; so are we. Many are angry with church officialdom, and some justifiably so. However, let's consider our own effort at such difficult transformation, and how long and tedious the process.

Peter, you rose from betrayal to embrace, from self-dependence to Christ-dependence, and from fishing to church leadership. We, as church, need desperately your transforming example. We resolve not to walk away from church because of some policies of control and insularism, and not to allow despair to overcome our dreams. Rather, we shall with God's grace help in its transformation into an assembly that replicates the freedom and compassion of Jesus ever more clearly. Blessed Peter, ask our mentor and hero, Jesus, to aid each of us and our church to journey on this, your road of transformation into the Christ of limitless love. Amen.

CHAPTER 56

LONG LIVE LAZARUS!

You will recall our mentioning previously that an excellent method of reflecting on God's Word is to imagine yourself as a character in the biblical story. This model fits powerfully in the story from John's eleventh chapter wherein Jesus raises Lazarus (and you) from the tomb. Be aware that, insofar as Christ does not reign in our hearts, we are spiritually dead. Therefore, to some degree, each of us truly fills the role of Lazarus.

Jesus was across the Jordan, safely beyond Roman and Judean police jurisdiction, when a messenger from Martha and Mary in Bethany of Judea arrived to say their brother Lazarus (you), *"the one you love is ill"* (John 11:3).

Discovering his friend had died, Jesus told his disciples *"Let us go back to Judea"* (John 11:7). The disciples, aghast at returning to where Jesus and they were "wanted men," objected vehemently, but Jesus insisted on returning to Lazarus (you) despite the grave danger. Thomas finally acceded, saying forlornly, *"Let us also go to die with him"* (v. 16). Thomas may have never realized he was giving a clarion call of vocation to himself and each disciple of Jesus forever.

"When Jesus arrived, he found that Lazarus had already been in the tomb for four days" (v. 17). Not so trivial a detail! The Judeans believed the spirit of a dead person hovered about the corpse for three days. This detail is John's way of stating that Lazarus was certainly dead. You and I shall experience this fourth day, but just as certainly, our Lord will arrive.

Learning of the approach of Jesus, Martha rushed out to greet him. Jesus told her, *"Your brother will rise"* (v. 23). Martha responded, *"I know he will rise, in the resurrection on the last day"* (v. 24). She was referring to the belief of most Jews that the people as a nation will somehow rise on the "day of the Lord." Jesus then uttered one of the most hopeful and insightful lines in all scripture, and exposed the heart of Christian belief: *"I am the resurrection* [to be experienced] *and the life* [to be lived] *"* (v. 25). Jesus, our savior, proclaimed resurrection is found only in living his life (in the spirit), which surely leads to living forever, and its correlative: that resurrection gives birth to living in Christ, and living in Christ gives birth to resurrection.

Jesus, seeing Martha and Mary and the Jews weeping, became deeply troubled within himself. *"And Jesus wept"* (v. 35). We see a man deeply sensitive to Lazarus (you) and his friends. Jesus courageously allowed without shame his emotional weeping to be observed by others; a sensitive male of courage and trust is a rare find!

Jesus arrived at the tomb, a shallow cave on the hillside. He cried out, *"Lazarus,* [insert your own name], *come out!"* (v. 43). It's his ageless command to each of us to rise from our daily tomb to symbolize and preview our final rising into his embrace. *"The dead man came out"* (v. 44).

John intended this rising as a sign to symbolize not only Jesus empowering us to rise from our daily tombs of pain and discouragement by leading his life, but also to rise permanently through and beyond death. Jesus is truly our savior!

Lazarus (you) came from the tomb, still bound by bonds. Jesus ordered, *"Untie him and let him go* [free]*"* (v. 44). Yes, Jesus sets us free: free of depression, evil, apathy, and especially death insofar as we embrace his person and live his values. None of these can harm us any longer. We are ultimately and fully "safe and sound" forever. This sudden return to earthly life (the resuscitation of Lazarus) symbolizes our lifelong journey to heavenly spiritual life (resurrection).

Let's reflect for a moment on Abba's great gift of life especially as portrayed in three outstanding scenes in the Bible.

1. Moses, atop Mt. Nebo, overlooking the Promised Land, addressing his beloved Hebrews for the final time before he dies. He raised his eyes toward heaven, summoned all heaven and earth to be his witness, and exclaimed, *"Choose life, then, that you and your descendants may live, by loving the LORD, your God"* (Deut. 30:19–20).

2. Jesus standing before the Pharisees to summarize the reason for his presence: *"I came so that they might have life and have it more abundantly"* (John 10:10*).*

3. Just before raising Lazarus to life, Jesus exclaimed to Martha, his sister, *"I am the resurrection and the life"* (John 11:25).

   The Bible champions the value of life throughout. If we profess to be of the Judaic-Christian tradition, we must protect and nurture life above any claim by tradition, nation, or principle. Therefore, abortion, war, capital punishment, nationalism, poverty, and all else that threatens human life and the quality thereof, constitute our common enemy.

O Divine Gift-giver,
I stand beneath the endless waterfall
of your abundant gifts to me.
I thank you especially for the blessing of life,
the most precious of all your gifts to me.

Grant that I may never greet a new day
without the awareness of some gift
for which to give you thanks,
....
And may constant thanksgiving
be my song of perpetual praise to you.[1]

CHAPTER 57

CHOOSE YOUR COMPANY: GOATS OR SHEEP

I was saved on June twenty-fifth of two thousand five," says one Christian. Another says, "For me it was August eighth, two thousand four." They both agreed their salvation was assured because they both enjoyed on those days an experience of ecstasy and decision for Jesus. Ever since, they have attended church services, read their Bible, and improved their lifestyle. It appears these two Christians "have it made."

They have certainly made wise choices, but their decisions for Jesus and those choices do not guarantee their salvation; that is, not according to Jesus of Nazareth. He never mentioned a spiritual experience or a decision for himself assuring anyone of salvation. Nor does he even require belief in certain teachings or membership in a particular church (despite what certain churches might state). In other words, no experience or church has the power, jurisdiction, or wisdom to determine one's eternal fate. That is God's "call."

Jesus provides his standard for salvation in Matthew 25:31–46. This is the famous Judgment of the Nations. It represents the climactic finale of the fifth and final discourse of the gospel, and so occupies a highly authoritative position. Jesus describes the Son of Man in verse 31 as the judge. Does this refer to himself? Perhaps, or perhaps we will be judged by each other in terms of how we have reached out to each other. Accordingly, Edward Schillebeeckx, esteemed theologian, writes, "Jesus and the oppressed are identified by Matthew. Therefore, not only Jesus, but the oppressed will judge us."[1] Both understandings might well cast fear among us who are relatively affluent, and does dramatically introduce the core meaning of the story to follow.

All the nations will assemble before him: Jews and Gentiles, those of all religions and those who profess none. We will, in this court, finally be equal, for earthly power and status, whether civil or ecclesiastical, will be absent. The Son of Man will separate the sheep from the goats. Notice his standard for salvation is not attending church services, reading the Bible, a change of morality, or a religious experience, although these have value. Nor does Jesus ever mention sexuality, upon which our churches often focus. Jesus' standard is more elevated. The goats in his scenario comprise those who live for themselves, who don't reach out to the marginalized. Perhaps they're "too busy," or perhaps they are religious types who define their faith in terms of church, mosque, or synagogue attendance, or maybe they're simply apathetic. Whatever the reason, these goats are guilty of evil by default, of not bearing responsibility for sisters and brothers who are impoverished, strangers, or sinners. Jesus is not saying you shouldn't provide for those close to you. Rather, he is taking us beyond, to the rejected. We have noted many Christians think of themselves as saved, but honestly, we Christians are not known today by our love for the despised and downtrodden. We are better known for our political influence, beautiful churches, pageantry, clericalism, and doctrine, though Jesus never called for any of these. Some of this has its place, but the fact is, Jesus has identified himself with the poor and rejected (in Hebrew, the *anawim*). Mother Teresa commented, "We are touching Christ's body in the poor. It is the hungry Christ we are feeding; the naked Christ we are clothing; it is the homeless Christ we are giving shelter."[2]

The goats and sheep in the story didn't know they were neglecting or serving him in those oppressed; today, sadly, we also don't seem to recognize his presence in these anawim. The goats failed to reach out, and only later realized Christ was present therein. We have already been told of his presence, and if we fail to embrace them, our guilt is even greater. Oscar Romero, the martyred Archbishop of El Salvador, exclaimed, "The Christian who does not want to live this…solidarity with the poor is not worthy to be called Christian."[3]

We began this chapter by referring to those who believe they were saved at a particular moment of inspiration. The truth is we are being saved moment by moment, day by day if we are, in the name of Christ, supporting the lives of the oppressed. To these, and only to these, he exclaims, *"Come.…Inherit the kingdom prepared for you from the foundation of the world. For I was hungry and you gave me food, I was thirsty, and you gave me drink, a stranger and you welcomed me, naked and you clothed me, ill and you cared for me, in prison and you visited me"* (Matt. 25, 34–36).

Truly, salvation is not something attained but a lifelong maturing, a journey into love and compassion for other sheep and goats. This journey hangs on the conscious decision of the traveler to whom Antonio Machado refers as quoted by Robert Bly:

You walker, your footprints are
the road, and nothing else.
There is no road, walker,
you make the road by walking.
By walking you make the road,
and when you look backward,
you see the path that you
will never step on again.
Walker, there is no road,
only wind-trails on the sea.[4]

One final reflection: Jesus embraced the rejected with his entire being throughout his life so that in his last dying cry, he could demonstrate full trust in Abba: *"Father, into your hands I commend my spirit"* (Luke 23:46). What a gigantic leap in faith: to give your life to the anawim and then trust fully and finally in your Abba. In contrast, sadly, some claim and clamor for their own salvation.

Lord Jesus, we realize you desire us, not only to experience a vertical relationship between ourselves and Abba, but also a horizontal one of care and compassion for our suffering brothers and sisters. You envision all of us helping each other to a more productive and fulfilled life under our beloved Abba. This depicts the truth of which you dreamed, and my life for which you lived yours. Help me to focus therefore, not on my own salvation, but in losing myself by serving my desperate sisters and brothers. Amen.

CHAPTER 58

LOVE IS YOUR NAME!

D o you recall that popular song entitled "Love Makes the World Go Round"? Probably not; most likely, you're too gloriously young. However, for me, that old song title still carries much truth. We discussed in chapter 39 that Abba is not an elderly man with a flowing beard, but a Spirit of evolving, involving, and revolving love. This love penetrates and permeates through every cell of this universe, summoning us to participate in what truly makes the world "go round."

Some years ago I joined a community club called Sertoma (acronym for service to mankind). We met monthly, "passed the hat," and selected a worthy cause to support that month. After one such meeting, several of us were questioning the need for Christianity in the light of multiple charitable organizations such as Sertoma. Jack, a former priest, betrayed his theological background by proclaiming that Christianity's role is not mere charity but to imbue us with God's spirit. I complimented his comments, and we agreed that, for Christians, life consists of growth into this all-pervasive cosmic love-spirit through an ongoing commitment to compassion for all in our lives. Laughingly, we concluded this was a long way beyond Sertoma or any other philanthropy. Jesus understood this universal love clearly and lived it fully: his most outstanding achievement. Toward the end of his life, he was therefore able to proclaim his only commandment, *"Love one another. As I have loved you, so you also should love one another"* (John 13:34).

Author Scott Peck defines love as the will to extend oneself for another's spiritual good. Accordingly, our loving is not a mere emotional surge, or even the desire to aid our beloved, although these can greatly help. Love begins with decision and finishes "in the doing." If you wish to gauge who loves you, or whom you love, don't consider so much his or her wonderful words as much as what he or she is doing for you or you for him or her. Further, this action must be for your beloved's spiritual good; for example, your spouse is alcoholic and begs you to supply him or her regularly with a bottle of scotch. If you accede, you are not loving your spouse's spiritual good but enabling him or her, thereby indicating that you are both ill. These two standards, giving yourself and for another's spiritual good, clarify quickly this difficult discernment.

Many theologians claim the most common destructive religious attitude is God's nearly exclusive residence in heaven, and/or in some other tabernacle. This exclusive emphasis on an objective location tends to separate God and neighbor, thereby allowing us to love God while ignoring or abusing our neighbor. We referred in chapter 18 to the outrageous example of the documents belonging to Mohammed Atta and the other terrorists of 9/11: "When boarding the plane, say, 'this raid is for Allah!' Seconds before hitting the target, shout, 'There is no God but Allah!'"

Karl Rahner responds for all thoughtful religious women and men: "When one really understands the unity of the love of God and neighbor...We have expressed the single totality of the task of the whole human being."[1] To express love for Abba means to love my brother and sister because of Abba's identifying presence within that person. Nothing separated fully from Abba is loveable so that when you love someone you really love the Holy Spirit's person and characteristics (his presence) within your beloved.

Every one of us is called from our divine origin and destiny not merely to love but to be love, just as our God is love. Abba (love) summons each of us to love each other as Abba loves us. Each man, woman, or child, indeed every creature, expresses Abba (love) for me and you. Whether a person is Iraqi, Native American, Oriental, or Haitian; whether saint or sinner; whether heretical or orthodox, nothing can reduce Abba's love for him or her one iota. A. N. Wilson, the acclaimed English journalist, wrote, "God's forgiveness is not dependent upon human virtue at all, but rather on a free outpouring of divine love for the human race regardless of its moral behavior."[2] We refer to this free outpouring of divine love as the Holy Spirit, who is also identified with the fire of love burning within our triune God. Abba is purely and wholly love and can offer us only him or herself. Therefore, he sends us, in Jesus, love in human form who teaches us how to respond in kind.

Because Jesus is Abba on earth, he is love on earth, the Holy Spirit in human form. The Holy Spirit could fill Jesus because Jesus embraced him fully despite the cost. The Holy Spirit also seeks to fill us who embrace him, but we "play our games" at varying times and to varying degree. Thus, we can describe our lives as an ongoing quest to embrace and live the Spirit of Abba just as Jesus did.

Recent generations have been trained to follow law rather than love; for example, we must attend church on Sunday; we must not read certain books; we must not use birth control, etc. Laws, doctrines, and sacred books have value, but have you noticed, Jesus left us none of that. He left us the Holy Spirit of love and trusted us to embrace each other therein. *"If I go, I will send him to you"* (John 16:7). Therefore, as Christians, we determine to speak, behave, and love in the impassioned Spirit of Abba, and not as much in the boredom of an uninspired legalistic existence. Assuredly, it's time for us to broaden our vision beyond the easy written word of book, law, or principle, and enter the boundless, more difficult freedom of living and loving divinely without restraint. Your hour of decision beckons!

How often we tell each other, "I love you," but do we really mean it in terms of "doing" for our beloved? Our love, however, assumes an entirely new and sublime dimension when we intend to love another as Abba loves him or her. You and I, as Christians, are being asked today by Jesus to love as he loved. Although I do not know you physically in time and space, I declare to you today in the Spirit of Abba, "I love you."

Blessed Spirit of Love, ignite me and my treasured readers with your fire of love for the people in our lives. Help us to rise from our apathy, embrace your passion, touch all your beloved, and thereby set our corner of the world afire with your embrace. Amen.

CHAPTER 59

TABLE O' PLENTY

The multiplication of loaves represents the sole "miracle" story of Jesus that appears in all four gospels; in fact, the tale is told not four but six times. This sign then bears unique importance, but I do wonder why the Lord who multiplies bread so easily can't relieve the widespread hunger in the world today by simply repeating this miracle a few thousand times. I don't mean to be flip with such a comment, but it does illustrate the childlike fundamentalist interpretation some adults still apply to the story. Jesus was "up to something more" than just a fish story.

To support a more profound meaning than the literal interpretation, consider the following: These six versions contain differing numbers of loaves and locations, numbers of people, the presence of the boy, the length of time they had been together, the proximity of the Passover, which disciples brought the boy, how many in the groups, and the numbers of baskets containing the leftovers. Such discrepancy hardly suggests a literal understanding.

Matthew alludes to a deeper meaning when introducing his version: Jesus *"said, 'My heart is moved with pity for the crowd, for they have been with me now for three days and have nothing to eat. I do not want to send them away hungry, for fear they may collapse on the way'"* (Matt. 15:32). The Greek word *splagchnon*, translated here as "moved with pity," has no adequate English translation. Actually, the word means the whole being of Jesus reaching out to others with compassion. Matthew writes they had been with him three days. The number three refers, like many other biblical references, such as the three days of redemption, to the spiritual impacting of the divine in our human lives. Jesus wanted the crowds (us) to remain spiritually with him, not three days, but for theirs and our entire lives. If he left us hungry for our spiritual journey, we might well collapse "on the way." He must give us himself as spiritual sustenance.

Jesus instructed the disciples to feed the crowd, but as usual, they responded on a physical level and objected, saying they didn't have the money to buy so many loaves. However, no funds were needed for the food Jesus gave. *"Taking the five loaves and the two fish and looking up to heaven, he said the blessing, broke the loaves, and gave them to* [his] *disciples to set before the people"* (Mark 6:41). Notice the near identification of these words to his at the Eucharistic institution. Remembering the real spiritual presence of Jesus in Eucharist, we discover the true meaning of the story: Christ is giving himself through his disciples to all who come to him. He is really saying he wants to grow in more intimate communion with us, and we, therefore, with each other. Those communities who have retained this Christian Tradition of real presence are accepting the spiritual reality of Christ under the appearance of bread and wine. Just as Jesus multiplied the loaves, so the presider multiplies the spiritual Christ really present under the appearance of bread and wine. Christ, through his presider, blesses, breaks, and gives it to his disciples of all eras to distribute. Finally, several versions note that sufficient bread is left over to fill twelve baskets, symbolizing the twelve tribes of Israel. Today, the twelve baskets refer to the whole world. Jesus is giving us our ministerial marching orders: take me (the spiritual Risen Christ) through and in yourselves to all people.

This is a feeding story for sure, but the food (the loaves) is not merely physical but the spiritual Christ multiplied for all people. John quotes Jesus stating this succinctly: *"I am the bread of life"* (John 6:35). We, his ministers, are called to distribute him, but the question is, how do we accomplish this? By being him, so that when people experience us, they experience him in us. St. Teresa of Avila wrote of this in the sixteenth century: "Christ has no body now on earth, but yours; no hands, but yours; no feet, but yours; yours are the eyes through which Christ looks out with compassion upon the world."[1]

Lord Jesus, arching over the centuries, you are still multiplying the loaves by calling us to spiritual oneness with you. You are still sending us out to those in our lives who are searching for love and truth. Grant that each of us may realize how privileged we are to walk in your sandals and become, like you, food for others. Help us to multiply the loaves of your presence by living your life for all those we touch. Amen.

CHAPTER 60

TEMPLE TENDERS

Don't imagine the temple at the time of Jesus as similar to our Jewish temples of today: sizeable but not massive, pleasant but not eye-catching, different but not unique. The Temple in Jerusalem, the seat of organized Judaism, was all these and more: a unique wonder of the world both in size and grandeur. It occupied over thirty acres and consisted of a series of courtyards, one within the other, shimmering in limestone and gold plate. A massive altar of sacrifice, surrounded by steps of nearly thirty feet, assumed a prominent position before the temple's central building. This building housed the Holy of Holies (the residence of Shekinah, God's reflected glory on earth) and the holy place with its altar of incense.

More importantly, the temple was the source of a vast socioeconomic system of caste and control. The priests directed this religious oligarchy from their positions of honor and affluence. They used law and ritual to maintain their establishment and to justify extreme taxation of the Jewish people. The temple thus stood, in one sense, as the symbol of the positives and negatives of the Judaism of that day. It's not surprising this hierarchical institution, parading as the true Judaism, would draw the ire of Jesus of Nazareth. One wonders how he would respond today to those who worship him in multilayered, hierarchical, nearly inaccessible strata.

Jesus enjoyed a deep understanding of the Hebrew Testament. He had fully embraced the commandments of love of God and neighbor and rejected passages of religious preferential caste and power. He revered among other texts Hosea 6:6, *"For it is love that I desire, not sacrifice,"* and Zechariah 14:21, *"There shall no longer be any merchant in the house of the LORD of hosts."* Jesus dreamed of the house of Israel purified of these atrocities.

So, toward the end of his ministry, Jesus and his disciples entered the temple of Yahweh and found merchants selling, at exorbitant profit, animals for sacrifice, while the money changers were exchanging, for a price, forbidden tokens for accepted Hebrew shekels. The mayhem that accompanied such commerce was deafening. This, in the house of the Lord!

Despite his personal human fears, the commitment of Jesus to Yahweh overpowered him and ignited his passion. He fashioned a whip of cords and, together with his disciples, drove them angrily from the sacred corridors. We can picture this physical happening, but the event has deeper meaning. This is Jesus striking out against the injustices perpetrated by this and every oppressive religious economic system. He revered the temple and the people but hated the evils and excesses of those who exploited the people in the name of Yahweh. God help those of any era who use religion for profit or control.

Jesus and his disciples had literally occupied the temple, and this could not be tolerated by the priests. Therefore, they approached Jesus, and demanded, *"What sign can you show us for doing this?"* (John 2:18).

Instead of understanding the meaning and truth of the Hebrew Testament and the corresponding actions of Jesus, they asked him for a sign, some miraculous proof that would justify his action. Jesus would never acquiesce to such a self-serving demand and so he ignored their question. Rather, he exclaimed, *"Destroy this temple and in three days I will raise it up"* (2:19). It is not surprising that these rulers of Israel would quickly conspire to murder him as soon as possible! We ask ourselves whether we also ignore the biblical wisdom of God's Word.

Jesus was certainly not speaking, however, of rebuilding the physical temple or even his physical body. Rather, John tells us in 2:21 that Jesus was speaking of his own spiritual person and his rising after they try to destroy him. In other words, "If you try to destroy me, I will rise and return"; and so he does in the spiritual body of the Risen Christ (1 Cor. 15:44). Jesus was also, therefore, anticipating his disciples forming such an intimate union with him that he was referring to himself and them as one body. This body of Christ forms the new temple: he the cornerstone, we the building stones; he the vine, we the branches; he the head, we the body. Jesus, by his response, was declaring the old temple of social strata, sacrifice, priestly ritual, commerce, and social injustice, abolished. He and we, his disciples, have become the new temple. All this is possible because of his courageous passion, such that his disciples recalled the words of scripture from Psalm 69:10: *"zeal for your house consumes me."* We must ask ourselves, "Does my church reflect more the socioeconomic oppression of the temple, or the justice, love, and zeal of the Christ? What am I doing to overcome the former and promote the latter? If such zeal consumes Jesus, then we are called to have it consume us.

Let's reflect with total honesty on our own denomination or parish. Does my religious institution oppress or exclude others on spurious grounds of legality or "divine right"? Does it prioritize principles, books, or teachings before people? Do we or our leaders seek to defend positions or status rather than seek truth and live lives of loving service? If so, have I been excessively fearful and apathetic toward such grave injustice while neglecting to take appropriate steps to confront my religious institution with the ideals of its founder, Jesus the Christ?

Lord Jesus, give me the courage to resist undo control and oppression, especially when it comes in the name of religion. Help me to support, in your name, justice and compassion, particularly because of my participation in your Body. Grant that, like you, I may have such zeal for the house of Abba that it might consume me. I shall reject all measures opposing you, whether in society, church, or my own heart, and promote your presence in all three. Amen.

CHAPTER 61

THAT "THEY MAY ALL BE ONE!" (JOHN 17:21)

Our nation's motto, *E Pluribus Unum* (from many comes one), refers to our fifty states speaking in one united voice. Buddhism, Christianity, Hinduism, Islam, and Judaism comprise the five major religious ways of life in our world today, but they do not speak with one voice. Their very separateness has generated competition, multilateral hostility, and wars through the centuries even to this day—naturally, in the name of our God of peace. Worse, each of these five admits to numerous internal divisions; for example, nearly 21,000 Christian denominations claim today some degree of autonomy. They justify their independence on their supposed unique and superior teachings, morals, and/or practices. Such arrogance is negative of itself, but the competition and the aforementioned hostility it breeds are far worse. Meanwhile, the earnest prayer of Jesus, *"That they may all be one"* (John 17:21), echoes plaintively down through the ages.

If Jesus walked physically among us today, one wonders what denomination he would choose, if any. Somehow, I believe he would do what he did the first time; that is, select how he could best serve all his sisters and brothers regardless of today's churches or their claims. Incidentally, we religionists would probably respond similarly; that is, we would take his life again, out of fear he would choose another denomination or seek to reform ours. Perhaps, that's what our denominations are doing to him anyway by asserting that our principles and doctrines are superior to others' despite his soulful plea for sisterhood and brotherhood.

There can be no doubt that our physical "lone ranger" behavior rejects his stated prayer for unity. However, all is not lost! We have repeatedly seen in these pages Abba's desire through Jesus and his inspired Word to draw us into his spirit, which has no division. Could it be that in these Christian and non-Christian denominations, a spiritual unity abides that overshadows the divisive fences we have erected in the name of God, Christ, Mohammed, Moses, and the like? If so, what comprises this unity? I suggest such a unity already exists on two levels.

First, all of us by our human nature seek what is true, desire what is good, and work in some fashion (admittedly often bizarre) to achieve these ideals. Each of us perceives them differently according to our unique genetics and experience. For example, most of us appreciate God, his truth, and goodness, but a Baptist, a Catholic, a Muslim, and a Jew might disagree on their specifics. A Buddhist and others might deny God altogether. Nevertheless, because of our common aforementioned human commitment to truth and goodness, all have a foundation for communicating. All of us share common universal goals of truth, goodness, peace, and justice. This constitutes of itself a towering unity that justifies ongoing mutual respect, communication, and even love.

Second, beyond these natural human considerations lies the magnificent schema of our divine parent: that supernatural plan by which he envisions all people as his children. *"You received a spirit of adoption, through which we cry, 'Abba, Father'"* (Rom. 8:15). This does not represent a pious platitude but rather our feeble effort to describe his universal love in its ineffable excess. Because of that love, he draws us into his family, and we dwell in our earthen home as brothers and sisters.

Our bonds are not merely familial, national, or legal, all of which can imply competition or division. Our unity in his Spirit transcends these dividers, and in his plan, we have no competitors or human walls but only beloved. This is the supreme unity to which Jesus refers when he prays that we may be one as he is one with his father. This sounds like an impossible dream, but Jesus treasured this grand vision and gave his life for it. To the degree, we answer his call to do the same, we will achieve his ideal, and heaven and earth will kiss.

This unity does not mean uniformity. We will always profess our unique perspectives, disagreements, and perhaps religions, but these differences wilt before the aforementioned inseparable human and spiritual bonds.

Finally, among us of differing denominations, rather than overpowering or criticizing others, we recall the wisdom of three outstanding proponents of Christian unity. We begin with Thomas Chalmers, the first moderator of the Scottish Free Presbyterian church, who believed that a church should be judged not because of its numbers, doctrines, or governance, but on it's giving birth to people in love with Christ.

As for the possible union of our Christian denominations, listen to Fr. Paul Wattson, founder of the Franciscan Friars of the Atonement, who dedicate their lives to Christian unity.

> Heresy and schism have gone too far...Rome, too proud and unbending; England, too self-satisfied; the East, too

orthodox; Protestantism, too enamored of letting everybody do and think just as they please. They never can, and never will come together. Christian unity is hopeless! Our answer is....Patience must be allowed time to do her work perfectly. She cannot and will not be hurried: the fabric exceedingly delicate, the pattern most elaborate, the robe of unity she is weaving for the Son of God will be of matchless beauty. And it is the work of many generations.[1]

Mother Teresa herself exclaimed, "I convert you to be a better Hindu, a better Catholic, a better Muslim or Jain or Buddhist. I would like to help you find God. When you find him, it is up to you to do what you want with him."[2] Embrace and live this message until that day when there will be no division among us, for we shall be *"one body and one Spirit"* (Eph. 4:4).

Will you seek to support your earthly brothers and sisters in their search for love and truth? Will you today select one person of another Tradition and decide what you can do to support her or him in her or his search for truth and love, not as we, but as she or he views them?

Adonai, Allah, Brahman, Abba, God of many names and no name, alert us to your urgent struggle to unite us—each in our uniqueness, all in our diversity. Fill us with awe and joy at your presence in our sisters and brother, and with energy and passion to work for blessed peace—that they all may be one in you, and you may be glorified in all of us. Amen. Alleluia!

CHAPTER 62

COME DINE WITH ME!

C ome on over for dinner!" said Bob to his friend.
We have all issued this type of pleasing invitation, but its meaning pales when compared with its Judean counterpart twenty-one centuries ago. When any Jew of that time invited his friends to supper, he was opening his heart and home to them. They were welcome in his family and in his life. Further, Jesus the Jew suspected a particular year's Passover supper (probably 30 CE) carried "life and death" significance for him, and so he cherished deeply the disciples he invited that night, and spiritually we are among them.

However, as his guest disciples climbed the outside stairs and entered the upper room (possibly belonging to the mother of Mark), they noticed Jesus had uncharacteristically failed to provide the first courtesy: a slave to wash their feet, dusty from the roads. This was tantamount to insult, and they murmured about this neglect. Then, after being seated, the unbelievable happened: he, their leader and host, approached each to wash their feet as their slave. He also seeks to wash your feet, to serve you. Have you ever menially served another with such sincerity and intensity?

Simon Peter resisted, but Jesus remarked, *"Unless I wash you, you will have no inheritance with me"* (John 13:8). Peter, thinking Jesus was referring to the physical washing, responded, *"then* [wash] *not only my feet, but my hands and head as well"* (v. 9). Jesus answered, possibly with a chuckle, that he was not speaking of mere physical washing, but spiritual commitment. Then he emphasized his point: *"If I, therefore, the master and teacher, have washed your feet, you ought to wash one another's feet"* (v. 14). Jesus intends this washing not to convey mere physical meaning but to symbolize the life he and his followers are to lead. For us, this life stems from our identifying with Christ that reaches its liturgical zenith in the celebration of Communion.

During the meal, *"He took bread, said the blessing, broke it, and gave it to them, and said, 'Take it; this is my body.' Then he took a cup, gave thanks, and gave it to them, and they all drank from it. He said to them, 'This is my blood of the covenant, which will be shed for many'"* (Mark 14:22–24).

Hours before his death that he surely by now realized was imminent, Jesus affirmed the meaning of his passing over; namely, that he would not persuade, intimidate, or force himself on anyone, but offer himself in love to all who would accept him. Have you considered allowing those close to you the freedom to choose and live their selected lifestyle without your interference?

For centuries, theologians have discussed whether he intended his presence under the appearance of bread and wine to be real or symbolic. Theologically it carries importance, but his message remains the same either way: that Christ becomes us that we might become him. I, myself, agree with the tradition of real presence, with which Paul concurs in 1 Corinthians 11:23–29. Others, however, have denied this "real presence"; some even call its believers cannibalistic. If one insists on his physical presence, that conclusion, though absurd, seems valid. However, if Jesus stood for anything, it is that we must view physical reality as a window through which we perceive the spiritual. Teilhard de Chardin was right, "We are not physical beings having a spiritual experience; we are spiritual beings having a human experience."[1] Jesus was and you and I are spiritual beings. Therefore, the U.S. Conference of Catholic Bishops states, "It was Christ's will that this sacrament [Eucharist] be received as the soul's spiritual food…This is what the Church means when she speaks of the real presence of Christ" (June 15, 2001).

However, his pivotal message for us became manifest the following day when he lived the intent of his words and actions from supper the previous night. He gave his physical life that we might live his spiritual life. Yes, this was an agape, a love feast in the finest sense of that word. He would give himself to each of us so that we would give ourselves to all. Jesus becomes our food so that we can become food for others. Jesus hereby proves his surpassing desire to remain even after his death with his beloved as an inseparable companion.

One final remark on this love feast: he invited all twelve to that supper, even Judas. He washed their feet, even Judas, and offered the bread and cup to all, even Judas. Jesus did not exclude or excommunicate anyone contrary to the practice of some churches today. If Judas did not wish to be with him, he could depart, and so Judas *took the morsel and left at once. It was night"* (John 13:30). Jesus frees us to accept or reject his lifestyle in our lifelong journey.

The synoptic gospels, Matthew, Mark, and Luke, depict Jesus instituting the Eucharist, but John never mentions it. As we have seen, he describes Jesus washing the disciples' feet. According to John's gospel, the last to be written, he is declaring to us that as a result of our consuming the spiritual person of Jesus the Risen

Christ, he is sending us out to serve others in oneness with him. Would you resolve that, whenever you are dining with Jesus in Eucharist, you will select a certain service in his name that you will provide for a specific person or community? Do that and you begin to fulfill his love command, *"do this in memory of me"* (Luke 22:19). You will then be leading a Eucharistic life.

Lord Jesus, you found a way to remain sacramentally with us even after your death. Your dynamic presence urges us to give ourselves to each other even as you did. Nurtured by your invitation to dine with you, we promise to seek out a particular sister or brother today, and live as a Christ in their presence. Amen.

CHAPTER 63

DO WE SLEEP IN GETHSEMANE?

Would you agree with psychiatrists, and has it been your experience that the most devastating pain for us humans is that of the psyche? Physical pain is one thing, but anguish, desolation, and desperation are worse; thus, many spiritual writers feel Jesus suffered most deeply, not on Golgotha, but in Gethsemane. Perhaps this is why in that garden Jesus turned plaintively to Peter, James, and John to beg them to *"keep watch with me"* (Matt. 26:38).

Luke depicts vividly what follows in chapter 22, verse 44 when he wrote, *"his sweat became like drops of blood falling on the ground."* To the Hebrews, blood indicated life, suggesting the very life was draining from Jesus. Was he suffering a suicidal trial (not as rare or pejorative in those days)? At any rate, this passage (disputed by some) certainly illustrates the soul-filled horror of "his hour." Jesus himself described this torture: *"my soul is sorrowful even to death"* (Matt. 26:38). In such moments of desperation, we turn to beloved for needed support. Blaise Pascal, in the seventeenth century, pondered Jesus' grave disappointment: "Jesus seeks some comfort at least from his three dearest friends and they sleep."[1] Before our denouncing them, let's apply the utterance of Pascal to our own slumbering. Christ's desperate cry for help echoes through the centuries as we apathetically drowse in our own "Gethsemane sleep" No wonder, the grieving Jesus uttered his profound and poignant prayer, *"Father, if you are willing, take this cup from me; still not my will but yours be done"* (Luke 22:42). Amid the throes of his deathly struggle, he humanly begged for relief, but accepted from the roots of his ravaged soul the decision of his divine Abba. If only you and I could summon his courageous trust, our problems would also meld into the security of Abba's loving providence.

Finally, a trusted comrade approached Jesus and embraced him. Jesus asked him a pivotal question: *"Judas, are you betraying the Son of Man with a kiss?"* (Luke 22:48). We, like Judas, are his disciples, and still, we also betray him when we fail his command to love each other. Judas ignored the question of Jesus and planted a polluted kiss on his cheek. As the soldiers rushed in to seize Jesus, Simon Peter, in typical headstrong fashion, struck with a sword the right ear of Malchus, the high priest's servant. Jesus eschewed this vacuous, violent response by ordering Simon to replace his sword in its scabbard, *"for all who take the sword* [physically] *will perish* [spiritually] *by the sword"* (Matt. 26:52). Jesus was pointing out that all who live by violence and oppression have already been spiritually slain.

In the darkness of night, soldiers bound his wrists and led him down the mount across the Kidron Brook and up toward Jerusalem, the city of death. Jesus had suffered extreme loneliness and desperation in Gethsemane. Still, by trusting in the unseen and unfelt Abba, he modeled human courage at its best. He had not allowed pain to alter his conviction and behavior, but had risen through and above it. He left a Gethsemane message for us: that we, like him, can overcome in Abba whatever pain or desolation we suffer.

The following lines provide a modern story illustrative of Jesus' Gethsemane experience. In 1945, an American soldier entered warily a burnt-out building in Cologne, Germany. The empty rooms were dark, frightening, and exuded the stench of death. Suddenly, he saw scribbled on a pot-holed concrete wall the following words:

> *I believe in the sun even when it's not shining,*
> *I believe in love even when I don't feel it.*
> *I believe in God even when he's silent.*[2]

> *The Author: A nameless Jew hiding from the Nazis.*

Lord Jesus, most of our hospitalized today reside not in general hospitals but in mental and psychiatric institutions. Tortured by depression, paranoia, and schizophrenia, they are mocked and forgotten. Few of these have experienced the compassionate power of your presence. Do inspire us to reach out to these rejected with your grace and kindness.

Grant, Lord, that when the agony of mental anguish overcomes light in our spirit, we may realize that remaining loyal to your unseen spirit will ensure for us secure passage into the gentle caress of your Daddy and ours, now and forever. Amen.

CHAPTER 64

OUR ROYAL SCAPEGOAT

Jesus was a loyal Jew who preached the love of God and neighbor, and went about "doing good." Why would anyone seek to murder him, especially those of his own faith? As we seek to answer this question, we remember that he stands now as a "spiritual everyman": he stands for each of us, Jew or Gentile.

The religious overlords at the time of Jesus had "a good thing going." They commandeered, through the temple, a massive economic establishment. They offered expensive sacrifices, collected high taxes, and occupied the top rung on Judea's social caste system. Importantly, they had worked out the political arrangements with the Romans by which they could wield such power, and they seemed destined to retain it perpetually; after all, they ruled in the name of Yahweh.

Jesus walked one day from the hill country into this very profitable comfort zone. He railed against their organized oppression, denounced their fundamentalism and legalism, and to the consternation of their pietism, seemed to accept the titles of prophet and savior. Worse still, this upstart was gaining great popularity. The religious leaders sensed acutely his threat to their position and set out to discredit and destroy him. Why wouldn't they reexamine their understanding of the Hebrew scriptures, or enter into honest discussion with him? Perhaps, like many today, they prioritized their social and economic position and had therefore lost sight of their search for truth. Moreover, Jesus told them as such: *"If you were blind, you would have no sin; but now you are saying, 'We see,' so your sin remains"* (John 9:41). Today, do our political and religious leaders and we behave differently? Are we also blind while proclaiming our superior churchy vision? Consider your response carefully, and you will see that the flaws and excesses of human nature, not just the Jews and Romans, killed Jesus, the ultimate paradigm of human love and compassion. This is murder in the first degree.

Why didn't he escape? Instead of fleeing, Jesus returned from safety across the Jordan to the environs of Jerusalem, the hotbed of hostility against him. *"Let us go back to Judea"* (11:7). He deliberately returned, not with a martyrdom complex, but to teach his saving message to the crowds he loved. He endangered his own person so that his beloved Jewish brothers and sisters might understand the wisdom of Abba as taught in their Hebrew Testament. His love for men and women would drive him all the way to his death on the cross, but not because he desired it. No threat or event could quench his passion for Abba and his beloved. This is why Jesus lived, and died, the way he did. No matter how horrific the pain or crushing the defeat, Jesus continued to love and to trust Abba, himself, and his sisters and brothers. This represents the prime lesson from Golgotha for each of us. Where, oh where is our passion for seeking divine wisdom from the Hebrew and Christian Testaments and then living their lessons?

The Day of Atonement was the most profound Jewish religious day of the year. It was the only day in which anyone could enter the temple's Holy of Holies, and then, only the high priest. The room was totally empty, because the Jews believed this was the home of Yahweh on earth. The high priest wore a seamless garment and spread the blood of a goat about the room in atonement for his personal sins. Outside, in the courtyard, another goat was brought before him. The priest kicked and spat on the goat, smashed a crown of thorns atop its head, and ordered it brutally scourged. Finally, the goat was driven outside the walls to its death. The Jews believed the goat was removing the sins of Israel, from which we derive the term *scapegoat* (chapter 44). Today, individually and nationally, we project our own apathy and shadows on others, and thereby create our own scapegoats, whom we then punish. Have we made today's Jews scapegoats? Jesus, the Jew, reversed the traditional role by absorbing the abuse and accepting the role of scapegoat. His wisdom and courage are incredible, but reflect that our calling is also to accept the role of scapegoat and not to create others.

Rather than blame the Jewish aristocracy and Roman rulers for their shocking ignorance, we must look within our own hearts, where we find the same brutality in differing form and degree. We have failed to feed the hungry, give drink to the thirsty, welcome the stranger, clothe the naked, and care for the ill and imprisoned. In this sense, we are just as guilty of murder. Worse, in our listless apathy, we observe our sins dispassionately from the lairs of our own denial. By following Christ on his path of care and compassion for the oppressed, we make resurrectional success of his tragic death.

Lord Jesus, even as the priests and elders of the temple abused you in every physical way, so we torture you spiritually by our blind agendas of selfishness and apathy. Stir us from within our hearts to rise from these ashes. Lord, help us to see what we are doing, and not doing, in your service. Rescue us from our blind denial. Inspire our souls with the stark truth that our sisters and brothers wither and die while we debate our doctrines. Pierce our hearts with your passionate love even toward those who reject us. Help us to understand from our depths that in order to live in love forever, we need only follow radically your one commandment: "Love one another. As I have loved you, so you also should love one another" (John 13:34).

CHAPTER 65

HE'S RISEN!

Sister Rose taught us in the eighth grade that when we died, our souls would be judged. Later, our bodies would rise and join the soul, and both would go to general judgment. As a boy, I wondered about all this but finally accepted it.

As an adult, however, this scenario has led to numerous apparent inconsistencies; for example, how can a soul leave a body and later find it, and why? Because the physical body will participate in heaven, does this mean heaven and hell are physical places? What appearance would the body assume? All this and more: very confusing! I don't expect comprehensive answers to all my questions, but surely Christianity could offer adults more reasonable explanations, and it does.

We reflect first on the reality of resurrection. There is no proving absolutely the fact of Jesus' resurrection (that lies beyond empirical science), but powerful arguments do indicate our faith is well founded. First, we know that you as a whole person represent a unique, reflective energy. However, the laws of physics tell us no energy is ever totally nullified. Rather, it's changed: as wood into ash, water into steam, or apathy into passion. Postmodern physics also argues against our classical division of body and soul; rather, it posits matter and spirit as two manifestations of one reality: energy. One, which is matter, dissolves; the other, spirit, transcends. Einstein's famed formula, $e = mc^2$, reflects this. Therefore, resurrection serves as an example of the ongoing existence through death of the same energy (person).[1]

Second, our best functional description of God casts him/her as love creating us gratuitously, holding us in existence, and gifting us beyond imagination. Can such a God of pure love suddenly abandon us and will our annihilation?

Finally, Jesus' disciples endured horrendous trials and finally martyrdom. Did they suffer for something they knew never happened, or for something they themselves had manipulated? If considered carefully, these arguments are more than sufficient for us to rejoice in believing that Jesus survived death and implores us to join him forever.

What really happened, however? The gospel appearances of Jesus after his resurrection would convince any reasonable person that the same person, Jesus, lived through death, because he was recognized in many varied scenarios by hundreds of different people (1 Cor. 15:5–9). However, because he was not recognized at first, he was also different. Jesus the person had conquered the limitations of time and space and entered into an altered spiritual state. This is why the spiritual Risen Christ can dwell and live within you two thousand years later. Paul calls this Risen Christ the *"spiritual body"* (1 Cor. 15:44).

Because Jesus loved fully, and God who is love is greater than death, Jesus subsisted fully through death. Likewise, to the degree you love, you will rise and survive death in your spiritual body.

The question immediately arises, what is your spiritual body? The renowned scripture scholar, Jerome Murphy O'Connor, tells us it is "a mirror image of your present body; [that is], everything is reversed. The qualities which make the present body a burden in this life are simply negated, and replaced by their opposites." O'Connor lists four changes you will experience:

Physical to spiritual: You will no longer be subject to change or disintegration. The spiritual has no material makeup and therefore no parts. It lies beyond dissolution.

Perishable to imperishable: You will never again suffer illness or death. You will have already conquered and superseded death.

Dishonor to glory: You will reflect, to your full capacity, Abba's splendor.

Weakness to power: You will participate, to your capacity, in Abba's power to love.[2]

In summary, you are destined, to the degree you have chosen, to be "oned" with Abba, who is spiritual, imperishable, glorious, and love. Your heaven originates in love, consists of love, and grows in love into its destiny of love.

Paul presents a clarifying analogy. Picture a farmer sowing his small seed of wheat. The seed, desperate for sun and water, struggles to grow midst rocky soil, suffocating weeds, and hungry rodents. Eventually, this seed overcomes its torments to blossom in a fertile field of "wheaten" gold. The seed has changed (risen) into its full glorious possibility by the transforming action of Abba, but still maintains its radical essential identity.

The Bible describes your resurrection, like the seed, not only as a state of being, but also as a daily journey in your growth through the pain and joy of life: from slavery in Egypt to freedom in the Promised Land; from the blindness of Bartimaeus to his clear vision; from paralysis to "take up your mat and walk." The Bible is filled with many transforming experiences, and each beckons us on our continuing journey of resurrection.

Resurrection becomes, therefore, a daily growth-event, a plunging into the wonder of God present in our every homey enterprise. You are living a daily resurrection with Christ, and will be forever. Victory is yours over any and every obstacle. Even death, supposedly our most challenging enemy, succumbs to Abba's power of resurrection in you. Death becomes your friend by ushering you through resurrection's vestibule. O child of Abba, nothing can stop you! You are a winner in Christ, rising now and forever!

Lord Jesus, we know yours is the only resurrection. Ours participates in yours insofar as our love in life replicates yours. It is you who rises in us. Therefore, help us to live your life in ours, to live your love and truth in ours, and thereby to live our resurrection in yours. You have gifted us with a "once in a lifetime" opportunity, and we shall seize it. Our spirit rises in thanksgiving to you through all eternity. Amen. Alleluia!

CHAPTER 66

JOURNEYING IN FIRE, WIND, AND TONGUE

Imagine yourself, as a fundamentalist, present at the first Pentecost, the events of which Luke describes in Acts 2. Your hair is singed by fire. You are nearly blown away by a powerful wind, and you're understood in foreign languages that you have never heard or spoken. They who were present, experienced, most likely, none of these, and neither would you. Instead, Luke is using these images to convey stupendous truths of divine wisdom designed for each of his readers through the ages.

Luke employs fire as did the author of Exodus in chapter 3. That chapter describes Moses encountering a burning bush atop Horeb, the mountain of God. This fire does not consume the bush because its flames are not physical, but represent an intimate, spiritual encounter with Yahweh. Luke even expands on Exodus by having Jesus proclaim to his followers, *"I have come to set the earth on fire!"* (Luke 12:49). Therein, Jesus seeks passionately to mediate Abba's spirited presence on earth by using symbolically the consuming power of fire. Luke also implies that, as a disciple of Jesus, such mediation is your role also. Whatever your occupation, age, ethnicity, or religion, you are called to present Abba appropriately to your family, friends, co-workers, and every person you meet. In a real sense, the Spirit of Abba seeks to ignite you to become a spiritual torch of love and light to your world.

As for your being blown away, Luke describes a power-packed wind filling the entire house. The author of Genesis writes in the first two verses of the Bible, *"In the beginning, when God created the heavens and the earth...darkness covered the abyss, while a mighty wind swept over the waters."* This signaled the creation, the ordering of the disordered primordium. The Hebrew Testament words for wind (*ruah*) along with the Christian Testament Greek word for wind (*pneuma*) both mean "spirit" as well as "wind." Therefore, the author is intending to say the Pentecostal wind is generating a new creation of people dedicated to the spirit of Abba and each other. No wonder creation is often called the first Pentecost! Reminiscent of Abba blowing life into mankind in Genesis 2:7, the wind of Acts 2 symbolizes Abba's propelling us on our journey home to himself. Residing in the hurricane alley that is Florida, I often reflect on the gale-like gusts of Abba seeking to carry us with power to his bosom. So, in our life journey, we must become like autumn leaves trusting in Abba's Spirit to blow us where it wills.

Finally, Luke depicts his spirit-filled disciples speaking in different tongues and being understood by peoples from throughout the known world. Truly, despite our differences, we all recognize the language of love, Abba's language. If we believed from our depths and not just from our lips that Jesus had risen from the dead, we also would be telling everyone who would listen of this shocking intervention by the Spirit of Abba. Thereby, Pentecost becomes our daily celebration of Abba's impassioned impact in our world through us.

Imagine: the same irrepressible Spirit of truth and love resident in Jesus seeks to dwell also in us! This Spirit is not an objective, occasional, nearly magical impulse from God. Actually, the Holy Spirit is our decision, driven by the Risen Christ seeking to come alive in us by adoption as he did in Jesus by nature. You and I are not called to wait for Abba to descend to correct our evils, whether personal or societal. The Holy Spirit is far too intimate, too "oned" with us. Our decision to love as Jesus loved marks the presence of God's Spirit in us and our living out that Spirit-filled decision to transform our world. We conclude this chapter with the earth-shattering vision of Teilhard de Chardin that only we can effect: "The day will come when, after harnessing the air, the winds, the tides and gravity, we shall harness for God the energies of love. And, on that day, for the second time in the history of the world, human beings will have discovered fire."[1] On that day, perhaps today, God's Holy Spirit will have triumphed in you. This victory depends on your spirit-filled effective decision.

> *O wind that blows when and where it will,*
> *teach me to reverence the Wind of Heaven.*
> *O mover of tree tops and tall grasses,*
> *you who are the servant of no other forces,*
> *open me up to the mysterious Breath of God.*

> *O Divine Wind, blowing with the Spirit's sweetness*
> *through a chant-filled mosque in Arabia*
> *or causing a silent heart to dance*
> *in a hidden hermit's cave high in the Himalayas,*
> *or caressing with compassion*

an abandoned packing crate in an urban slum,
wherein sleeps a homeless drifter;
let me feel your loving touch.

Lift me up above my selfish interests,
spreading my concerns wider than myself.
exhale a gale of your grace into me
and set me under full sail
as your servant of life and of love.[2]

CHAPTER 67

THE BATTLE LINES ARE DRAWN

The truth is, it is not Jesus as is historically known, but Jesus, as spiritually risen within people, that is significant for our time,"[1] writes Albert Schweitzer, the gifted Lutheran theologian.

A titanic battle rages today beneath life's surface, and you are a forceful, though perhaps unknowing, combatant in it. I'm not speaking of any personal struggle with your supervisor or mother-in-law, or even of the seeming global confrontation of East and West. I refer rather to the savage encounter between the forces of good and evil that we have been fighting through human history in all earthen lands, and which seems to be approaching a crescendo.

Evil, the enemy, has tremendous powers, which flow chiefly from our own human failings, regardless of nationality, race, or religion. These include grasping for power, depression, ignorance, violence, discrimination, war, and addictions. Add to that illness and death, and we have a partial list of the massive task challenging us. Notice this list never mentions any person or nation. People do not comprise our enemy, evil does, in its entire dimension in all of us. To understand the magnitude of this struggle, we must visualize all humanity of every race, nationality, and religion joined together in one integral body. So, the battle lines are drawn, and the two forces face each other: evil and its minions on one side and all humanity on the other.

Our objective begins with the crushing of evil wherever we find it: in ourselves and in our cultures. Our gravest difficulty arises from our confirmed belief that what I, my religion, my political party, or my nation stands for is always good and true, while the other side is always corrupt or false. However, the scenario to which we refer is more than "we against them." This is Christ in us rising up against evil wherever and whenever found. Andrew Harvey, noted spiritual author, wrote recently of this struggle: "Only a vast army of...beings who have consciously chosen the path of Christ...can effect the changes that are needed in every arena of life for the planet to be saved."[2]

By selecting the cause of the Risen Christ, we humans choose him and his voice spoken by our conscience. We are continually forming this conscience from our core human principles and spiritual ideals. For Christians, these arise from the historic Jesus. For others, Jesus may not be their Christ. Mohammed, Moses, Buddha, or another could provide their core truths, moral principles, and spiritual ideals. The role of all religions is to help us in this momentous struggle for goodness.

The Christ represents, for all of us, the fulfilling of our God-given person and talents in the service of our human neighbors and our planet. Hopefully, all will prioritize their brothers and sisters of every persuasion over holy books, principles, politics, laws, or teachings, despite their worthiness. Thus, we humans reject violence, war, vengeance, and profit in favor of peacemaking, compassion, forgiveness, and justice, and choose our savior and our religion according to how effectively they promote these causes.

For us Christians, goodness is rooted and flows through Jesus the Christ; therefore, this battle against evil is really his battle through us. Without us, he has no body, hands, feet, or voice, as we quoted previously from Teresa of Avila. Apropos of this, we have weapons, but they are not bullets, nukes, or dollars. Paul lists our weapons: *"Put on the armor of God....stand fast with your loins girded in truth, clothed with righteousness as a breastplate, and your feet shod in readiness for the gospel of peace"* (Eph. 6:13–15). The use of these weapons ensures success for us in this titanic struggle, for these are what attract humanity.

The Risen Christ calls us to overcome in our struggle with evil and to journey beyond into the love and life of Jesus. He, Jesus, urges us to be willing to sacrifice all, even our comforts and lifestyle, in the cause of goodness, compassion, and love, as he did. His living, as described on the biblical page, becomes our life principle, and according to T.S. Eliot, "The still-point of [our] turning world."[3] Each of us is empowered to speak, with our life, his words of life: *"I came so that they might have life and have it more abundantly"* (John 10:10). The prolific scripture scholar Raymond Brown reminds us that we are asked to love and identify with our founder. Evil is, however, so deeply embedded in the psyche of mankind, we can't expect to win this battle in our lifetimes, just as Jesus didn't, but we can contribute our resources in this life-and-death struggle as fully as possible. That contribution alone constitutes and measures our personal human success and helps to realize the eventual victory of mankind over evil.

Lord Jesus the Christ, when looking into a mirror, I see myself in reverse physical position, an apparent new person. I know this symbolizes the daily resurrection of my becoming you, a whole new person. I resolve that whenever encountering my reflection in a mirror, I shall consider this new person, the Christ, whom I am called to become.

Lord, please lead me to a new lifestyle grounded in your wisdom. Grant that I may thereby express you more vigorously in our clash with evil, and help me to perform heroically in this war against all wars. Risen Christ, rise within me in this titanic struggle of all humanity against evil. Amen.

CHAPTER 68

PAUL JOURNEYS
FROM LAW TO SPIRIT

It was a cold, wintry night in Jerusalem, about the year 20 CE; Saul, an eighteen-year-old student of the Jewish law, was engrossed with the most fundamental text for all Jews: *"Hear, O Israel! The LORD is our God, the LORD alone! Therefore, you shall love the Lord, your God, with all your heart, and with all your soul, and with all your strength. Take to heart these words which I enjoin on you today. Drill them into your children. Speak of them at home and abroad, whether you are busy or at rest"* (Deut. 6:4–7). Saul reverenced this text and vowed to follow it, and the entire Torah, to the letter. Saul was a fundamentalist. His intensity was such that he committed the entire Torah to memory, just as Gamaliel, the renowned Pharisee, his teacher, had taught. He resolved to dedicate his life to fulfilling every law and nuance of the Torah and would tolerate nothing to deter him from this mission. Already, we observe the powerful passion of this man of God that would consume his life.

Years later, Saul encountered members of that Jewish sect who claimed that a nondescript from the hills, Yeshua from Nazareth, was a prophet and messiah for all Jews. How outrageous! The law promised salvation, but not from some simpleton who broke the law, encouraged others in the same sin, and was then crucified for it. Some prophet was he! Saul needed no persuasion to seek the destruction of this insidious heresy. He would defend orthodoxy and temple even to executing Stephen, that blasphemer who accused the most sacred court, the Sanhedrin, of crimes and even murder (Acts 7:52). Luke summarizes that tragic scene in which Stephen was cast outside the city, stripped, and backed against a wall. Temple police under Saul stoned Stephen to death. He fell in his own blood. Saul approached and saw the destruction of the man that he had wrought. Then, he heard the dying man cry out, *"Lord Jesus, receive my spirit...Lord, do not hold this sin against them"* (Acts 7:59–60). Saul was shaken to his very core. "How could this impious Gentile, this sinner, have such trust in this Jesus? What right does he have to forgive me and my men? We are the ones who are following the law! I must root out these blasphemers!"

Saul set out angrily Damascus to find and punish others of them, but a spiritual detour lay just ahead. Saul was brooding within himself and questioning the law for the first time in his life. He mused, "The law can't ever give me the faith and courage in life or death that Stephen had. Where did that heretic get it? I try and try to follow the law, but find it impossible. Is my life a waste? My God, help me!" One person, Stephen, proved crucial in the life of Paul.

Then, as a desperate questioning and searching Paul descended from the cold heights of Mt. Hermon toward the heat of the desert, thunder struck: storm, lightning, and a clarion call, *"I am Jesus, whom you are persecuting"* (Acts 9:5). Call it divine intervention, a vision, or the crash of conscience, but spiritual cosmic thunder had struck! Blindness for three days ensued, and finally, the resurrection of enlightenment. Paul was beginning to see with a spiritual eye, and was baptized. You and I could become a Stephen, a Paul, or even a Jesus, and through our goodness impact the people in our lives. Are we beginning to see through our third eye?

Paul (Greek for Saul) visited Peter in Jerusalem, undoubtedly to question him concerning this Jesus: who he was and what he preached in detail. Paul then spent several years reflecting not on laws or doctrines, but on Jesus, his community, and their new relationship. Whatever the cost or pain, Paul would refocus and follow Jesus the Christ (the Messiah) with even greater passion than he did the law. For Paul and for us, law has value only when it leads to Christ.

Eventually, Barnabas, a loyal follower of Jesus, traveled with Paul to the Gentile provinces northwest of Antioch. Many of the Jews to whom they preached believed Jesus was the Christ, but some could not accept the Good News of Jesus and his resurrection. Even today, in their own lives, some can't believe that brilliant, joy-filled light can rise from ashen darkness.

In Acts 15, Luke spotlights a major dissension among the believers. Must Gentiles be circumcised prior to Baptism? This question carried immense implication; namely, whether this new "Way" would grow autonomously from its Jewish roots or remain in some way a Jewish sect. Paul and Barnabas traveled to Jerusalem for a plenary meeting in 47 CE to decide the issue. After listening to the heated debate by many and noticing the consensus, James, the conservative leader, declared this requirement of circumcision did not apply. Even Peter, listed traditionally as the first pope, consented, thus seeding Christianity with roots of collegial governance.

Energized by this liberating decision, Paul expanded his missionary efforts to wherever he was led. He toiled tirelessly in Ephesus, Philippi (his first European venue), Athens, Corinth, and countless

315

other communities in the Mediterranean basin. Jewish tradition-alists in the law punished him relentlessly. He suffered beatings, scourging, stoning, shipwreck, cold and exposure, sleepless nights, hunger, and near-death experiences for Christ, whom, like us, he had never known physically but in whom he believed fully (2 Cor. 11:23ff.). He also wrote countless letters, some of which form much of the Christian Testament. The passion of Paul never languished. What of mine and yours?

As the years blurred by, Paul developed an amazing theology. The resurrection formed its foundation. He told us that, were it not real, our faith is in vain, and we would be the most pitiful people of all (1 Cor. 15:16–19). Nevertheless, Paul asserts it truly did happen, and we also shall rise (Rom. 6:4). Because of this personal resur-rection of Jesus, he, the Risen Christ, overcomes physical time and space. He lives again in each of us individually and communally.

Individually, the Risen Christ lives in you and me, dwelling not as one separate, but as "oned" with us, in the totality of our persons. Thus, even your dreams, motivations, and actions flow from his residence within. Mental health professionals assert that we act from what we have derived genetically and experientially, but even in this process, one still discovers the presence of the Risen Christ.

"As a body is one though it has many parts, and all the parts of the body, though many, are one body, so also Christ. For in one spirit we were all baptized into one body" (1 Cor. 12:12–13). Our community of believers forms therefore the one body of Christ, and our inti-macy with him and each other surpasses all human affection and bonds us in Abba's spirit of love forever. This is the spiritual body of Christ that transcends our denominational walls.

Most students of Paul seek to understand his physical travels through three journeys. This does help our study, but we must remember his spiritual journey from the law to the spiritual Christ marks one of the greatest journeys in all human history. It builds to the climax by which even Paul's person changed: *"I have been crucified with Christ; yet I live, no longer I, but Christ lives in me"* (Gal. 2:19–20). Further, by his writing, Paul calls each of us to the same transformation: to be open to change fearlessly, day by day, into a new person who is Christ living in us in our daily circumstances.

If Paul were alive physically today, would he impact society? Would narrow minds still seek to silence him? No doubt, the answer is yes to both questions, and he would just as certainly wield as great influence now as then. The reason? He was a man of fierce passion that was fed by his invincible commitment to Christ. Do we need a Paul today? Absolutely, and he would add that you and I form the raw material.

Blessed Paul, although I know what you knew—that Jesus rose from the dead and seeks my commitment to his cause—still I falter. You started a great journey, and I hesitate; you gave your entire person, and I cling to self; you became a Christ, and I only dream of it. Help me to decide for Christ as you did, to draw others to the individual and universal Christ, one by one. Help me especially to bond with you in Christ and become a person who is caught up with you into paradise. Amen.

CHAPTER 69

REVELATION REVEALED

C able News Network reported on July 30, 2006, that 17 percent of Americans believe the end of the world, with all its attendant fear, is imminent. Perhaps this explains, in part, the dominant negativity so prevalent today. How shameful for religious leaders to ignore the certain hope to which the book of Revelation summons us. Not to say this last book of the Bible does not receive attention. Indeed, it ranks first in that department despite Revelation's never addressing the life of Jesus, being the most difficult biblical book to understand, and including hate-filled language of divine revenge. Still, some very visible preachers, authors, and televangelists center their message on its mysterious symbolism and project their own fanciful and often terrifying interpretations of the text rather than search out the meaning the author intended. They truly have no excuse for their musings, for scripture scholars have already completed much of the symbolic spadework. Why do these sensationalist preachers display such recklessness? Could it be that their dramatic interpretations lend themselves easily to ensuring handsome economic rewards? Let's search out the authentic meaning of this inspired work.

Jerusalem had been destroyed. Peter, Paul, and the twelve were martyred. Domitian, the Roman emperor, had just ordered a violent persecution of Christians in 90–95 CE. The Christian call seemed doomed, and many disciples cowered in hopeless disarray. Suddenly, an unknown from the Johannine community took quill in hand. He authored a book depicting with vivid imagery the desperate conditions of the time, but, more importantly, God's ultimate victory that lay ahead for the faithful. Because the Romans might discover copies of this anti-Roman material, he wrote for Christians in coded symbolic language that, if found, the Romans could not understand. Therefore, Revelation is really an underground leaflet designed to give hope to battle-weary Christians of the late first century. This background is a "long way" from those fundamentalist preachers of today who insist the biblical author of two thousand years ago is deftly referring to our current cast of international villains or future cataclysmic disasters.

The author, purported to be John the Apostle, wrote to seven churches in Asia Minor. Incidentally, archaeologists have found evidence of these seven in the geographical order the author presents. He described a vision in which the Son of Man holds seven stars symbolizing his universal dominion. His readers can feel secure; evil shall not conquer. The author wrote in chapter 3 to the listless Laodiceans (one of the seven churches), which finds certain application in our contemporary society: *"I know that you are neither cold nor hot....I will spit you out of my mouth....You say, 'I am rich and affluent and have no need of anything,' and yet do not realize that you are wretched, pitiable, poor, blind, and naked....Behold, I stand at the door and knock"* (Rev. 3:15–17, 20). Could that be our door on which the Lord knocks?

Chapter 5 presents an electrifying vision. God is holding a scroll that no one can open or examine. The tears of many flow because God's word can't be understood or embraced. What was true then remains true today. The lamb with seven horns (full power) and seven eyes (complete knowledge) steps forward to open the scroll, for he alone has lived its content. With that, the twenty-four elders and four living creatures (heaven, earth, and all creation) bow and acclaim the lamb just as they did God himself. Breathtaking in scope and supreme in praise is this scene!

Chapter 7 represents an interlude before the Lamb's opening the seventh and final seal in chapter 8. God is restraining all evil until 144,000 (the square number of twelve tribes multiplied by 1,000, symbolizing the new and utterly complete Israel) are sealed with an imprint of God. All are wearing the white of victory.

An elder asks, *"Who are these wearing white robes, and where did they come from?"* (7:13). The Lord says, *"These are the ones who have survived the time of great distress; they have washed their robes and made them white in the blood of the Lamb"* (7:14). They have lived the life of Christ and are declared victorious, *"and God will wipe away every tear from their eyes"* (7:17). Ah, the sublime and joyous company to which we are called!

Chapter 13 is famous for its reference to the beast whose number is 666. Fundamentalist preachers have for generations applied this number to terrorists such as Stalin, Hitler, Saddam Hussein, and Osama Bin Laden. Actually, Hebrew and Aramaic, like Latin, have no numbers, but rather letters to signify numerical values. The number 666 stands not for a terrorist of today, but in Roman numerals, to Nero Caesar, the first emperor persecutor of Christians. Roman oppression is symbolized by seven heads, the number of emperors from Nero to Domitian. Every individual and society are called to struggle against the force and hostility of their own Nero dimension.

The Messiah is pictured in chapter 14 standing gloriously atop Mt. Zion in Jerusalem with the 144,000 righteous at his side, and you stand among them. The author is cryptically proclaiming that all those who remain faithful to the Lord shall reign with him forever: this, our glorious future!

Chapter 16 recalls the last, great, famous battle at Armageddon, which these same shortsighted preachers have dated as occurring next week or next year. In reality, the author is describing that huge symbolic final battle at Megiddo where many pivotal conflicts had already been waged, but no place called Armageddon ("the hills of Megiddo") has appeared on any ancient map. This battle portrays all the forces of evil pitted against God. The truth is, you and I are fighting daily this battle of Armageddon in our own souls, and this encounter represents the supreme struggle of our lives. Wicked forces in our hearts and in society are symbolized today by what the author calls the great harlot. The author consciously used this term to signify the evil forces of Babylon that lay already in ruin and Rome, which would one day be destroyed. The name of the conqueror of these destructive powers is "King of Kings and Lord of Lords," who reigns within each of us. Vindication and reward shall come to the Christian community. Martyrdom has its reward, and "alleluia" (praise to the Lord) is their cry and ours!

Satan is chained for one thousand years, and then released. He gathers forces of evil but is defeated and cast into fire forever. Then, the final judgment occurs and God dwells in those whose names are written in the Book of Life. He wipes every tear from their eyes, for death and mourning are abolished. God's city, the New Jerusalem, descends in glorious magnificence in which you are invited to reside in personal and communal intimacy with Abba and the Lamb. Nothing else is needed, for that, my friend, is heaven.

John concludes this fascinating encoded letter of hope with the cry from the Lord, "Maranatha," *"'Yes, I am coming soon.' Amen!"* (22:20). Just as sure as the Lord dwells in us already, so he wishes to come to us more deeply, filling us with his Spirit—not next week or next year, but today. Now is the moment for each of us to banish hostility, apathy, and depression, and thereby bond with the Lord. Until we meet in the Jerusalem of the Lord, let us live with maranatha, ever in our hearts and on our lips.

Lord God, this life on earth is difficult for us, and our churches are burdened with pain, rejection, and discouragement of every kind. However, your book of Revelation promises us final victory if we pursue faithfully your Son, the Lamb. Your promise gives us hope no matter what evil, even death, besets us. We know, with your presence in us, we shall overcome every evil, including death, forever, and so we proclaim today, "Maranatha, come Lord, Jesus!"

CHAPTER 70

GOOD-BYE TO GOOD-BYES

Chances are you have never heard of Luiz Scolari. He coaches the Portuguese World Soccer Team and, previously, the Brazilian team. His success has been unbelievable in World Cup competition, winning twelve consecutive games against the world's greatest soccer stars. When asked his secret, Scolari said of his players, "They're overcoming limits. When you do that, the limits fall away, and you can start dreaming." Scolari has fingered the pulse of mankind's greatest dream: to overcome all limits; we add, even the limits of death.

Jesus also dreamed, but his vision was supreme: that of eternal oneness with the author of this universe, Abba. He conceived brilliantly the truth of personal afterlife, into which we now inquire.

As we have seen, Jesus viewed Abba as ultimate truth and love (chapter 39). He judged all values and behavior by these two standards. Truth and love cannot adequately describe the indescribable Abba, but they draw the best rendering we have.

Jesus reasoned a person is destined to reside in Abba if he or she seeks, in good and growing conscience, his truth, and then loves in accord with that truth. These two, with their offspring of varied transcending virtue, empower one to participate in the life of Abba (following rules and doctrines may be helpful but insufficient of themselves). All conduct that offends truth and love, or ignores truth and love, chooses, by that very choice, not to be of Abba. Hence, the degree to which I respond to the truth of my own conscience (impacted by my spiritual tradition) and exercise genuine love is the degree to which I participate in Abba (heaven). The degree to which I refuse to respond to these virtues is the degree to which I do not so participate in Abba (hell).

A man was once seeking answers to those eternal questions: what is hell, and what is heaven? He asked the wisest monk in a nearby monastery, but the monk didn't know. However, the abbot directed him to a wise woman who lived by herself outside town. Following the abbot's instructions, the man walked hastily through a deep, dark forest and emerged to behold a magnificent green meadow with a cheery, white cottage in the center. As he approached, he saw a lady working in her garden within a surrounding picket fence. He opened the gate, introduced himself, and declared, "I have been told to seek your answer to a most pressing question: 'What are hell and heaven like?'"

After a long, awkward moment of silence, she looked up and retorted, "How dare you enter my property without permission? Get out immediately!" He responded, "I was told you have wisdom and you—" She interrupted, shouting, "I told you, get out!" Now the man became angry. "Who do you think you are? You're not wise; you're a fraud!" His neck and face reddened with fury, and he began moving threateningly toward her. Suddenly, she verbally disarmed him. "My friend, now you know what hell is like." He stopped, refocused, fell to his knees, and stammered, "Thank you, now I understand, and I'm eternally grateful." The woman of wisdom then responded, "And now you know what heaven is like."

Because of genetic and experiential differences among all of us, we seek truth and love with differing degrees of spiritual insight and psychological freedom, for we are all captive in some manner. Abba alone, not church, synagogue, mosque, or even ourselves, can fully determine the authenticity of that search with total accuracy. Abba can pierce beneath our personal and communal masks and motivations to the fundamental spiritual ground of our beings. He discovers that core truth and love, which he alone recognizes because he alone is truth and love. This explains Jesus' refusing to believe Abba sends anyone to hell. Pope John Paul II agreed, "Damnation cannot be attributed to...God because in his merciful love He cannot want anything but the salvation of the beings He created. So, eternal damnation is not God's work but is actually our own doing."[1] The darkness of eternity fades into the light of reality.

How distressing it is that so many Christians and others still believe from their youth that Abba does dispatch people to hell. This belief, springing fundamentally from Matthew's gospel to the Jews who believed in Gehenna, imagines God as a severe, judgmental punisher and helps form our theologies of guilt. Actually, Abba is our impassioned lover and reward (chapter 45).

Because of his unique oneness with Abba, Jesus could speak authoritatively of heaven and describe it as a joy-filled paradise. *"I will see you again, and your hearts will rejoice, and no one will take your joy away from you"* (John 16:22). Astounding is the eternal depth and breadth of the joy Jesus has promised, and Abba has prepared for you: *"What eye has not seen, and ear has not heard, / and what has not entered the human heart, / what God has prepared for those who love him"* (1 Cor. 2:9). John Paul II presented an even greater theological description when on July 21, 1999, he exclaimed heaven is "Our definitive meeting with Abba that takes place in the Risen Christ through the power of the Holy Spirit."[2] This spotlights our destiny insofar as we prepare for it. Our heaven is, therefore, our union with Abba insofar as we allow the Risen Christ to rise in us. All this transformation is accomplished through the impact of the Holy Spirit.

We may biblically describe all of life as Abba's clarion call to his embrace. *"Go out, therefore, into the main roads and invite to the feast whomever you find"* (Matt. 22:9). This call from the numinous mystery of Abba resounds in every human psyche, ever drawing us through our tears and joys to his twin spires of love and truth. May you, each of my readers and all whom you touch, concur in this glorious privilege of seeking his truth and living the love his truth proclaims.

The memory of these pages may falter, but all of us are called to participate in a certain spiritual relationship that will steadily mature through and beyond all ages as we approach Christ (who is truth and love), each on our own path. Our destinies, here and beyond, are joined, for as we draw ever nearer to Abba, we converge so that we can truly say to each other, "Good-bye to good-byes"!

Blessed Abba, we, your beloved, have given ourselves to these pages as witness to the wisdom of your word. However, we also understand your richness exceeds infinitely beyond words and the insights of our efforts.

With full gratitude, we shall begin each day with your word and live that day in its exalted meaning. May this be our guide through our deserts to your bosom, our promised land. Amen. Alleluia!

EPILOGUE

Once there was a traveler who was urgently seeking a village named Celestia but who was woefully lost. The more he searched, the more confused and desperate he became. In a panic, he suddenly spotted a happy sign with an arrow: Celestia, one mile. His heart leapt for joy, and he realized he would soon find his destination.

The wisdom of the Bible may be likened in the story not to Celestia (for the Bible is not the destination) but to the sign, for the Bible points the way to our divine destiny. This does not mean the Bible is the sole signpost. Other signs for different people in different languages on different roads point in the same direction to the same exquisite destiny. Just as no one recognizes the signpost as our destination, so no one ought to judge another's salvation by one's own signpost.

This saving signpost called the Bible does not resemble a Band-Aid approach, a kind of positive thinking or mere book of inspiration. Rather, we have seen it addressing the core of our relationships: the archetypes of the pains and joys of our total human experience. These biblical characters and events, when understood in-depth, respond to our questions and doubts with wisdom. They summon us to the heights of human behavior and beyond. This is why we have objected in the text to the pitiful pabulum of fundamentalism that represents, at best, a fringy footnote in our Christian Tradition—that is, until the twentieth century. Now, fundamentalism presumes to speak *for* Christianity. It has no such right, for it ignores the soul of Christianity, this biblical Wisdom Tradition that we have discussed here. The followers of fundamentalism are legion and deserve more robust, spiritual nutrition. Story, symbol, and myth free us from mundane limitations and free our hearts for the breathtaking, limitless expanse to which the Word of God points. No longer are we bound to one fixed understanding of a text. Rather, guided by our particular tradition, we are free to explore the biblical Word for its bountiful, transcending wisdom. I have suggested numerous insights and applications of these texts, but they represent just a mere beginning. The inexhaustible depths of biblical wisdom, shrouded in numinous mystery, invite now your exploring with the help of a fine commentary. Mine the wisdom of the Lord, and experience free flight into his heart.

John Shelby Spong, former Episcopal Bishop of Newark, writes, "These [biblical] stories and symbols are open ended, only if they are vehicles through which one journeys into the mystery, the wonder, the wordlessness of God. It is, and will be eternally so, only if one is able to resist the perpetual human tendency to think that literal words capture truth, when all they can ever do is point toward [it]."[1] Karl Jung adds, "The history of symbolism shows that everything can assume symbolic significance…The whole cosmos is a potential symbol. Man with his symbol-making propensity, unconsciously transforms objects or forms into symbols…and expresses them in both his religion and visual art."[2] Still, our literalist friends seek to deny us this universal world of wonder.

Why ignore divine wisdom that's portrayed with such boundless beauty and artful imagery by the sacred authors? Why not allow the profound meanings of the lives of Abraham, Jeremiah, and the others—especially Jesus—to continue summoning us to profound meaning and human heroism? Why deny or deplore this surpassing symbolism that God himself approves in his human authors?

Conservatives and progressives have important roles to play in maintaining religious balance, but fundamentalism has no role for the adult Christian. Its motives are suspect; its theology, specious; its political and scientific relationships, disastrous. Further, fundamentalism provides an easy straw-man target for the invective of self-declared enemies of spirituality. For example, Christopher Hitchens, an avowed atheist, wrote recently, "Reflecting on the nonsense story of Adam's fall...that forbidding Adam to eat from one tree lest he die, and from another lest he live forever, is absurd and contradictory."[3]

Christopher, seek to destroy spirituality and Christianity if you must, but 'tis futile, for you are really attacking human nature as it seeks meaning beyond itself. As for Christianity, you have targeted its straw-man imposter: fundamentalism. Try ingesting true biblical wisdom that challenges you, with all men and women, to the fullness of forgiving, sharing, and loving, even to death on your own cross.

True Christians love divine wisdom, for which they spend their lives in search. Recall my introduction in which I referred to a double-fibered thread weaving through these chapters. The first reflects our ever-increasing understanding of the Word of God. We have experienced this by exploring prominent facets of the included biblical characters and events. In this search, I pray you will dedicate at least ten minutes each day to "Lecto Divina" (divine reflection). Your commitment to this practice will help to ensure the success of your life journey to Christ. Keep in mind the three outstanding presuppositions we have traced (chapter 3):

1. that we reverence the author's in-depth intended meaning of the text from an astute biblical commentary,

2. that we are free to explore its wonders within our Tradition, and

3. most importantly, that the biblical wisdom of which we have written motivates and energizes our daily transformation into other Christs. If such transformation does not occur, all is lost. To the degree it does occur, all is gained. This relates to the second fiber that recalls Abba's effort to draw you to his heart by the values and lifestyle Jesus and the others lived. Jesus was consumed with his love for you and uttered it plaintively as John records it: *"That they all may be one, as you, Father, are in me and I in you, that they also may be in us, that the world may believe that you sent me"* (John 17:21). Yes, Abba is also journeying in quest of our hearts to identify with us even as he did with Jesus. It is no surprise that Rabbi Abraham Heschel entitles his classic *God in Search of Man: A Philosophy of Judaism*.

Jesus tries to control no one, not even his betrayers. He accepts, supports, and challenges all whom he touches and models for his sisters and brothers an intimate, indestructible bonding of himself with Abba. This provides the foundation of biblical wisdom that may be summed up by the desire of Jesus that you transform into another Christ in your corner of the world. Thereby, you continue in your person the glorious spiritual incarnation of Jesus of Nazareth. Incredibly, you and I live in the same Spirit by which he lived; we're called to the same destiny as he, and assume his identity as Joan the Christ, Mark the Christ, Joy the Christ, or Dawn the

Christ, etc. This leads us to our final gratifying conclusion: Jesus was the full human expression of divine wisdom, and to the degree the Risen Christ lives in us, we become a growing personification of that same wisdom. It's not surprising that each of us is called to serve each other, bonding with the divine wisdom of Abraham, Isaiah, Jeremiah, the Baptist, Magdalene, Paul, and all the others, especially Jesus, as they served heroically in their day the people in their lives. Truly, we live spiritually on the biblical page.

Could in-depth wisdom be drawn from biblical characters and themes other than our seventy? Absolutely! Even more importantly, one can find God's wisdom by exploring your response to the trials, pains, and joys of life. God so inspired the sacred authors that they might inspire us to become transformed expressions of his wisdom. Therefore, we resolve to live the certain truth of that "purple patch" of biblical wisdom: "You may be the only Bible some will ever read."

Dear Abba, many of us are enamored with the words of the Bible. You have gifted us, however, with the desire to "dig down" through them for your deeper wisdom, and you have empowered us to perceive it more clearly. Because of wisdom's female dimension, we acknowledge both masculine and feminine in you. You are wisdom present in the events and persons on the biblical page and truly also in us.

The heroes/sheroes in these pages struggled with apparent disaster and defeat just as we do. Still, nearly all persevered until their final reward in you. We are privileged to learn from all of them. From this moment and through the journey to come, we shall in faith walk with them in the unbounded freedom of your eternal wisdom. Amen.

POINT/COUNTERPOINT

I have included this section not to state the exact declared position of the fundamentalist, the nonbeliever, and the Christian scholar, but to provide a representative summation of their varied opinions. Moreover, these positions are not intended to counter one or the others' statements, but merely to present a likely objective thinking of each. I leave the critique and preference of one rather than another to you, my reader.

Chapter 1: Spirituality and Religion

Fundamentalist: Religion and spirituality are identified, and my particular religion is the true one.

Nonbeliever: Religion and spirituality are distinguished, but the former leads imperiously to an unbelievable dead-end, which is the latter.

Christian Scholar: The two are distinct, but religion, when healthy, serves spirituality, which represents the mutual embrace of divinity and humanity.

Chapter 2: Tradition, Mother of the Bible

Fundamentalist: We have never heard of religious tradition. We follow only the Bible.

Nonbeliever: Religious tradition consists of fairy tales passed down by church-goers.

Christian Scholar: Christians had no Christian Testament for nearly four hundred years and were giving their martyred lives for Tradition. Eventually, some of the Tradition was written down and gave birth to the Bible.

Chapter 3: How to Interpret the Bible

Fundamentalist: The meaning of the Bible is obvious from the clear meaning of the words.

Nonbeliever: At Times, the Bible can provide a "good read."

Christian Scholar: We seek first the meaning the author intended by using an informative commentary. Then, we determine that our derived interpretation agrees with Tradition. Finally, we seek to incorporate its message into our daily living.

Chapter 4: Dig Down: Fundamentalism Exposed!

Fundamentalist: Why search for some clever meaning foreign to the text? Anyone can understand the Bible.

Nonbeliever: The Bible resembles any other fiction. It surely contains symbolism, but what it symbolizes is not necessarily true.

Christian Scholar: God's wisdom is reflected in the authors' intended meaning, whether an event carries historical truth (as it sometimes does) or not.

Chapter 5: Abba's Breath of Inspiration

Fundamentalist: Every biblical word is inspired and therefore absolute.

Nonbeliever: The Bible can claim no additional inspiration than any other book.

Christian Scholar: God did inspire the biblical authors, but from within their culture, attitudes, and literary style. God's inspiration was only affirmed later by the church as guardian of its foundation document.

Chapter 6: In the Name of Yahweh

Fundamentalist: God directs this universe in a hands-on style.

Nonbeliever: God does not exist, or if he does, does not engage with our world.

Christian Scholar: God is inherent in all that is, in a sublime unitive relationship that we call love.

Chapter 7: In the Beginning, When God Created...

Fundamentalist: Genesis states unequivocally that God created the universe (obviously from the external) in six days. That is the absolute truth.

Nonbeliever: This universe originated with a "big bang," or something similar and not with a god who is somewhere.

Christian Scholar: The author of Genesis weaved a story from and for his culture that told of God's creative action. Science explains that the universe exploded into being over fourteen billion years ago and continues its expansion even today. It adds that such dynamism is evident in us as evolving earthlings. We Christians accept scientific truth with

a caveat that our creating God is present in and
presides over this continuing process

Chapter 8: Eve and Adam, Alive and Well

Fundamentalist: Adam and Eve walked in a garden, ate forbidden fruit that devastated humanity forever, and talked with a serpent and with God.

Nonbeliever: This is a story of a pleasant garden with two residents eating fruit and thereby disobeying a god. This god overreacts to this innocent dalliance. Its negatively affecting all humanity is utter nonsense.

Christian Scholar: he story is mythic and designed to teach many lessons. For example, God created all and the seventh day should be reserved for God. Eating the fruit of the tree of the knowledge of good and evil bespeaks their attempt to assume God's authority. Having disturbed the order of nature, shame and guilt arise, with all their attendant consequences.

Chapter 9: Cain and Abel: Brothers in Blood Only

Fundamentalist: Cain murdered Abel and God punished him. Therefore, we must punish any disturber of peace.

Nonbeliever: All of us should know we should not murder, not because of a god but because we are brothers and sisters.

Christian Scholar: This mythic tale demonstrates the potential for violence in human nature, and that God seeks our rejection of all violence in ourselves and society.

Chapter 10: Noah the Mariner

Fundamentalist: God saved Noah from the flood because he was obedient.

Nonbeliever: A flood over the entire planet? Impossible! This presents additional evidence that the Bible is fable.

Christian Scholar: This story is patterned on the Epic of Gilgamesh, a well-known ancient story of flooding. The author adapts the story to convince mankind to choose goodness and avoid evil.

Chapter 11: Abraham, Our Father in Faith

Fundamentalist: Abraham was apparently a man of God who fathered the Jews. Because he was not Christian, we pray he was saved.

Nonbeliever: God orders Abraham to slay his son, and Abraham follows orders. Who can believe any of these three players would realistically fulfill these roles?

Christian Scholar: The story of Abraham nearly slaying his son, Isaac, was planned to show that God did not accept human sacrifice as other nations did. More important for today, the Abraham stories depict the common familial origins of Islam, Judaism, and Christianity. The stories cry out for mutual love and honoring of these peoples.

Chapter 12: Isaac, the Passive Patriarch

Fundamentalist: Isaac was an obedient son of Abraham, a patriarch of Israel, and chosen by God. He was, therefore, a great man.

Nonbeliever: Isaac is initially traumatized by his father trying to sacrifice him. Then he is betrayed on his deathbed by his wife. He hardly seems like a man favored by a god!

Christian Scholar: The author depicts through this story that God can draw greatness even from a member of such a dysfunctional family. This story brings more evidence that resurrection is a central theme of the Bible.

Chapter 13: Jacob and Rebekah, Family Conspirators

Fundamentalist: Jacob's ladder to heaven, his all-night wrestle with God, the bitterness between Jacob and his brother Esau: this is a difficult story to understand but true.

Nonbeliever: These events stretch beyond the absurd.

Christian Scholar: These stories portray the Hebraic style of dramatic writing, which points to deeper meaning.

Chapter 14: Our Judaic-Christian Covenants Endure

Fundamentalist: The Hebrews and God formed an everlasting covenant.

Nonbeliever: God chose one small people with whom to covenant. Incredible!

Christian Scholar: The Hebrews created this covenant with their God to consecrate their mutual and permanent bonding. Christians then superseded it with their new covenant.

Chapter 15: The Exodus: Bon Voyage!

Fundamentalist: The Hebrews journeyed forty years to freedom in the Promised Land.

Nonbeliever: Others have also sought and gained their freedom from oppressive governments.

Christian Scholar: The Hebrews saw uniquely the saving presence of God in all their desert desperations.

Chapter 16: Moses, the Transformed Journeyman

Fundamentalist: Moses works many astounding miracles in the Hebrews' forty-year trek through the desert.

Nonbeliever: Moses: one in a long line of resourceful liberators.

Christian Scholar: Moses personified his people journeying from their being despised to their being revered, all with the aid of God's grace.

Chapter 17: Hail, the Ark of the Covenant!

Fundamentalist: The lesson is clear: fear God.

Nonbeliever: A people worship a box they themselves constructed. How bizarre!

Christian Scholar: The ark symbolized God's presence (shekinah) to the Hebrews; therefore, they reacted to the ark always with fearful awe.

Chapter 18: Our Warrior God?

Fundamentalist: If one disobeys God, he or she will pay a fearful price.

Nonbeliever: Their God was one of vengeance, fury and murder, not love as some claim.

Christian Scholar: The Hebrews conceived of God as always supporting them in battle, but God is a lover not a warrior. Humanity must continue to mature in understanding God in that universal light and not in the darkness of parochial competitiveness.

Chapter 19: Singing Psalms and Living Liturgy

Fundamentalist: Sing to the Lord! Praise the Lord! Alleluia!

Nonbeliever: Religionists use liturgy and song to bond their followers together in subjection to God.

Christian Scholar: The Hebrews were so filled with commitment to the Lord that they erupted in sacred song. This embodied the exultant human heart when it encountered the divine.

Chapter 20: Wisdom and Her Children

Fundamentalist: Wisdom refers to the omniscience of the Lord.

Nonbeliever: Human wisdom would surely not include a remote, fanciful God.

Christian Scholar: Human wisdom respects the evolving spiritual inheritance of humanity that views God as the seat of wisdom and humanity as participating in it.

Chapter 21: Joshua, the Four-Star General

Fundamentalist: Joshua exemplifies defending our faith even with arms.

Nonbeliever: Religion is finally exposed as constructing a kind of empire and then defeating its enemies in battle.

Christian Scholar: Truly, Joshua commanded Israel's military forces, but he gradually learned also to trust in the Lord—a lesson for all humankind.

Chapter 22: Samuel, Our Wise Ancestor

Fundamentalist: Like Samuel, we need only trust in the Lord and goodness will prevail.

Nonbeliever: The Hebrews were just another nation needing an earthly king.

Christian Scholar: Despite his leadership in military affairs, Samuel never forgot that the Lord was ultimately responsible for his success and that of Israel, whether they had a king or not.

Chapter 23: The Tragic Saul

Fundamentalist: Saul was a sinner whom the Lord punished.

Nonbeliever: Saul responded as all of us do to events, not because of the God of Israel.

Christian Scholar: The story of Saul appears in the Bible because it reflects a dangerous archetype for all; namely, by placing our entire trust in worldly success, we become vulnerable to ultimate disaster

Chapter 24: A Shepherd Boy: The True Goliath

Fundamentalist: David was the great king and ancestor of Jesus.

Nonbeliever: This man enjoyed much success and suffered many failures. These do not justify a godly explanation.

Christian Scholar: David's defeat of Goliath signifies our conquering the mammoth challenges we encounter in our daily living.

Chapter 25: Solomon, Son of Wisdom?

Fundamentalist: Solomon was shrewd and powerful, just as our Christian leaders must be to defend faith, nation and family.

Nonbeliever: Solomon was clever, ruthless, and eminently successful without the help of a god.

Christian Scholar: His fame and power provided Solomon stature among his royal peers, but do these reflect divine wisdom? An age-old question for each of us to ponder.

Chapter 26: Elijah, A Man of Conscience

Fundamentalist: God can do anything; even cause fire to consume water, for which Elijah prayed. You can believe it!

Nonbeliever: Elijah may have been a wise man, but fire does not consume water and a god does not answer prayer.

Christian Scholar: This story of Elijah need not be accepted as historical truth, but the spiritual truth to which it points is clear: the Lord alone is God.

Chapter 27: Ah, For a Jeremiah Today!

Fundamentalist: Jeremiah was a man of conviction, but Judah had to defend the homeland.

Nonbeliever: Political maneuvering is needed in times of international trial.

Christian Scholar: Jeremiah's suggestion from God was to surrender Jerusalem in the hope it would not be destroyed and also to promote justice. This was neither radical nor foolish, but reasonable and wise. It also proved prophetic.

Chapter 28: Ezekiel, A Prophet Among Us

Fundamentalist: Ezekiel has symbolic dreams and visions, but such are unreliable.

Nonbeliever: This man was a visionary with opinions that proved accurate, but a god was not necessarily involved.

Christian Scholar: Ezekiel declared that his entire career sprang from God's Word as symbolized in his vision of the chariot. Ezekiel uses even his wife's death to symbolize to Israel God's plea for justice.

Chapter 29: "Here I Am: Send Me!" (Isaiah 6:8)

Fundamentalist: We fundamentalists acknowledge the importance of Isaiah.

Nonbeliever: These men who claim to be prophets are actually informed kingly advisors: politicians.

Christian Scholar: The book of Isaiah stands in its three components as a masterpiece of allegory and symbol. Isaiah asserts clearly that he speaks for God, and later Jesus believes in him by modeling his career on Isaiah's four servant songs.

Chapter 30: Jerusalem: Tragedy and Triumph

Fundamentalist: Jerusalem has a sacred history and must be defended at all cost.

Nonbeliever: Jerusalem does have a storied history, but like all cities, the history is one of victories and defeats and not related to a god.

Christian Scholar: Jerusalem's history is intertwined with prophets and others who speak and live in the shadow of God. More than any other city, Jerusalem reflects humanity's tortuous journey to the Lord.

Chapter 31: The Four Evangelists: Why Can't They Agree?

Fundamentalist: The evangelists differ only in details. Their versions can be easily integrated.

Nonbeliever: These differences provide evidence that the Bible is fiction.

Christian Scholar: The evangelists' numerous disagreements derive from the authors' objectives, resources, and culture.

Chapter 32: Herod to Christ: The Great Divide

Fundamentalist: Herod proved himself an evil monster who massacred the babies of Bethlehem.

Nonbeliever: King Herod is historical, but the events ascribed to him in the Bible are not.

Christian Scholar: Herod stands for the force of evil that attacked Jesus from his beginning to the cross.

Chapter 33: Merry Christmas!

Fundamentalist: Jesus lived forever in God and miraculously was born as a human being.

Nonbeliever: No evidence, no witness, no truth to this impossible claim of theology.

Christian Scholar: The significant details of this birth might not reflect historical truth, but the incarnation does express God's supreme humility to raise humanity on earth to his dizzying heights.

Chapter 34: The Colorful Visitors

Fundamentalist: Three magi followed a miraculous star that stopped over the spot of Jesus' birth while angels from heaven spoke to the shepherds.

Nonbeliever: The exact movement of a star is scientifically impossible, and there is no evidence of the existence of angelic beings.

Christian Scholar: The story of the magis' gifts symbolizes the baby's future, and the star refers to Numbers 24:17. The shepherd represents the poor and sinners. Matthew's and Luke's literary skills present outstanding examples of Hebraic pictorial depiction.

Chapter 35: John, Mentor and Baptizer

Fundamentalist: Neither John nor anyone could mentor Jesus, the Son of God.

Nonbeliever: John displayed courage and, like many other outspoken witnesses, paid the price.

Christian Scholar: The story of Jesus' baptism by John suggests these authors believe that Jesus fulfills the promises of Psalm 2:7 and Isaiah 61:1; 63:19b. By his life and death, John journeys from being an itinerant desert man to a martyr for the one whose coming he proclaimed.

Chapter 36: Will You Marry Me?

Fundamentalist: Jesus begins his ministry by miraculously changing water into wine to aid an obscure couple at their wedding.

Nonbeliever: No one can accomplish this, and even if Jesus could, there is no significant reason for his doing so.

Christian Scholar: John tells the story to depict that, in his opinion; Christ has fulfilled and superseded Judaism (symbolized by the previous wine having run out).

Chapter 37: "Behold the Man!" (John 19:5)

Fundamentalist: Jesus is my divine savior, and I would protect him from all attacks by this society.

Nonbeliever: Jesus was a great man, perhaps even a human prophet.

Christian Scholar: Jesus wept, rejoiced and loved. He was fully a human being, one of us except for sin. However, this absence of sin and his fullness of love give unique and surpassing evidence of his being the human face of God (love) on earth.

Chapter 38: Prayer: Embracing the Divine

Fundamentalist: God answers every prayer, often in ways we do not request.

Nonbeliever: Prayer reflects the pray-er merely talking to himself or herself and is therefore totally futile.

Christian Scholar: Prayer assumes the pray-er enters intimately into God's unifying presence. He or she thereby absorbs something of God, and that union far exceeds whatever else could be requested.

Chapter 39: His Secret Passion

Fundamentalist: Jesus, being God, needed no additional motivation or energy.

Nonbeliever: At best, Jesus was a man of courage.

Christian Scholar: Jesus was a man who maintained such intimate "oneness" with God that as God and man, he could overcome spiritually every human distress with indomitable love.

Chapter 40: Mary, His First Disciple

Fundamentalist: Mary, his mother, was a special woman.

Nonbeliever: His mother certainly taught Jesus well the lessons of life.

Christian Scholar: Because Jesus was divine and was her son on earth, Mary became the mother of God; however, could her greatest asset be that she became also the greatest disciple of her own son?

Chapter 41: The Challenge of Family Living

Fundamentalist: This story demonstrates Jesus' determination and courage.

Nonbeliever: So this supposedly holy family has severe dysfunction. Hardly exemplary!

Christian Scholar: Let's forever remember that true holiness resides not in the perfect (that doesn't humanly exist) but with those who journey from dysfunction to healing.

Chapter 42: The ___ of Abba

Fundamentalist: Jesus instituted a kingdom to be defended and spread throughout the world.

Nonbeliever: He failed to initiate any kingdom, for his death by the state renders him an obvious and total deceiver.

Christian Scholar: Jesus initiated a spiritual kingdom in himself and invited all to participate in it; that is, to love Abba and each other without restraint.

Chapter 43: The Constitution of God's Kingdom

Fundamentalist: We will always defend Jesus and his teachings.

Nonbeliever: These beatitudes bespeak humility and compassion which other outstanding leaders through the ages have also espoused.

Christian Scholar: These fundamentals of his teaching breathe of life in God's Spirit and stand as essential pillars of the true Christian.

Chapter 44: Shalom Aleichem!

Fundamentalist: We Christians must "stick together" in protecting our faith and each other.

Nonbeliever: There are evil people in this world who must be defeated. Peacemaking is not always practical.

Christian Scholar: The true Christian renounces not only war but every form of violence. Defending our faith lies not in defeating our accuser but embracing him or her.

Chapter 45: Evil: Our Stepping Stone to Success

Fundamentalist: Offer your pain to God in atonement for your sins.

Nonbeliever: Evil is crushing for all of us, so accept it and try to move on.

Christian Scholar: God is love in transcendent purity and thus pain that dwells in every relationship offers the richest opportunity to choose love and become like unto Christ, unto God.

Chapter 46: Seeds of the Final Conspiracy

Fundamentalist: I am saved, and thus conflict loses its sting.

Nonbeliever: We must persevere through conflict with confidence in our position but retain open minds.

Christian Scholar: Christ approached every conflict with foundational love for even the offender and with trust in the pervasive presence of Abba.

Chapter 47: Jesus Challenges Capitalism

Fundamentalist: Possessing money measures worldly success, providing we don't hurt anyone in acquiring it.

Nonbeliever: Having money translates into power that can be used for good.

Christian Scholar: Money has value insofar as we use it for others. Hoarding money constitutes the sin of greed. Jesus understood that wealth (the capitalist standard of success) presented a great danger to one who lives to serve others.

Chapter 48: John 5 and John 9: A Stark Contrast!

Fundamentalist: Jesus works miracles whenever and on whomever he pleases.

Nonbeliever: One cannot say these are miracles. They could represent exaggerations or redactions if they ever really happened.

Christian Scholar: John contrasts opposite reactions to healing. The lame man in chapter 5 is only physically healed because he refuses to believe in Jesus. Jesus also heals the blind man in chapter 9, but he professes faith in Jesus and is spiritually healed, which is far more salutary.

Chapter 49: You Can Walk on Water!

Fundamentalist: Jesus, as God, is the author of nature and therefore can easily walk on water.

Nonbeliever: The reality is that no one can walk on water.

Christian Scholar: Did Jesus walk on water? Perhaps, but the synoptic authors are really saying Jesus supports us in our swirling, muddied waters of trouble and desperation.

Chapter 50: The Canaanite Teacher

Fundamentalist: Jesus can even heal a person who is not present to him.

Nonbeliever: Why didn't Jesus just heal everyone? Then we would believe.

Christian Scholar: This story focuses not on the healing but on the broadening lesson of universal love this woman teaches the Jewish Jesus.

Chapter 51: A Woman En Route from Magdala

Fundamentalist: Jesus also forgives the sin of this woman.

Nonbeliever: This lady admirably turned her life around.

Christian Scholar: Because of Christ, Mary journeys from a demonic life in Magdala to the tomb of the Risen Christ. Not only Jesus, but Mary also rises, and her resurrection is just as radical.

Chapter 52: A Tale of Two Sisters

Fundamentalist: Prayer is essential to the Christian calling.

Nonbeliever: The author simply tells the story of two sisters as they interact with Jesus.

Christian Scholar: This tale suggests that Christian activity must flow from prayer, and that prayer shapes the activity. Christian living requires both dimensions.

Chapter 53: The Good Samaritan Lives On

Fundamentalist: Jesus seeks to expand the Judeans' appreciation of their mortal enemy, the Samaritans.

Nonbeliever: This story contains real value: that international enemies must reconcile.

Christian Scholar: Jesus indicates with this story that his followers have no human enemy, only the prejudice and hostility within human hearts.

Chapter 54: The Greatest Short Story Ever Told

Fundamentalist: The parable states we must honor our father.

Nonbeliever: Family ties are stronger than familial dysfunction.

Christian Scholar: Jesus illustrates the father (representing God) loving his sons and daughters despite whatever evil they may commit. We recall all three characters present in each of us.

Chapter 55: Simon Peter at the Helm

Fundamentalist: Simon Peter was first among equals.

Nonbeliever: This story seems unimportant to me. Whether he or John or James is their leader has little meaning for my life.

Christian Scholar: Peter might have been the disciples' leader, but he had a lot to learn of himself and Christ. His journey is one of self-reliance to Christ-reliance, and becomes the model for everyone's journey.

Chapter 56: Long Live Lazarus!

Fundamentalist: Jesus even raises people from the dead. Certainly, he is God's Son.

Nonbeliever: I doubt this ever happened.

Christian Scholar: Some insist on asking the wrong question; namely, did this really happen. Instead, we should question the story's meaning. In this case, John prepares us for Jesus' resurrection and ours, both daily and beyond our final tomb.

Chapter 57: Choose Your Company: Goats or Sheep

Fundamentalist: Thank God, I was saved on January 18 of last year.

Nonbeliever: There is no judgment except among human beings on earth.

Christian Scholar: We cannot be saved on a particular day when our salvation depends on our continuing efforts in behalf of the needy and oppressed.

Chapter 58: Love is Your Name!

Fundamentalist: Love is very important, but we must also follow the law.

Nonbeliever: Love stands as the most fundamental and energizing human relationship.

Christian Scholar: Christ calls his disciples to a most profound and sacrificial love that embraces the entire creation of Abba. Christ embodies this love on the cross.

Chapter 59: Table O' Plenty

Fundamentalist: There can be no doubt that after multiplying loaves and fish, Jesus proves he is the Son of God.

Nonbeliever: This is the best magic story I ever heard.

Christian Scholar: This story serves as an overture to the Eucharist: same words, same matter, and same spiritual nutrition for our long spiritual journey.

Chapter 60: Temple Tenders

Fundamentalist: Even Jesus defended his faith.

Nonbeliever: Jesus lost his temper. He was a mere man like the rest of us.

Christian Scholar: Jesus was truly a human being, but he loved Abba so fully he would symbolically rid the needy Jews of their false religionists who sought to control them through their religion.

Chapter 61: That "They May All Be One!" (John 17:21)

Fundamentalist: I genuinely grieve for those who are not Christian and can't be saved.

Nonbeliever: What silly competition among religions with each claiming to be the only path to salvation.

Christian Scholar: We seek not a mere physical unity of churches but the spiritual ideal of all humanity seeking truth and love to the fullest. When this begins in earnest, one can only dream of the magnificent fruit we will taste.

Chapter 62: Come Dine With Me!

Fundamentalist: I interpret the Bible literally but not his words at the last supper.

Nonbeliever: An unleavened morsel of bread can't sufficiently feed anyone.

Christian Scholar: The Christian Tradition asserts Jesus' true presence under the appearance of bread and wine. Ah, soul-food for the forty-year journey across the barren desert we all must tread!

Chapter 63: Do We Sleep in Gethsemane?

Fundamentalist: Jesus never surrendered in despair at the prospect of what lay before him.

Nonbeliever: He nearly gave up, which proves again that he was merely human.

Christian Scholar: His agony was extreme while his friends slept, but he overcame, while trusting Abba to the end. Are we still sleeping today?

Chapter 64: Our Royal Scapegoat

Fundamentalist: Jesus died for our sins, becoming thereby our savior.

Nonbeliever: He is no scapegoat; Jesus was simply executed by the state.

Christian Scholar: Jesus did not retaliate at his tormentors but forgave them and absorbed the pain. He thus personified for all to witness, the fullness of love "in the flesh." In this real sense, Jesus became our universal scapegoat and model.

Chapter 65: He's Risen!

Fundamentalist: Our physical body and soul shall rise and meet in heaven. Hallelujah!

Nonbeliever: No one can prove his so-called resurrection ever happened.

Christian Scholar: Paul refers to the "spiritual body" of Jesus that rose from the dead; that is, his spiritual person was so pervaded by Abba's Spirit of love that he would live forever in Abba. Love had conquered death for him and for us insofar as we choose him in life.

Chapter 66: Journeying in Fire, Wind and Tongue

Fundamentalist: Luke describes the presence of fire, wind, and understanding of foreign languages at the first Pentecost. This is what happened, and I believe it just as it's written.

Nonbeliever: If all these were present, there would have been some mighty conflagration.

Christian Scholar: These three symbolize the passionate presence of the Spirit of God seeking to draw us with full freedom into Abba's embrace of love.

Chapter 67: The Battle Lines Are Drawn

Fundamentalist: The universal struggle will continue until Jesus comes again to carry his followers into eternal life.

Nonbeliever: There is conflict between the forces of good and evil, but no god is involved.

Christian Scholar: Paul describes the worldwide spiritual combat between the forces of Abba (love and goodness) and evil. Each of us often unknowingly is mortally engaged in this cataclysmic battle that will terminate in a universal embrace (the omega point, the cosmic Christ).

Chapter 68: Paul Journeys from Law to Spirit

Fundamentalist: Paul was miraculously converted by the Risen Jesus and consecrated himself to Jesus for the remainder of his life.

Nonbeliever: Simply stated, Paul changed his attitude toward this Jesus sect.

Christian Scholar: The conversion of Paul must be viewed in the context of his passionate search for truth, first in the law and later in the Risen Christ. He never flinched from his radical commitment despite horrendous disappointment and suffering.

Chapter 69: Revelation Revealed

Fundamentalist: The book of Revelation is part of the Bible and must be taken literally despite its difficulty.

Nonbeliever: These bizarre descriptions prove the inanity of the book.

Christian Scholar: Revelation endures as a book of symbolic apocalyptic literature that brings, at moments of desperation, hope and assurance in the ultimate victory of our God of love.

Chapter 70: Good-bye to Good-byes

Fundamentalist: We wait for salvation in heaven.

Nonbeliever: All talk of heaven or deliverance from hell reflects wishful thinking from our fear-filled living.

Christian Scholar: Insofar as one loves, one will participate in eternal love because love is greater than death. We are free to choose love daily, and this constitutes daily resurrection that will finally grow into the Godhead of the fullness of truth and love.

NOTES

Preface: Essential Preambles

1. Raymond Brown, *A Retreat With John the Evangelist: That You May Have Life* (Cincinnati: Anthony Messenger, 1998), 28.

2. Ibid., 29.

Introduction: Fundamentalism, Deflecting the Search

1. J. N. D. Kelly, *Golden Mouth: The Story of John Chrysostom—Ascetic, Preacher, Bishop* (Ithaca: Cornell University Press, 1998).

2. *St. Irenaeus of Lyons Against the Heresies*, trans. Dominic J. Unger, vol. 1, Ancient Christian Writers Series (Mahwah, NJ: Newman, 1992).

Chapter 1: Spirituality and Religion

1. Abraham J. Heschel, *God in Search of Man: A Philosophy of Judaism* (New York: Farrar, Straus and Giroux, 1987), 3.

2. Tom Roberts, ed., "Elton John," *National Catholic Reporter* (Kansas City, MO: National Catholic Reporter Publishing Co., December 8, 2006.

3. Stephen Doyle, *Luke's Gospel For the New Liturgical Year*, Alba House, audiocassette, 2001.

4. Augustine, *The Confessions: (Works of Saint Augustine, a Translation for the 21st Century: Part 1—Books)*, ed. Maria Boulding, 2nd ed. (Hyde Park, NY: New City Press, 2002).

5. Edward O. Wilson, *On Human Nature* (Cambridge: Harvard University Press, 1978).

6. John Shelby Spong, *Jesus, For The Non-Religious* (San Francisco: Harper, 2007), 11.

7. Albert Nolan, *Jesus, Today a Spirituality of Radical Freedom* (Maryknoll, NY: Orbis, 2006), 12.

Chapter 2: Tradition, Mother of the Bible

1. Cyril C. Richardson, ed., *Early Christian Fathers: Letters of Ignatius, Bishop of Antioch* (New York: MacMillan, 1970).

Chapter 3: How to Interpret the Bible

1. Joseph Fitzmyer, *Scripture, the Soul of Theology* (Mahwah, NJ: Paulist Press, 1994), 42.

2. William Blake, "The Everlasting Gospel," in *The Oxford Book of English Mystical Verse*, eds. Nicholson & Lee (Oxford: The Clarendon Press, 1917).

3. Alex Ayres, ed., *Wit and Wisdom of Mark Twain* (New York: Harper & Row, 1997).

4. Pope Pius XII, "Divino Afflante Spiritu," originally promulgated September 30, 1943, Papal Encyclicals Online, http://www.papalencyclicals.net/Pius12/P12DIVIN.HTM (accessed September 7, 2007).

Chapter 4: Dig Down: Fundamentalism Exposed!

1. Ellyn Sanna, *Touching God* (Mahwah, NJ: Paulist Press, 2002), x.

2. Dietrich Bonhoeffer, *The Cost of Discipleship* (New York: MacMillan, 1963), 45.

3. Eugene LaVerdiere, *Fundamentalism: A Pastoral Concern* (Collegeville, MI: Liturgical Press, 2000).

4. Barbara King, *Evolving God* (New York: Random House, 2007), 220–21.

5. Abraham J. Heschel, *God in Search of Man: A Philosophy of Judaism* (New York: Farrar Straus and Giroux, 1955), 178–179.

6. Simon Parke, "Desert Warm," *Origins* (New York: Crossroad, 2001), 10. Used by permission.

Chapter 5: Abba's Breath of Inspiration

1. Austin Flannery, ed., "Verbum Dei," in *Vatican Council II* (Northport, NY: Costello Publishing, 1975), par. 11.

2. *Catechism of the Catholic Church* (Mahwah, NJ: Paulist Press, 1994), par. 106.

Chapter 6: In the Name of Yahweh

1. Dean Hamer, *The God Gene: How Faith is Hardwired into our Genes* (New York: Doubleday, 2004).

2. Marty Haugen, "Shepherd Me, O God" *Gather* (Chicago: GIA Publications, 1986). Used by permission.

Chapter 7: In the Beginning, When God Created…

1. Thomas Berry, *The Great Work: Our Way into the Future* (Los Angeles: Harmony/Bell Tower, 2000), 77.

2. Gerard Manley Hopkins, "God's Grandeur," in *The Top Five Hundred Poems*, ed. William Harmon (New York: Columbia University Press, 1992), 792.

3. Francis Thompson, "The Mistress of Vision," in *The Columbia World of Quotations*, ed. Robert Andrews and others (New York: Columbia University Press, 1996), #58107.

Chapter 8: Eve and Adam, Alive and Well

1. Oscar Andres Rodriquez Maradiaga, "Just A Thought," Nothing For Granted, http:// www.nothingforgranted.com/justathought. php?pageno=2 (accessed September 7, 2007).

2. Lawrence Boadt "Faith Alive—Does Evolution Contradict the Biblical View of Creation?" Texas Catholic (Dallas, TX: Texas Catholic Publishing Co).May 8, 2003.

Chapter 9: Cain and Abel: Brothers in Blood Only

1. Samuel Tayler Coleridge, *The Wanderings of Cain* (Geneve, Paris: M. J. Minard Lettres Modernes, 1963).

Chapter 10: Noah, the Mariner

1. David E. Graves, "Appointment of Canadian to Mount Ararat Archaeological Research Expedition," press release, Arc Imaging— Archaeological Imaging Research Consortium, May 16, 2005.

Chapter 11: Abraham, Our Father in Faith

1. Al-Hajj Muhammad Shakarzadeh, *The Meaning of the Glorious Koran*, trans. Mohammed Marmaduke Pickthall (New York: The New American Library), a lithograph copy written at the command of Sultan Mahmud of Turkey, 1246 AH.

Chapter 15: The Exodus: Bon Voyage!

1. Gerhard von Rad, *Wisdom in Israel* (Nashville: Abingdon, 1972), 62.

2. Oscar Romero, *The Violence of Love* (Farmington, PA: Plough Publications, 1998), 19.

Chapter 16: Moses, the Transformed Journeyman

1. Elizabeth Barrett Browning, *Aurora Leigh*, "bk.7", ed. Kerry McSweeney (Oxford, NY: Oxford University Press, 1993), 246.

Chapter 18: Our Warrior God?

1. Percy Bysshe Shelley, "To_____," in *The Top Five Hundred Poems*, ed. William Harmon (New York: Columbia Press, 1992), 508.

2. Mother Teresa of Calcutta, *Study Cassettes*, Jeffrey Norton Publishers EC #99, audiocassette, 1979.

Chapter 19: Singing Psalms and Living Liturgy

1. Austin Flannery, ed., "Sacrosanctum Concilium—December 4, 1963" *Vatican Council II—The Basic Sixteen Documents* (Northport, NY: Costello Publishing, 1996), par. 14.

Chapter 20: Wisdom and Her Children

1. Eleanor Rae, "Divine Wisdom for Significance for Today," in *Teilhard in the 21st Century: The Emerging Spirit of Earth*, eds. Arthur Fabel and Donald St. John (Maryknoll, NY: Orbis Books, 2003), 1989.

2. James Robinson, *The Gospel of Jesus* (San Francisco: Harper Collins, 2005), 191.

3. Gerald O Collins, *Following the Way*; Jesus, Our Spiritual Director (Mahwah, NJ: Paulist Press, 2001), x.

4. Monica Helwig, *Guests of God* (Mahwah, NJ: Paulist Press, 1999), 120.

Chapter 21: Joshua, the Four-Star General

1. William H. Shannon, ed., "An Open Letter to the American Hierarchy," in *Witness to Freedom: The Letters of Thomas Merton—In Times of Crisis* (San Diego: Harcourt Brace & Co., 1995), 89.

Chapter 25: Solomon, Son of Wisdom?

1. Bernhard Anderson, *Understanding the Old Testament* (Englewood Cliffs, NJ: Prentice-Hall, 1975), 194–95.

Chapter 29: "Here I Am: Send Me!" (Isaiah 6:8)

1. Lawrence Boadt, *The Book of Three Ages: Isaiah*, Alba House # 9531, audiocassette.

2. Etty Hillesum, *An Interrupted Life: The Diaries of Etty Hillesum 1941–43* (New York: Washington Square Press, 1981).

A Transition

1. John Shelby Spong, *Liberating the Gospels, Reading the Bible with Jewish Eyes* (San Francisco: Harper, 1997), 185.

2. John Paul II, "Address to Pontifical Biblical Commission April 11, 1997," in *L'Osservatore Romano* (Baltimore: Cathedral Foundation, April 23, 1997), 2.

3. Fred Holmgren, *The Old Testament and the Significance of Jesus* (Grand Rapids, MI: Wm. B. Eerdmans, 1999), 41.

4. Norbert Lohfink, *Option for the Poor: The Basic Principle of Liberation Theology in the Light of the Bible* (Berkeley, CA : BIBAL Press, 1987), 54, quoted in Fredrick Holmgren, *The Old Testament and the Significance of Jesus* (Grand Rapids, MI: Wm. B. Eerdmands, 1999), 99.

5. Cardinal Edward Cassidy, President of the Holy See's Commision For Religious Relations With The Jews, *We Remember: A Reflection On The Shoah* (Vatican City: Liberia Editrice Vaticana, 1998)

6. Karl Rahner, *Encyclopedia of Theology: The Concise Sacramentum Mundi* (New York: Seabury Press, 1975), 500.

7. Edward Hays, "A Prayer for Zeal," *Prayers for a Planetary Pilgrim: A Personal Manual* for Prayer and Ritual (Notre Dame, IN: Forest of Peace, 1989), 99. Used by permission.

Chapter 31: The Four Evangelists: Why Can't They Agree?

1. Thomas Browne, *Religio Medici, Hydriotaphia, and The Garden of Cyrus*, ed. R.H.A. Robbins (New York: Oxford University Press, 1972).

2. Martin Luther quoted by Tony Castle, *The New Book of Christian Quotations* (New York: Crossroad, 1988), 21.

Chapter 32: Herod to Christ: The Great Divide

1. Seneca, "On Saving Time," in *Seneca, IV, Epistles 1–65*, trans. Richard M. Gummere (Cambridge, MA; Harvard University Press).

Chapter 33: Merry Christmas!

1. Karl Rahner, *Foundations of Christian Faith: An Introduction to the Idea of Christianity* (New York: Seabury, 1978).

2. Angelus Silesius, "It Depends on You," in *The Enlightened Heart: An Anthology of Sacred Poetry*, ed. Stephen Mitchell (New York: HarperCollins, 1993), 88.

3. Austin Flannery, ed., "Lumen Gentium—November 21, 1964," in *Vatican Council II* (Northport, NY: Costello Publishing, 1996) par. 65.

4. St. Augustine, "In Johannis evangelium tractatus" (1568), quoted by Paul VI "Paths of the Church: Ecclesiam Suam," promulgated on

August 6, 1964, Papal Encyclicals Online, July 2007, http://www.
papalencyclicals.net/ (accessed September 8, 2007).

5. Henri LeSaux, Abhishiktananda, "The Cave of the Heart," in *Contemplative Companions Newsletter*, (San Diego, CA: Wellspring, the Center Contemplative Outreach of San Diego Contemplative Outreach) Vol 13: Issue 6, 4.

Chapter 35: John, Mentor and Baptizer

1. John Meier, *A Marginal Jew: Rethinking the Historical Jesus*, vol. 2 (New York: Doubleday, 1994), 116.

Chapter 36: Will You Marry Me?

1. Austin Flannery, ed., "Nostra Aetate—October 28, 1965," in *Vatican Council II* (Northport, NY: Costello Publishing, 1995), par. 4.

Chapter 37: "Behold the Man!" (John 19:5)

1. Mark Link, *He is the Still Point of the Turning World* (Niles, IL: Argus, 1971), 8.

2. Wolfhart Pannenberg, *Systematic Theology*, vol. 2 (Grand Rapids, MI: Eerdmans, 1994), 321.

3. Ron Seitz, *Song for Nobody: A Memory Vision of Thomas Merton* (Liguori, MO: Liguori Publications, 1995).

Chapter 38: Prayer: Embracing the Divine

1. Gene Walsh, *A Valuation of the American Liturgical Scene*, National Catholic Reporter no. A-678, audiocassette.

2. St. John Damascene, *De Fide Orthodoxae: An Exact Exposition of the Orthodox Faith*, 1.111 c24, trans. by Dom Vitalis Lehodey, *The Ways of Mental Prayer* (Dublin: M. H. Gill & Son, 1960), 1.

Chapter 39: His Secret Passion

1. Roger Haight, *Jesus, Symbol of God* (Maryknoll, NY: Orbis Books, 1990).

2. Elizabeth Johnson, Consider Jesus (New York: Crossroad, 2002), 57.

Chapter 40: Mary, His First Disciple

1. Gerard Manley Hopkins, "The Blessed Virgin Compared to the Air We Breathe," in *Penguin Classics: Poems and Prose*, ed. W. H. Gardner (New York: Penguin Putnam, 1985), 52.

Chapter 42: The ___ of Abba

1. John Paul II, "Redemptoris Missio—December 7, 1990," in *The Encyclicals of John Paul II*, ed. J. Michael Miller (Huntington, IN: Our Sunday Visitor, 1996).

2. James Finley, *Merton's Palace of Nowhere* (Notre Dame, IN: Ave Maria, 1999), 61.

3. Ursula King, *Spirit of Fire: The Life and Vision of Teilhard de Chardin* (Maryknoll, NY: Orbis Books, 1998).

4. Austin Flannery, ed., "The Church," in *Vatican Council II* (Northport, NY: Costello Publications, 1996).

5. Andrew Harvey, *Son of Man: The Mystical Path to Christ* (New York: Tarcher Putnam, 1999), 95.

6. United States Conference of Catholic Bishops "Dominus Jesus" in Congregation of the Doctrine of the Faith, August 6, 2000, par. III (15).

Chapter 43: The Constitution of God's Kingdom

1. Karl Barth, *Action in Waiting for the Kingdom of God* (Rifton, NY: Plough Publishing, 1969).

2. L.H. Sigourney, *History of Marcus Aurelius: Emperor of Rome* (Hartford: Belknap & Hamersley, 1836), 67.

Chapter 45: Evil: Our Stepping Stone to Success

1. Jim Manney, ed., *The Best Catholic Writing 2007* (Chicago: Loyola Press, 2007), 81.

2. Henri Nouwen, *A Retreat With Henri Nouwen: Reclaiming Our Humanity* (Cincinnati: St. Anthony Messenger, 2003), 76.

3. Barbara Reid, interview by Norman B. Carroll, January 17, 2007, St. John the Baptist Church, Fort. Lauderdale, FL.

4. Brian Kolodiejchuk, ed., *Mother Teresa, Come Be My Light* (New York: Doubleday, 2007), 281.

5. Thomas Merton, *Seeds of Contemplation* (New York: Dell, 1960), 40.

Chapter 47: Jesus Challenges Capitalism

1. Jonathan Luxmoore, "How an Unknown Text Could Throw New Light on John Paul II's Views on Economics," in *Houston Catholic Worker 26*, no. 2 (March–April 2007).

2. Stanley Vishnewski, *Meditations by Dorothy Day* (New York: Paulist, 1970), 82.

3. Edward Hayes, Prayers for a Planetary Pilgrim: *A Personal Manual for Prayer and Ritual* (Notre Dame, IN: Forest of Peace, 1989), 203. Used by permission.

Chapter 50: The Canaanite Teacher

1. Austin Flannery, ed., "Church in the Modern World,"in *Vatican Council II* (Northport, NY: Costello, 1995), par. 22.

2. Michael L. Cook, *Responses to 101 Questions About Jesus* (New York: Paulist, 1993), 57.

Chapter 51: A Woman En Route from Magdala

1. Elizabeth Schüssler Fiorenza, *In Memory of Her: A Feminist Theological Reconstruction of Christian Origins*, (New York: Crossroad, 1983), 123–124

Chapter 52: A Tale of Two Sisters

1. Barbara E. Reid, *Choosing the Better Part? Women in the Gospel of Luke:* (Collegeville, MN: Liturgical Press, 1996), 1.

Chapter 53: The Good Samaritan Lives

1. Gerald O Collins, *Following the Way; Jesus, Our Spiritual Director* (Mahwah, NJ: Paulist Press, 2001), 121.

2. Stephen R. Covey, *The 8th Habit—From Effectiveness to Greatness* (New York: Simon & Schuster, 2004), 314.

Chapter 56: Long Live Lazarus!

1. Edward Hays, *Prayers for a Planetary Pilgrim: A Person Manual for Prayer and Ritual* (Easton, KS: Forest of Peace, 1988), 9197. Used by permission.

Chapter 57: Choose Your Company: Goats or Sheep

1. Edward Schillebeeckx, *Consensus in Theology* (Philadelphia: Westminster, 1980), 31.

2. Mother Teresa of Calcutta, *A Gift For God: Prayers and Meditations* (New York: Harper & Row, 1975).

3. Oscar Romero, *The Violence of Love* (Farmington, PA: Plough, 1988), 191.

4. Antonio Machado, "Proverbs and Tiny Songs" in *The Soul is Here For Its Own Joy* ed and trans. Robert Bly (Hopewell, NJ: The Ecco Press, 1999) 248. Used by permission.

Chapter 58: Love is Your Name!

1. Karl Rahner, *The Love of Jesus and the Love of Neighbor* (New York: Crossroad, 1983), 84.

2. A. N. Wilson, *Jesus: A Life* (Columbine: Fawcett, 1992), 33.

Chapter 59: Table O' Plenty

1. Andrew Harvey, ed, *The Essential Mystics: Selections from the Worlds Great Wisdom Traditions*, (New York: HarperCollins Publishers, 1997), 206.

Chapter 61: That "They May All Be One!" (John 17:21)

1. Paul James Francis, *The Lamp* (Graymoor, NY: Graymoor Publications, 1903), 2.

2. Mother Teresa of Calcutta, *Come And See: A Photojournalist's Journey into the World of Mother Teresa* (Sanford, FL: DC Press, 2003), 32.

Chapter 62: Come Dine With Me!

1. Teilhard de Chardin, *The Phenomenon of Man* (New York: Harper & Row, 1965).

Chapter 63: Do We Sleep in Gethsemane?

1. Blaise Pascal, Pensees, Le Mystèrre de Jésus (The Mystery of Jesus), trans. A.J. Krailsheimer (New York: Penguin Putnam Inc., 1966), 289.

2. Miriam Chaikin, *In A Nightmare in History: The Holocaust 1933–1945* (New York: Houghton Mifflin, 1987), 17.

Chapter 65: He's Risen!

1. John Michael Perry, *Exploring the Resurrection of Jesus* (Kansas City: Sheed & Ward, 1993), 46.

2. Jerome Murphy O'Connor, *New Testament Message*, vol. 10, (Wilmington, DE: Michael Glazier, 1979), 147.

Chapter 66: Journeying in Fire, Wind, and Tongue

1. Teilhard de Chardin, *Toward the Future* (London: Collins, 1975), 86.

2. Edward Hays, "A Psalm To The Wind Of Heaven" *Prayers For a Planetary Pilgrim: A Personal Manual for Prayer and Ritual* (Notre Dame, IN: Forest of Peace, 1989), 145. Used by permission.

Chapter 67: The Battle Lines Are Drawn

1. Albert Schweitzer, *The Quest of the Historical Jesus* (Minneapolis: Fortress, 2001).

2. Andrew Harvey, *The Son of Man* (New York: Jeremy P. Tarcher/Putnam, 1999), 95.

3. T. S. Eliot, *T.S. Eliot and Our Turning World* (New York: St. Martin's Press, 2001), 62.

Chapter 70: Good-bye to Good-byes

1. John Paul II, "Inside the Vatican"(Vatican City: Urbi et Orbi Communications 1993).

2. Ibid.

Epilogue

1. John Shelby Spong, *Liberating the Gospels* (San Francisco: Harper, 1996), 309.

2. Karl Jung, *Man and His Symbols* (New York: Dell Publishing, 1975), 257.

3. Christopher Hitchens, *God is Not Great: How Religion Poisons Everything* (New York: Twelve, 2007), 157.